The Character of Kingship

The Character of Kingship

Edited by
Declan Quigley

Oxford • New York

English edition
First published in 2005 by
Berg
Editorial offices:
First Floor, Angel Court, 81 St Clements Street, Oxford OX4 1AW, UK
175 Fifth Avenue, New York, NY 10010, USA

Berg is the imprint of Oxford International Publishers Ltd.

Library of Congress Cataloging-in-Publication Data
The character of kingship / edited by Declan Quigley. — English ed.
   p. cm.
"Developed from discussions held during a conference on kingship
in St. Andrews, Scotland in January 2002"—Acknowledgements.
Includes bibliographical references and index.
ISBN-13: 978-1-84520-290-3 (cloth)
ISBN-10: 1-84520-290-2 (cloth)
ISBN-13: 978-1-84520-291-0 (paper)
ISBN-10: 1-84520-291-0 (paper)
1. Kings and rulers. 2. Chiefdoms.   I. Quigley, Declan.
GN492.7.C43 2005
306—dc22   2005018454

British Library Cataloguing-in-Publication Data
A catalogue record for this book is available from the British Library.

ISBN-13 978 1 84520 290 3 (Cloth)
            978 1 84520 291 2 (Paper)
ISBN-10 1 84520 290 2 (Cloth)
            1 84520 291 0 (Paper)

Typeset by Avocet Typeset, Chilton, Aylesbury, Bucks
Printed in the United Kingdom by Biddles Ltd, King's Lynn.

www.bergpublishers.com

Contents

Acknowledgements

This book developed from discussions held during a conference on kingship in St Andrews, Scotland in January 2002, which brought together a number of anthropologists and historians. I would like to make grateful acknowledgement to the Ladislav Holy Memorial Trust, the British Academy, and the Royal Anthropological Institute for providing funds to make the conference possible. The Ladislav Holy Memorial Trust also contributed to the costs of translation of one of the papers.

I was greatly assisted in the editorial process by Dr Anne McLaren, of the School of History, University of Liverpool. Dr McLaren gave a paper to the St Andrews conference and initially intended to contribute a chapter to this book but, because of various pressures, finally decided to submit her work to a history journal. I was very sorry to lose her contribution, but remain immensely grateful to her for the support she provided throughout much of the planning of the book. Without her help, the book might never have seen the light of day.

Declan Quigley

List of Contributors

Henri J. M. Claessen is Professor Emeritus of Cultural Anthropology, Leiden University, The Netherlands.

Susan Drucker-Brown is a research associate in the Department of Social Anthropology, University of Cambridge.

Luc de Heusch is Professor Emeritus at the Free University of Brussels, Belgium.

Marie Lecomte-Tilouine is Chargée de recherche at CNRS, Villejuif, France.

Emiko Ohnuki-Tierney is William F. Vilas Research Professor, University of Wisconsin, Madison.

Declan Quigley is an honorary research associate at the Institute of Social and Cultural Anthropology, University of Oxford.

Burkhard Schnepel is Professor at the Institute of Social Anthropology (Ethnologie), Martin-Luther-University, Halle-Wittenberg, Germany.

Lucien Scubla is a member of the Centre de Recherche en Épistémologie Appliquée of the École polytechnique (Paris).

Simon Simonse is an anthropologist working on peace building programmes in Sudan and Uganda.

Tal Tamari is a research fellow at the Centre National de la Recherche Scientifique (France) and a Lecturer at the Université Libre de Bruxelles.

–1–

Introduction: The Character of Kingship

Declan Quigley

Kingship's Leitmotif

Kingship is a unique principle of political organization in that it straddles societies of every type apart from the very simplest hunter–gatherer communities. Clearly not all societies where kingship is present can have historical or cultural connections to each other since they range from small Pacific islands through the classic cases of sub-Saharan Africa to the complex city-kingdoms of south and southeast Asia to modern European democracies. The structural basis of this kind of organization must therefore be found in conditions that are very widespread in human societies. It is undeniable that many countries today function perfectly well without a monarch. And yet, in a great many others, a sizeable proportion of the population clings to the idea that kingship provides an indispensable mechanism for transcending political division and underwriting stability and harmony. While some consider that the symbolic function served by kings and queens has become redundant in the contemporary world, for others this symbolic function is as indispensable as ever because no other form of political authority comes close to providing such a 'shared symbol of a sacred authority above politics or personal power'.[1]

Certain contemporary misconceptions impede the understanding of kingship and to get to the heart of the institution we must go beyond these. In our own historical experience and imagination we are so accustomed to the encapsulation of kingship within states that we can scarcely conceive of kingship as being something other than political. We see the modern monarch occupying a position within the overarching political machinery of the state and we thus conceive of this individual as playing a political role. But kingship has its roots in the pre-modern world, and it is only by looking at that world that we can see clearly that kings reign rather than rule, and that their function is as much ritual as political. As Scubla puts it below, paraphrasing Frazer: 'To reign does not mean to govern or to give orders, but to guarantee the order of the world and of the society by observing ritual prescriptions.' Kingship is an institution that develops its full reality in a world where the political has not emerged as an autonomous sphere from the ritual. With the skilful guidance of the contributors to this volume, the reader will be able to transport his or her imagination beyond the layer that the state – the agency that has a monopoly on the legitimate use of violence – has added to the societies with which they are likely to be more familiar.

Another common misconception about kingship is the idea that one country has one monarch. As the chapters below demonstrate, this is generally not the case in Asia and Africa and the Pacific, and indeed the norm is that there is competition and fragmentation with kingship being devolved throughout the society's nobility insomuch as the quality of kingship inherent in any particular office is relative to that office. This is seen particularly clearly in Drucker-Brown's chapter on northern Ghana, below, where she shows that the quality that is embodied in king-ship – *naam* – is transmitted to each chief by the king when they in turn are installed. The British concept of nobility, with all its dukes and marquises and so on, echoes this refraction of the monarchy. In fact, it is not just nobility that is in the image of kingship. The mechanisms, which permit the setting apart of the king, are replicated in *all* status positions. We are, perhaps, misled by expressions such as 'the divine king' and 'the king is dead, long live the king'. It is king*ship* – not the king – that is sacred (the divinity of kings is an ethnographic oddity), so the chant should be: 'The king is dead, long live the kingship' as Evans-Pritchard (1962: 84) and other anthropologists have pointed out.

A third misconception is the tendency to identify nobility and royalty with opu-lence that is beyond the reach of common people but which could, in principle, be accessible to others if only they had the means of generating sufficient wealth. Royalty is not fundamentally about material privilege. It is perfectly possible to be extremely wealthy and have no connection to royalty or nobility whatsoever – though it is an interesting fact that people who have accumulated wealth or power very frequently try to convert it into status through marriage to people of more noble pedigree.

Royalty and nobility are essentially about separation. While this may convey privilege from one perspective, the comparative ethnographic literature from Africa and elsewhere suggests a rather different picture. Simonse in this volume nicely describes kingship as a drama in which there are 'two principal protago-nists': the king and the people. More often than not the king is portrayed as a kind of prisoner of the people and of the institution of kingship, hemmed in by numerous taboos that severely restrict his behaviour (Evans-Pritchard 1962: 79; Fortes 1968: 6). It would seem that the idea is not just that the monarch's behav-iour should be seen to be distinctive: there appears to be a frequent desire to sep-arate him or her from the earth quite literally. The king of the Mamprusi in Ghana, for example, while called 'the owner of the world' (Drucker-Brown 1992: 75), is confined to his palace and forbidden from touching the earth: 'the skins of animals sacrificed at his enthronement must always be placed between the earth and his feet' (de Heusch 1997: 222). Indeed this separation is sometimes taken to its logical limit when, during the rites of enthronement, a form of symbolic death takes place. That is to say, the king is symbolically killed at the very moment he is installed, making him into 'a living dead man' (de Heusch 1997: 218; 1982: 24). He is thus categorically separated first from his own kin, then from all other mortals.

The underlying preoccupation here seems to be a desire to pre-empt the natural death of the monarch by making culture more powerful than nature. This idea is endlessly repeated during the king's reign. One does not simply assume the king-ship at the installation ceremony; one must continually live up to its heavy demands. Should the king evade, or fail in, his responsibilities, he can expect at least to be ostracized (a social or symbolic death) if not literally to be put to death. Other attempts to make culture override nature include being confined to the palace at night, being obliged to be carried everywhere, having the space around the royal personage as free as possible from contamination, being dressed in special clothes, being housed in special kinds of residences, and being prevented from talking or being addressed in the same manner as ordinary people. All of these features are, of course, still prominent in the way in which royals are treated today. Imagine, for example, that the Queen of England decided one day to go jogging in Hyde Park wearing a torn T-shirt, or if, on some great ceremonial occa-sion, she substituted a Harley-Davidson motorcycle for her Rolls Royce or car-riage and horses. There is no doubt that this would cause a great deal of upset, even panic. If she decided one evening to 'hang out' at a local bar for a few hours downing copious amounts of alcohol, this would also undoubtedly affront those who have a certain conception of the dignity of her office – which is most of us. Yet everyone else can go running in the park wearing whatever they want and nobody will pay the slightest bit of attention, and if anyone else has a pint of beer too many, nobody will be too upset. Why?[2]

The most common answer – because she is the queen and everybody else is nobody in particular – is tautological and gets us nowhere. Another common answer – that it is a question of heredity – does not get us any further. If the queen were *automatically* the queen because of her pedigree, then we would not need all the ritual palaver that surrounds her. We would not need archbishops and ministers and various 'people-in-waiting', all with their very particular roles. Conversely, in most places heredity is clearly not an automatic qualification if the heir is a lunatic. In the United Kingdom today, to be a Catholic or to marry a divorced woman pres-ents intractable difficulties to an otherwise legitimate heir. Clearly something more than heredity is at stake here.

The answer 'because she is the hereditary queen' would not explain why we need to make the monarch dress up in clothes which would look ridiculous on anyone else and which are so heavy that they impede her movement. It would not explain why she and her consort are made to eat sleep-inducing eight-course dinners. It would not explain why she has to open each session of parliament, nor why she has to do so in a very formal manner, surrounded by a great variety of functionaries. Why could not a famous actor, or comedian or glamour model or footballer be hired for the day to simply bang a gavel and shout, 'Right, let's get on with it!'?

The fundamental idea underlying kingship is the separation of one human being from others. Being set apart is the very crux of the institution. The ways in which this is achieved may appear ridiculous, and sometimes perversely deviant, because they depart so radically from convention. But this is the point: if kings could not be distinguished very easily from ordinary people, then how would we know that they were kings?

The leitmotif of this separation is the recurrence of a bundle of highly ritualized elements revolving around regicide. This bundle appears consistently wherever the institution is found, regardless of historical era or geographical location.[3] By 'bundle' is meant that these highly ritualized features are systematically related to each other as a package: each of the features only makes sense in terms of the others. In isolation they frequently appear so arbitrary as to be ridiculous to the outside eye – for example, that a monarch may only be addressed in an extraordinarily formalized way, must live in a kind of dwelling that no-one else would live in, and must, on occasion, wear clothes that clearly serve some purpose other than covering or protection. A nice illustration is given by Drucker-Brown below when she refers to a description of the Asantahene king: 'so weighted with gold objects that courtiers needed to help him move his body'.

The central issue in the anthropology of kingship is understanding how an individual is extracted from the kinds of economic, political and kinship relations that 'ordinary' people also find themselves in, and made into a person (or non-person) who is literally extraordinary – outside conventional society – by using the cultural device of an installation ritual. It is not difficult to see that culture consists of a never-ending series of rituals. It may be less obvious that all rituals are a kind of installation ritual, though this is less obscure than might at first appear. The purpose of all ritual is either to transform a person from one status to another or to maintain him in that status. It amounts to the same thing – the overriding of nature by culture. Without ritual – which is inherently transformative and repetitive – changes of identity and their maintenance are impossible. The process begins for all human beings immediately following birth when the newborn baby is immediately transformed from being a natural entity into a social/cultural entity. Thereafter, successive rituals progressively add new social/cultural identities or seek to deny natural change by recharging an established identity, i.e. repeating the initial installation. A status change made through an initial transformation will lapse unless it is continually reinvigorated by a repetition of the original ritual.

The mechanisms involved in establishing and maintaining everyday identities are often opaque both because of their complexity and because they frequently involve a great deal of concealment and deception. This is partly because changes in social status always involve shifts in power, and partly because such changes are generally embarrassing for the parties involved because of the readjustment in relations that is brought about. With royal installation ritual, however, the transformative process must be clear. Because the kingship belongs to all the people, the inauguration is necessarily very public. And because this particular installation is of concern to all, the steps involved – such as the placing of a crown on the monarch's head by a bishop, or a proclamation to the effect that the king belongs to all the people and not just to his own family – are transparent.[4] Few people care if, one day, I cease to regard my brother as my brother by failing to observe the appropriate rituals that distinguish him from other males around me – i.e. which repeatedly install him in that role. However, most people in any given society *will* care if, one day, the prime minister announces that henceforth there is to be a new king but that there will be no ceremony to mark the installation and no further ritualized markers to keep reminding us who the king is. And most people will mind even more if an individual one day proclaims himself king simply by virtue of his greater force – unceremoniously, as we say.

In either of the above eventualities, people will express their concern for the simple reason that the king is that individual who is uniquely connected to everyone in the society. *That* is the king's function. Unlike everyone else, who connect only to *some* people through kinship and marriage or via various political and economic mechanisms, the king has a relationship with everyone. In order for this to be possible, the mechanism that connects the king to his people is unlike the mechanisms that make other relations possible. It transcends kinship and marriage as well as conventional politics and economics. The essence of the identities given by religion, economics, politics or kinship (without a 'g') is that some people are united to each other by separating them from yet others. The essence of kingship, however, is that everyone is united by his or her common relation to the king.

All relationships depend on ritual in order to make those connected into something that they were not before. But the king's relation to his people is unique in relying on ritual alone to separate him from the world since his function requires him precisely to stand apart as a perfect being who is separated from the contaminating concerns of ordinary people and the political and economic mechanisms which allow these concerns to be acted out. It is not for nothing that kingship is surrounded by constant ritual and it is a mistake to perceive this as 'mere pomp and ceremony' in the sense of a superstructural gloss on materialist realities, or icing on the cake. It *is* the cake. The ritual must be continually repeated because as soon as it stops the king becomes sucked into the mundane world of intrigue and poison.

All royal ritual thus flows around two interconnected paradoxes. The first is that the king is simultaneously united to, yet separated from, all of his people. To be made king through the transformative act of an installation ritual is to be made into a figure who is at the very centre of society and yet must simultaneously be removed from it. The second paradox is that the king should always be pure yet can only be so for the instant after a purification ritual is performed. Since the king is, as a matter of fact, immersed in social relations like everyone else, he partakes of the inauspicious qualities of social life like everyone else. Indeed, since his function is to be related to everyone, he is a conduit for everyone's inauspicious qualities. Purification ritual provides an escape from this, but only at the moment of expiation. As soon as the ritual finishes, the king re-enters the world of compromising relations.

Modern society has become so caught up with material explanations of social life that many professional social scientists – let alone the average lay person – have lost sight of the fundamental role that ritual plays in all our lives every second that we are engaged in relations with others. Yet it is obvious that we continually have to re-make the statuses that link us to others – both ours and theirs – and we do this using a variety of ritual mechanisms. Mostly we take our relationships so much for granted that we are incapable of seeing how they are made. When I talk to my mother, I do not consciously say to myself every second: 'this is my mother; therefore I must address her in the appropriate way'. I just say, 'hi'. When I interact with a friend, I do not have to question myself about the appropriateness of using his first name, as opposed to behaving formally and addressing him with a title and his surname. I just know how to behave. But *how* do I know how to behave, and indeed how do I know that this woman is my mother, and this other person is my friend? Of *course* I know, you may say: the question is absurd. But is it?

Consider that I go to a community where I know no one. How am I going to work out who is related to whom? To me they are people with no particular identity. I may see that some are older, some younger; some are differently dressed from others; some look poorer, some richer; some appear to live in one house, others in another house; some in one part of town, others in another area. However, to take just one example, if there are a number of adults living in a particular house, I cannot know which, if any, are the parents of the children with whom they live (perhaps the children are adopted). I need additional information. But how do I work out how exactly they are related to one another? I can only do this by observing the ritualized ways in which they interact. Another way of saying this is that I need to observe the ways in which they distinguish individuals from each other by assigning them with qualities and characteristics they were not born with. Once learned, we come to associate these attributes with the persons concerned as if they always had them even though we know perfectly well, if we think about it for a second, that this is impossible. Even the 'most obvious facts' of kinship are not given. One person is another's 'brother' not just because he was born to the same parents, but because there is general agreement in that society that males born of the same couple stand in a particular relation to each other that is significantly different from other people's relations. This becomes clear when we see that what constitutes 'brotherhood' is not the same in every society.

Nature never creates cultural relations, notwithstanding the fact that most of humanity refuses to admit this most of the time. Culture – the investment of meaning in social life – is always a creative and arbitrary business. We see this if we look at other people's relations because they often seem peculiar to us. And yet we have great difficulty in seeing the arbitrary character of our own most fundamental relations, and even some of those that are not fundamental. Many people simply cannot conceive of this at all, so imbued are they with the idea that their images of the world are natural rather than cultural. In modern European society we can undoubtedly see this arbitrariness more easily by looking at kingship than at kinship or ethnicity because of the increasingly marginalized character of the king as opposed to the taken-for-granted nature of family relations and ethnic identity. Yet this arbitrariness is a feature of all statuses since all statuses require a contrived setting apart.

It is not only with respect to kingship, then, that something very curious takes place as the arbitrary is made to appear natural. But the king's installation ritual makes particularly clear the most significant fact of all ritual: that it separates us from those we were joined to in the way that we were connected to them before the ritual took place. In this sense royal installation ritual provides a means for illustrating how all relationships are made and unmade. It provides a paradigm for all ritual because all ritual is a means to underpin the mechanisms of symbolism, which make the separation of people possible.

The royal installation ceremony strips the new king of his erstwhile identity, divesting him of his previous clothes and taking him through a rite of investiture in the literal sense – a robing ceremony – where a form of dress signifying permanence and separation from others will be presented to him. One might more accurately say that this dress, and the behaviour that goes with it, is *forced* upon the new king. At the least, he will forever after be surrounded by taboos which prevent him from being connected to the world in the manner of ordinary mortals. In some cases the break with the individual's past identity is enacted in a dramatic fashion, as illustrated in the following account by Fortes of installation among the Tallensi of Ghana:

> The king's messengers come and wake [the chief elect] and immediately shave his head … They strip off his clothes [and] the next day present him with a new tunic, … a new

red fez on his head and ... new sandals on his feet. Thereafter he may never step on the earth barefooted ... [Should he do so – i.e. behave like ordinary men by walking bare-foot], it is tantamount to a curse which will destroy him and the land and the people. This is but the first of a number of avoidances and restrictions he will have to submit to in fulfilling his responsibility of conducting his life and activities so as to ensure the well-being of the country and the people. [Following this the chief-elect will take a new name, and] it is a taboo for him to be referred to by his former name. (1968: 13 & 15)

It is difficult to imagine a more complete transformation than erasing one's former name.

Comparison lends itself to the conclusion that a king is only able to establish his credentials by standing apart from everyday cultural rules with regard to speaking, eating, moving, sexual activity and the ordinary rules of kinship (without a 'g'). Kinship and kingship are in some sense fundamentally opposed. Sometimes this is demonstrated in a banal way. For example, at the installation the king-maker will simply advise the new king that now he belongs to all the people and must not treat those of his own family or lineage with any favouritism: he has effectively been deprived of normal kin relations. But this rupture must be unambiguous, and commonly enough the symbolic breaking with normal kinship rules is achieved in a dramatic fashion – through some kind of strange and violent transgression of normal rules. Typically this transgression involves incest or cannibalism – the victim on occasion being a member of the new king's own lineage. By performing an act that is (often literally) unspeakable in conventional society, the new king transforms his very being and places himself 'in an ambiguous zone where he is looked upon either as a sacred monster or as a dangerous sorcerer' (de Heusch 1997: 217). Simonse shows that the logic can be reversed while retaining the same message: ' [w]hile the Lokoya and Lotuho humanize a monster from the wild to become their king, the Bari and Lulubo deliberately turn their king-elect into a kind of monster, a receptacle of evil'.

Underlying the ethnographic variations of transgression there is, according to de Heusch, a central unifying theme: 'what does one do with that human being who is charged with articulating the social order and the natural order? Does one place him at the centre of the society or outside it? Or inside and outside at the same time?' (de Heusch 1997: 219). By breaking with convention in some deeply shocking way which goes right to the heart of what it is to be a human being, the king is placed outside normal society – at the bridgehead between the social and the natural (or heavenly) world. And yet, for all that, he must remain tied to all the members of his kingdom. That is his role.

Frazer and Hocart

Two figures stand out in the development of the comparative explanation of king-ship: Sir James George Frazer and Arthur Maurice Hocart.[5] Earlier attempts to dis-credit their respective contributions by focusing on their theoretical weaknesses (Frazer's evolutionism, Hocart's diffusionism) now seem rather shallow given the suggestive richness of their observations and the comparative scope of their approaches. Recently Frazer has been championed by a number of Africanists,[6] while Hocart's insights have tended to figure most prominently among those working in the Pacific and in the caste-organized societies of South Asia, caste organization being a particular form of kingship.[7] The respective approaches of Frazer and Hocart are closer than is commonly acknowledged and one should not be misled into believing that geography somehow dictates the essential qualities of royal formations. The most striking feature to emerge from the literature is the way in which the same elements appear so consistently, albeit with different permuta-tions, in societies that have no obvious historical connection.

In a spirited defence of Frazer that draws on a wide range of ethnography, de Heusch has pointed out in a number of publications (including his contribution to this volume) that Frazer's *magnum opus*, *The Golden Bough*, contains two quite different hypotheses. In the first – positive – hypothesis (often mistakenly identi-fied as Frazer's *only* theory of kingship), kingship is identified with fertility, and the well-being of the kingdom is identified with the monarch's bodily perfection. Since the kingdom represents the cosmos for the people who live in it, the king's health is seen as guaranteeing the continuity of the universe. For this reason, the king must be removed before his physical degeneration endangers everyone – and in many societies some such provision is enshrined. In *all* monarchical societies, including contemporary industrial societies where rational beliefs allegedly prevail, any serious illness that befalls the king or queen is regarded with great foreboding. This is not some empty sentimentality, as contemporary commentators often mistakenly conclude, but reflects the crisis that will come about following the demise of the one figure who is related to everyone and whose death will thus mean a rearrangement of everyone's relations.

In Frazer's second hypothesis, which portrays kingship negatively, the king is held to take upon himself and absorb the sins/evil/inauspiciousness/death of his subjects. He must therefore find a means of perpetually ridding himself of the con-tagion that is an integral element of his function or he will imperil both himself and the kingdom. From this perspective, the king is a vehicle for carrying away all of those poisonous qualities that are the inevitable product of social life. Frazer himself does not appear to have seen that this second perspective on kingship makes his first view redundant. If the king is a vessel for carrying away inauspi-ciousness regardless of his health, then he is *always* in a potentially dangerous condition – not just when he is ill or near death. On this latter view – though Frazer himself does not spell this out – the ritual that surrounds kingship appears to be a Sisyphus-like attempt to continually re-purify the king. Once any particular ritual has concluded, the king automatically reverts to his 'normal' everyday dangerous state of absorbing inauspiciousness, and the ritual procedures must be reactivated. It is for this reason that royal ritual is never-ending.

The main emphasis in the approach of Hocart (who regrettably did not refer to Frazer explicitly) is on kingship as a form of ritual, rather than political, organization. Drawing parallels between traditional Fiji and the caste societies of South Asia, he argues that 'the king's state is an organization for prosperity by the due observance of traditional rules' (Hocart 1950 [1938]: 97). Primary among these rules is the repetitive performance of sacrificial rites the purpose of which is to regenerate the kingship by removing any pollution that accumulates at the royal centre. As a particularly illuminating example of kingship, Hocart looks at caste organization. In caste-organized communities, he argues, the function of the families that are attached to the court is to ensure the purity of the king. Contrary to the most commonly accepted theory of caste – in which the priest is seen as the acme of purity – Hocart states that the priest is always a vessel for removing the pollution of kings and nobles.[8] Without the purificatory mechanism of his priests, the Hindu king simply accumulates the evil and death of his people to become a kind of cesspit.

If Frazer and Hocart are correct, the paradox at the heart of kingship that de Heusch draws our attention to would appear to be irresolvable. To be made king through the transformative act of an installation ritual is to be made into a figure who is at the very centre of society and yet must be removed from it – who, as Durkheim might have put it, collapses 'good sacred' and 'bad sacred'. On the one hand kingship represents the most auspicious qualities – life and fertility. It forms the 'exemplary centre' (as Geertz 1980 calls it) and encapsulates a transcendent force, normally given material form in the regal appurtenances of relics, pieces of jewellery, thrones and palaces, all of which outlive any particular king and are typically thought of as the property of the ancestors. On the other hand kingship also appears to embody the most inauspicious social qualities, which can only be expiated through ritual, specifically sacrificial ritual. The literature on caste, with its never-ending preoccupation with purity and impurity, illustrates this particularly well. So too does the symbolic regicide which is typically enacted during the very rites of enthronement everywhere.

As we have seen, de Heusch (1997) argues that all of the ethnographic variations on the intensely problematic status of the sacred king derive from his unique function among humans of articulating the social order and the natural order. Of course this is rarely apparent in contemporary kingship since monarchs in modern democracies are no longer expected to harmonize the natural and social worlds, nor to be responsible for general fertility, health and prosperity, in the way that is widely reported in the anthropological literature. Nevertheless, vestiges of this idea remain, particularly in the association between monarchy and death – the required presence at national ceremonies of remembrance of the war dead, for example, or the way in which a royal death is often likened to a natural calamity. On such occasions, ordinary time stands still and a ritualized absence of temporality prevails, signalling the capacity of kingship to transcend even death. Normal television and radio programmes are suspended, a public holiday is declared and there is a general preoccupation with the royal death at the expense of focusing on ordinary everyday activities. Ritual always carries this quality of reverting to timelessness, an index of the sacrificial moment of perfection found in many religions, when the beginning of the universe is symbolically re-created.

Understanding Kingship

Even a relatively superficial survey of the study of kingship reveals certain core themes that marked the emergence of the academic discipline of social anthropology and the comparative study of humankind – in particular, the understanding of sacrifice, ritual and scapegoating. In spite of this conceptual centrality, however, and the extraordinarily rich literature on traditional kingship ranging across the globe throughout known history, the institution has been sorely neglected by the social sciences in recent decades. Where it is taken up, it tends merely to extend the popular media's trivializing, voyeuristic and vicarious obsessions with the privilege and peccadilloes of 'royalty' and 'monarchy'. This emphasis on the comings and goings and doings of particular kings and queens contrasts sharply with the rather abstract, timeless idea of king*ship* set out in anthropological writing.

In the pages that follow, the themes I have sketched out above are given flesh in a variety of settings. The contributors adopt different theoretical approaches but each links theoretical questions to historical and ethnographic evidence. The idea for this book first emerged several years ago following a public conference on the future of monarchy organized by the Royal Anthropological Institute. Three of the contributors in this volume – Luc de Heusch, Susan Drucker-Brown and myself – were speakers on that occasion, and I subsequently went on to translate an edited version of Professor de Heusch's talk for the *Journal of the Royal Anthropological Institute* (de Heusch 1997). As will become obvious on reading through the various chapters, a number of the contributors draw heavily on the work of de Heusch and some of his erstwhile collaborators at the CNRS team in Paris studying systems of thought in black Africa.

It seems particularly appropriate that the first chapter in this volume should be by de Heusch since he has laboured so hard to keep kingship to the fore in anthropology – against the intellectual fashion that has destroyed the core of anthropological theory. In 2000 I published an article linking earlier work I had done on caste to the Frazer–de Heusch connection of kingship with scapegoats. Around the same time, Lucien Scubla sent me a paper he had been working on which pursued very similar themes and I translated this for publication (Scubla 2002). That article served as a precursor for Scubla's paper in the present volume, where he sets out a radical alternative to the neo-Frazerian approach of de Heusch.

There are fundamental disagreements between de Heusch and Scubla revolving around the question of the king's scapegoat status. Scubla is convinced that this is the key to the interpretation of kingship, and in a highly innovative manner he draws on Girard and Freud to support the basic thread of his argument linking Frazer and Hocart. De Heusch, however, remains resolutely attached to a more orthodox Frazerian interpretation whereby 'the positive function of kingship is to ensure prosperity and fertility, and ... ritual regicide provides the corresponding negative aspect of this'. It is not that de Heusch is against the conception of the king as scapegoat *per se*. Commenting on the installation of a new king among the Samo in the Upper Volta, he writes:

> The status of his body is now profoundly changed. He may only move about very slowly; he cannot touch the earth, or walk barefoot or dance, etc. ... He has effectively become the scapegoat of the group; he is 'the pile of filth', the one who picks up and takes everything upon himself. He is held responsible for all the evil happenings in the village, the principal cause of which is the badness of its 'head'. (de Heusch 1997: 225)

However, for de Heusch this scapegoat quality is a negative quality that cannot be invoked as the mainspring of kingship. He strongly criticizes Scubla's adherence to Girard's (1988 [1972]) insistence (which draws heavily on the Christian story) that the surrogate victim provides the key not only to the explanation of kingship, but of culture more generally.

De Heusch also takes issue with Scubla regarding Hocart's stunning formula that 'the first kings must have been dead kings' (Hocart 1954: 27). De Heusch argues that the idea that regicide precedes kingship is completely untenable. Here I am unreservedly with Hocart and Scubla. One must be careful, however, as Scubla makes clear while criticizing Freud, not to imply that symbolic regicide indicates a surrogate for some real killing in humankind's long forgotten past. The issue is not historical (or speculative historical), it is morphogenetic. That is to say, regicide occurs when certain conditions occur or recur. Scubla himself is sometimes confusing about this when discussing Girard, for example when he talks about the latter's distinction 'between the founding murder and the ritual killing'.[9] But we do not need a concept of founding murder at all. Nor do we need to adhere to Girard's speculation, from which it derives, that mimesis is the unique human trait from which 'it is possible to deduce all of the other traits which characterize humanity ... [and that] [m]imesis triggers the sacrificial crisis' (Scubla, this volume). How one could provide the evidence for such a metaphysical claim is not at all obvious. It is certainly not provided by Girard himself.

The socio-logic of the predisposing conditions for scapegoating is, I believe, much more straightforward and demonstrable and can be stated in a small number of propositions. Human communities are only possible through symbolism and ritual. Symbolism is a set of arbitrary devices which are made to appear in every human community as if they are not arbitrary – i.e. as if they are natural. But since they actually are arbitrary, the only way they can be made to appear natural is through a violent deception. By symbolically killing a member of the society who represents values that are totally antithetical to those of the community, the community can be saved and reinvented. But it must be someone who can be linked to everyone, or he would not truly represent the whole society. This is why victims typically either come from among the ancestors or originate from outside the society. And it is why, if the victim is from inside the society, he must first be disengaged from his existing family ties.

Whether the king is killed to provide a scapegoat or a scapegoat is killed to provide a king is a matter of some dispute. As Scubla puts it below: 'For Frazer, the king is killed. For Hocart, a man is killed so that he can become king. In *The Golden Bough* the reign ends with an execution. In *Social Origins* it commences with one.' It is surely Hocart's insight that reveals the underlying mechanism, even if it appears that the scapegoat must be made into a king preparatory to being killed. The scapegoat's death is preordained from the moment he is chosen. As Hocart and others have demonstrated persuasively, the installation ceremony always involves a ritual death before a re-birth. We would not recognize a king unless he had already been symbolically 'killed' – i.e. made to appear as non-human. He may then be really killed, but this would only make sense if he were first killed symbolically.[10] There is a difference between murder and sacrifice.

It may seem to be an oxymoron that the fact that ritual killing or sacrifice is symbolic does not make it any less real. But it is symbolism that makes human society possible. What we are considering here is a very meaningful kind of killing. It is not something blind or caused by rage. The Christian story, which will be familiar to most readers of this book, illustrates the general principle perfectly. Christianity could not have existed had it not been for the sacrifice of Christ, the King. Christ was made king precisely in order to be sacrificed and there would have been no point in making him king if he were not going to be sacrificed. Conversely, there would have been no point in sacrificing him if he had not been king. To ask whether the killing of Christ was real or symbolic would be to miss the point entirely. The point is that it is not generally regarded as 'just another killing'. It is not, therefore, the death itself which is of significance but the symbolism attributed to it. In that sense the symbolism *is* the reality, whether or not the actual killing ever took place.

To lay emphasis on the scapegoat theme is not to suggest that it explains everything cultural and social – as de Heusch interprets Scubla and Girard as suggesting. It is rather that culture and society cannot be explained adequately without reference to the scapegoating mechanism because it is only by understanding this mechanism that we can see how the cultural is made to appear natural in any community. This can be seen by looking at pollution beliefs, which are a particular form of scapegoating. All societies use pollution beliefs as a means, if not the only means, of creating seemingly permanent social distinctions, and their members generally take these beliefs so much for granted that they construe them as natural rather than cultural. As a rule, we find other people's pollution beliefs absurd but are completely incapable of seeing the absurdity in our own. It is in the nature of symbols that our own symbolic devices appear indisputable and natural to us, while those of other people appear peculiar – manufactured, unreal and dispensable. In fact, as I have already suggested, symbols generally, and pollution beliefs in particular, are perfectly real in every society, they are not an optional extra that a society could do without and an explanation of culture must come to terms with this.

There is another way of looking at this. Anthropologists long ago showed how an individual comes to be identified with a particular office or social status through the transformative capacity of ritual, and that this transformation always brings with it a heavy responsibility – one might even say a terrible responsibility.[11] As Fortes puts it, 'installation ceremonies fix upon the tenant accountability to society for the proper exercise of the functions vested in his office' (Fortes 1968: 6). Once installed, should the incumbent behave 'improperly', he inevitably encounters a sanction. Depending on the nature of the impropriety, the sanction typically takes the form of ostracism – i.e. a social or symbolic death – and in some cases he may find himself facing a literal death.

De Heusch, in the powerful closing words of his reply to Scubla in this volume, argues against what he sees as the Hocartian view that 'the origin of all rituals is the royal installation rite'. This thesis, he says, smacks of evolutionism and, 'ignores the fact that there are societies which have rituals but which know nothing of the sacralization of power. The sacred chief emerges from a society based on lineages or clans as the result of a breakdown of the domestic order.' One could argue that the 'emerges' in de Heusch's argument is significantly more evolutionary in tone than Hocart's morphogenetic or structuralist position. More importantly, perhaps, it implies that there was once a kind of human society where kinship alone – the domestic order – was a mechanism sufficient unto itself. But it is difficult to see how this could be so. Different groups could have been internally regulated by kinship, but some other mechanism must always have regulated relations between them even if it was only unmitigated violence. In this sense, the seeds of kingship are found already in lineage-based societies. In any case, the idea that kingship is essentially about the sacralization of power only makes sense if we first understand this process as deriving from a separation of functions that is not given by nature.

Simonse underlines the purificatory processes surrounding kingship from installation until death and beyond. He examines the scapegoat theme historically in the eastern Nilotic communities using a fictional account of regicide as a back-drop. Making an interesting parallel with the feuding character of segmentary societies, Simonse argues that actual regicide is a drama connected with rain-making which ' [i]n its last stages of escalation ... is a necessity imposed on the community'. This leads him to the conclusion that where the king is really killed in the communities of his ethnography, this is 'not a ritual' since it would have been avoided if rain had fallen. But of course the escalating conflict that Simonse describes does not have to take the form of regicide and the opposition between the suspense-laden, 'tragic' model and ritual is not, perhaps, so clear cut. Simonse writes that the king is killed in revenge because he is 'an incarnation of evil' and this fits perfectly with the ritual model produced by Hocart and others. The projection of evil onto a scapegoat figure is precisely a ritualized way of dealing with a real problem. Nevertheless, Simonse's description of the dramatic build up to the sacrificial moment is rich and captivating and leads us to look at the historical factors underpinning this kind of 'solution' to political problems.

Simonse then turns to the scenario where regicide becomes ritualized and hypothesizes that it results from a search for political stability. Too many students of royal symbolism and ritual, he argues, lose sight of the 'realpolitik' of kingship while those with a political economy platform tend to relegate ritual and symbolism to false consciousness.

Ohnuki-Tierney, taking a broad sweep of the history of Japanese kingship, cautions against a universal application of Frazerian ideas. The political power of the early emperors, she says, depended on the ability to ensure a bountiful rice crop and the core imperial rituals were all connected to the rice harvest. Rice symbolism and ritual remained central to political ideology even when the shoguns took military and political power from the emperors and such was the supernatural power of the emperors that the shoguns did not dare to appropriate the role of officiant in rice rituals.

According to Ohnuki-Tierney, the symbolic opposition between purity and impurity has always been 'the most important principle in Japanese culture'. However, it was only in the twelfth century that the concept of impurity became 'radically negative', and not until the late sixteenth century that groups dealing in impurity were placed in caste groups. Comparing the Japanese situation with India, Ohnuki-Tierney observes that while there were scapegoat groups to carry the burden of impurity, 'at no point in [Japanese] history was there a social group of ritual specialists, equivalent to Brahmans. Instead, unlike Frazer's divine king, the emperor represented the principle of purity'. The impure aspect of kingship that we find in the accounts of Frazer and de Heusch is assigned in Japan to stranger-deities and the emperor represents only the positive forces of production and reproduction. Nevertheless, the death of the emperor unleashes the forces of impurity that are always associated with death in Japanese cosmology, and this impurity must be ritually dealt with before a new inauguration.

Ohnuki-Tierney lays great emphasis on the absence of violent killing in the Japanese case: 'animal sacrifice and violent death, either of the king himself or the sacrificial animal, are absent'. Yet there would appear to be some ambiguity in the offerings of rice, which play a central part in Japanese installation ritual. Every grain of rice, we are told, is a deity. Yet rice is also 'the gift of self' and of course rice is consumed. Ohnuki-Tierney asks at the end of her chapter: 'Why kill a king whose role is to guarantee good crops of rice and who is not a repository of impurity?' But equally one might ask: why lay so much cultural emphasis on impurity; why make rice offerings; and why eat your gods? It seems to me that there is a greater tension between cultural exegesis and comparative explanation here than Ohnuki-Tierney's attack on Frazer allows for.

Tamari explores the connections between caste and kingship in a broad swathe of societies from Nigeria to Ethiopia and lays great emphasis on the process of diffusion. She is careful not to claim that there is an absolute causal relation between caste and kingship, but nevertheless shows convincingly that when the two institutions are found in the same community, they are symbiotically joined. Specialists, typically endogamous or nearly so, often have an important role in a king's installation or death ceremonies, or in legitimating his reign in some way. In the African situation, as in the Indian, there is a connection between kingship and untouchability: '[t]he relationships between kings and specialists are most intense precisely in the societies where the latter are subject to the severest segregation'. A number of specialisms recur again and again of which blacksmithing undoubtedly heads the list. Tamari makes several references to blacksmith kings whose status appears to have been transformed as a result of struggles between different kings, the ensuing encapsulation of one kingdom by another, and the process of state formation whereby groups of different origin are brought together in the same polity. Similarly, a number of other occupations frequently involve some kind of transformative activity – e.g. leatherworking, pottery, woodcarving – or an association with funerary ritual. Musicians of certain kinds are also typically segregated.

Whereas in India the whole society is conventionally regarded as being divided into castes, in the African case specialist castes typically form a small segment of the population. Another way of looking at this might be to regard the majority population as a very large caste – the 'kingly' caste in Indian communities is invariably a very large group and frequently the largest by a very significant margin. As in India, African caste involves restrictions on intermarriage and various kinds of avoidance behaviour, for example in relation to commensality.

Schnepel examines small jungle kingdoms in India whose populations contained a high percentage of tribal groups. He has a number of aims here. One is to show that these polities did not have fixed territories or even a fixed form of political organization. They were multi-centred and moved between acephalous and state-centred forms depending on a variety of circumstances, including the changing fortunes of the greater kingdoms around which they were organized. His observations have ramifications for the 'classical' anthropological theory of segmentary societies for they demonstrate that there is no clear boundary marking the end of an acephalous society and the beginning of a state society. Typically found in inhospitable locations which provided them with a good measure of autonomy, the jungle kingdoms of Orissa acted as buffer zones or as allies to the great kingdoms on the one hand, and as places of retreat for aspiring kings on the other. Study of these kingdoms also affords a means of studying various aspects of religious practice such as 'Sanskritization', and the nature of caste relations.

One must not gloss over the prosaic reasons for establishing kingdoms and Schnepel provides an alternative to de Heusch and Scubla on the ritual killing of kings. The foundation of jungle kingdoms is often linked to the ritual killing of a tribal chief in front of a goddess as a means of subordinating tribal peoples. Schnepel points out, for example, that many jungle kings began as traders who criss-crossed areas that tribal peoples did not, thus building up considerable power. Charismatic outsiders were sometimes able to settle tribal disputes in a way in which indigenes themselves could not. Superior military power facilitated this and was often absorbed in a religious manner with outside rulers establishing themselves as the patrons of local goddesses.

Lecomte-Tilouine puts the theme of transgression at the centre of her chapter, which compares the forms of kingship found in two different groups in Nepal: the Shahs – who rule to this day – and the Mallas – indigenous inhabitants of the Kathmandu Valley, long famed for its wonderful royal architecture, who were overrun by the Shahs in the second half of the eighteenth century. The first thing we notice about Hindu kingship, she says, is that it reverses the process that occurred at the beginning of the universe according to Hindu mythology. An initial sacrifice of a primeval god–man led to the creation of four kinds of human being with different functions. In his installation ceremony the Hindu king uniquely overrides this differentiation and is made to partake of all four kinds, thus establishing a new unity. But while this sets the king apart from all other human beings, he is, nevertheless, a human being and, as such, subject to pollution as other human beings are. Lecomte-Tilouine shows that the king contends with this situation by producing 'monstrous doubles' of himself who deal with impurity.

Much of Lecomte-Tilouine's discussion revolves around cultural transgressions in the connected institutions of royal funeral ritual and installation, the latter inevitably following from the former. For example, the Shah king should not see death and this leads to an anomalous situation because the incoming king takes no part in the mourning of his predecessor – whereas among Hindus generally all members of the patriline of the deceased are touched by death and are required to mourn publicly. The new king is thus doubly detached – from his kin, and from normal pollution. Perhaps more striking is a further anomaly, which is created by the employment of a Brahman priest who is degraded by consuming some part of the dead king. This priest is subsequently dressed up in the dead king's clothes and ritually expelled from the kingdom. It would be hard to come up with a category that more confounds caste divisions than 'a monstrous untouchable brahmanic king' who is desacralized and socially killed by his expulsion.

Drucker-Brown recalls Valeri's thesis that sacred kingship is 'the first stage in the emergence of a type of polity antithetical to kinship' because the fraternal ideal of amity is undermined by exploitation and violence. She and others point out that African kingship is commonly associated with 'confrontations of diverse people' – another manifestation of the inadequacy of kinship once a certain kind of political organization is required. Paradoxically, however, the king's role is to be related to everyone else and this 'kin-like status' may be an aspect of his capacity to resolve conflict among unrelated groups.

This leads to the very tricky question of the demarcation of kingdoms from states. No one offers a satisfactory solution to this, and it is difficult to avoid asking whether one could ever produce a hard and fast set of criteria for delineating these two political forms. Clearly there has been an irreversible historical movement in favour of the state. For a number of the contributors in this volume, this movement appears to originate in a splitting of the king's function. Scubla puts this best: 'Kingship is an unstable compound which tends to break apart into its component elements in order to stabilize … Everything happens as if political power emerges thanks to an internal dynamic in the system of kingship, which leads it towards a more stable state through the separation, and balanced deployment of its constituent elements.'

Claessen, drawing on a wide survey of Polynesian sources, is the most hostile to a view of kingship which deals exclusively in ritual and symbolism and indeed opens his account with a definition of 'king' which many of the other contributors would take issue with: 'a king is the supreme, hereditary ruler of an independent stratified society, having the legitimate power to enforce decisions'. Claessen is, of course, the master comparative historian of the early state and throughout his article there seems to be little distinction between the kingdom and the early state, though he acknowledges that they are not the same thing. Using the neo-evolutionist work of Service and others as a platform, Claessen is concerned to distinguish kings from headmen and chiefs rather than to see kingship as a quality that might be found wherever political functions are made sacred. That said, he acknowledges that in Polynesia the kinship structure (i.e. kinship, not kingship), whereby everyone's position was determined with reference to primogeniture and seniority, was coupled with another principle whereby chiefly lines were sacralized and, as elsewhere, this was tied to a notion of guaranteeing fertility, plentiful harvests and the welfare of all.

In contrast to many of the other contributions, Claessen ties his argument to demography. Kings were not found in the small Polynesian island societies, he writes, because 'except for some ritual activities, there were no tasks for which a leader was needed'. In the Marquesas, lack of a surplus – either because of poor soil, or climate, or because of constant warfare that destroyed crops – rendered impossible the emergence of a kingship tied to a guarantee of fertility. In the Samoan islands, by contrast, food production was plentiful but the population density remained low for reasons that are unclear. But the outcome was that 'the emergence of a complex, well-functioning sociopolitical system [was] unnecessary … the development of kingship … is a matter of sociopolitical scale'.

Interestingly, mirroring the ethnography from other regions of the world, Claessen finishes his account by pointing out that in the two areas of his discussion where kingship (in his terms) was most developed, ritual and political tasks were separated. In Tahiti a high priest 'took over' many of the ritual tasks while in the Tongan Islands the 'ruler' concentrated on ritual duties and his worldly obligations were 'handed over' to other functionaries.

This splitting of the royal function is a prominent theme in the African ethnography on kingship and is strictly paralleled in the Indian case. Kings cannot be priests (or ministers) and priests cannot be kings. Kings are made by priests, who represent both the people and some divine or transcendent force: 'The tenant cannot, by legal or moral or by religious prerogative, take possession of his office by his own unilateral action. Office is conferred by functionaries who do not and, often, may not, legitimately hold it themselves.' (Fortes 1968: 8). If kings could be priests and vice versa, this would result in terrible confusion since it might become possible to install oneself; kingship would become internalized in one individual and would no longer represent the society. Office is a question of legitimacy, and this is always a matter of consent, of sharing with the people, even – perhaps especially – in those cases where kings appear to be particularly remote from commoners. Similarly, the confusion of king and priest would introduce the possibility of being unable to channel one's inauspicious qualities to someone else, thus rendering impossible the purification of the kingship. A kind of bridge to the separation of functions between kings and priests is that the kingship is itself sometimes bifurcated with one figure held to represent the auspicious, life-giving forces while another figure represents sterility and violent, war-making forces. As Scubla puts it, '[k]ingship is always double, with a good face and a bad face, a positive aspect and a negative aspect'.

This splitting of functions reaches its apogée in caste organization, variants of which are reported from many parts of the world, as the chapters by Ohnuki-Tierney and Tamari, as well as my own, make clear. Castes are groups whose members regard themselves as fundamentally different from each other because of a combination of who they are descended from and the ritual functions that some of their members perform either for members of the noble caste or for the society as a whole. What they mean by this is that they think that their descent makes them in some fundamental way different from people who do not share their descent – as different as different species are. And in the same way that different species cannot mate, so too should different 'species' of people avoid each other. This preoccupation with difference leads to a pervasive concern with the possibility of being 'polluted' by contact with members of other groups. It is revealing that this highly structured system of differentiation owes so much to kingship and, as in the Africanist literature, a concern with the prevention of chaos. In my own chapter, which explores one of the most striking features of caste organization – untouchability – I attempt to illustrate how caste and kingship intertwine and how the same ambiguity – of belonging yet being set apart – is central to both.

If we compare modern kingship with its traditional counterpart, it would appear that the rupture of the heavily ritualized association between the 'exemplary centre' and a generalized sense of social well being is at the core of the predicament faced by monarchy in the world today. Where kingship is genuinely indispensable, the scapegoating mechanism that is at its core acts to protect and rejuvenate the kingship when an individual king fails in health or deed. In modern democracies, however, there are many other possible exceptional figures to choose among as convenient scapegoats for society's ills. The scapegoating of contemporary royal figures thus no longer serves to reinvigorate the kingship, but to underline the marginality of their ritual contribution to society's welfare and to the other symbolic devices of political legitimation. Since scapegoating is essential to political life, and indeed to culture generally, *some* scapegoat mechanism remains an intrinsic element of modern political systems. But we all know that this mechanism no longer needs to attach to kingship with all its regalia. The more that some insist that it must do so the more ridiculous monarchy appears. The members of contemporary royal families who are caught up in this historical metamorphosis face an impossible dilemma. On the one hand, they need to set themselves apart in order to be identified as regal. On the other hand, should they differentiate themselves in any situation outside of those where their political role is strictly required, they invite savage ridicule for failing to recognize and accept that this role is now severely reduced.

That the role of kings is now greatly diminished does not mean that it has become wholly negligible, or that the political institutions which have swallowed up the most important functions of monarchy have done so successfully, or could do. Following India's independence in 1947 and the dissolution of the princely states, caste organization, with its system of devices for expelling whatever inauspicious forces threatened the kingship, continued to thrive everywhere that Hindus predominated, if in a somewhat mutated state. The supreme figureheads had gone, but the institution of kingship was retained through the practices that had always bound members of patron castes to those who made their patronage legitimate.

The paradoxes of political legitimation will always persist and for many people monarchy clearly provides a solution to these paradoxes, the only transcendent solution that they can imagine. If they are deluded, the symbolic devices of kingship provide good reason for their delusion. As the papers in this volume make clear again and again, symbolism is not *merely* symbolic.

Notes

1. The quote is attributed to the United Kingdom's Prince Charles in the London *Sunday Times*, 24 March 2002, News, p. 11.
2. In democratic countries at the end of the twentieth century, there appears to be some attempt at removing these restrictions by certain royal figures who aspire to 'move with the times'. Examples include: riding bicycles in public and dining in restaurants with 'ordinary' people – as British journalists, who are sometimes incredulous regarding this informality, have reported from the Netherlands and Spain respectively in recent years. Just how far one can extend this process of liberation from royal restriction and remain royal is an interesting question. One can of course go too far – as the Duchess of York discovered. Her removal from the royal circle is hardly likely to be repealed.
3. An excellent series of bibliographies on kingship can be found in J.-Cl. Galey (ed.) (1990) *Kingship and the Kings*, Chur, Switzerland and London: Harwood Academic Press.
4. See Fortes (1968) for an analysis of the different stages in installation ceremonies.
5. See especially Frazer (1978 [1922]) and Hocart (1969 [1927]), (1970 [1936]). Kantorowicz (1957) is often drawn upon by historians, but his impact on anthropologists is limited – though see Schnepel (1995).
6. The CNRS team studying systems of thought in black Africa (published as 'Systèmes de pensée en Afrique noire' – has produced some of the finest work. De Heusch (1997) is a good place to start with this literature; it contains a strong neo-Frazerian argument and cites a number of the most important works of this CNRS team.
7. See, for example, Marcus (1980), Raheja (1988) and Quigley (1993). For a useful summary of Hocart's material on kingship, see Schnepel (1988).

8. I have argued in Quigley (1993) that Hocart's approach provides the basis for the most satisfactory explanation of caste.
9. See also Scubla's footnote no. 22, p. 60 in this volume where he refers to 'the founding murder and the rites which repeat it'.
10. By insisting on the symbolic nature of scapegoating, I do not in any way wish to trivialise those cases where scapegoating leads to death. However, even in those cases where scapegoats are actually killed, they must first be killed symbolically, to be made to appear as if they do not belong to society in the same way as everybody else. It is a fine line between regarding this 'not belonging' as a matter of awe and respect and regarding it as a matter of complete disrespect.
11. On the transformative nature of ritual, see, for example, van Gennep (1909); Goody (ed.) (1966); Bloch & Parry (eds) (1982); Cannadine & Price (eds) (1987).

References

Bloch, M. & Parry, J. (eds) 1982. *Death and the Regeneration of Life*. Cambridge: Cambridge University Press.

Cannadine, D. & Price, S. (eds) 1987. *Rituals of Royalty. Power and Ceremonial in Traditional Societies*. Cambridge: Cambridge University Press.

Drucker-Brown, S. 1992. 'Horse, Dog and Monkey: The Making of a Mamprusi King'. *Man* (NS) 27: 71–90.

Evans-Pritchard, E. E. 1962 [1948]. 'The Divine Kingship of the Shilluk of the Nilotic Sudan'. Frazer Lecture, reprinted in *Essays in Social Anthropology*. London: Faber & Faber.

Fortes, M. 1968. 'Of Installation Ceremonies', *Proceedings of the British Academy, 1967*. London: British Academy.

Frazer, J. G. 1978 [1922]. *The Golden Bough*. London: Macmillan

Galey, J-Cl. (ed.) 1990. *Kingship and the Kings*. Chur, Switzerland and London: Harwood Academic Press.

Geertz, C. 1980. *Negara: The Theater State in Nineteenth-Century Bali*. Princeton, NJ: Princeton University Press.

Girard, R. 1988 [1972]. *Violence and the Sacred*. London: Athlone Press.

Goody, J. (ed.) 1966. *Succession to High Office*. Cambridge: Cambridge University Press.

Heusch L. de 1982. *Rois nés d'un coeur de vache*. Paris: Gallimard.

—— 1997. 'The Symbolic Mechanisms of Sacred Kingship: Rediscovering Frazer', *Journal of the Royal Anthropological Institute* 3(2): 213–32.

Hocart, A. M. 1950 [1938]. *Caste: A Comparative Study*. London: Methuen.

—— 1954. *Social Origins*. London: Watts (1954).

—— 1969 [1927]. *Kingship*. Oxford: Oxford University Press.

—— 1970 [1936]. *Kings and Councillors: An Essay in the Comparative Anatomy of Human Society*, edited by R. Needham. Chicago: University of Chicago Press.

Kantorowicz, E. 1957. *The King's Two Bodies*. Princeton, NJ: Princeton University Press.

Marcus G. E. 1980. *The Nobility and the Chiefly Tradition in the Modern Kingdom of Tonga*. Wellington: Polynesian Society.

Quigley, D. 1993. *The Interpretation of Caste*. Oxford: Clarendon Press.

—— 2000. 'Scapegoats: the Killing of Kings and Ordinary People', *Journal of the Royal Anthropological Institute* 6(2): 237–54.

Raheja, G. G. 1988. 'India: Caste, Kingship, and Dominance Reconsidered', *Annual Review of Anthropology* 17: 497–522.

Schnepel, B. 1988. 'In Quest of Life: Hocart's Scheme of Evolution from Ritual Organization to Government', *European Journal of Sociology* XXIX: 165–87.

—— 1995. *Twinned Beings: Kings and Effigies in Southern Sudan, Orissa, and Renaissance France*. Gothenburg: Institute for Advanced Studies in Social Anthropology.

Scubla, L. 2002. 'Hocart and the Royal Road to Anthropological Understanding', *Social Anthropology* 10(3): 359–76.

Van Gennep, A. 1909. *Les Rites de passage*. Paris: Picard.

–2–

Forms of Sacralized Power in Africa

Luc de Heusch

Introduction

A great number of African societies – regardless of whether they are large or small, cover a vast kingdom or a modest chiefdom, or are organized into some sort of state – display a form of politico-religious power whose main features are remarkably constant.[1] They emerge from the same logic in various places and at different moments in history. The symbolic mechanism evolved – in circumstances unknown to us, and recorded only in myth – in very different cultures in western, as well as central and southern Africa. Most often, although not always, it assumes the political form of kingship, a form which has its own history and cannot be explained simply as the outcome of military conquest. Its constituting principles are of a ritual nature, and can be found in small societies with neither centralized power nor military ambitions. I will place my remarks in the tradition of Hocart, and more particularly of Frazer, while disassociating myself from the evolutionist perspective in which the latter pursued his exploration of the origins of kingship. But Frazer must be given credit for having drawn attention to an extraordinary phenomenon: that in Africa and other parts of the world there exists a remarkable category of political leaders whose power depends on the mystical control which they are believed to exert over nature (Frazer 1911).

Frazer was mistaken in calling this institution 'divine kingship'. The king is not assimilated with a divinity in traditional black Africa as he was in ancient Egyptian civilization, which presents a variant type of sacred kingship that can be found elsewhere in the Middle East. In black Africa, it would be truer to say that through a special ritual of investiture, a particular person, whose political power varies enormously, is endowed with a unique property, best understood by considering that the holder is transformed into a 'fetish-body'. I am aware of Mauss's injunction to eliminate the notion of fetishism from the vocabulary of anthropology (1969: 244–5). But must we sweep away the concept of 'fetish' with the same broom? The transformation by which a particular ritual sacralizes the body of a king comes into the category of those 'god-things' described by Bazin when referring to the Bambara *boli*: that is to say, 'those things which, in their sovereign, mute independence, refer only to themselves' (1986: 258). The efficacy of fetish objects, such as the *boli*, depends on the sacrifices that feed them and confer upon them their vital energy (Cissé 1985: 14). One sees, then, the originality of the royal fetish-body – a living person whose mystical capacity is closely tied to the integrity of his physical being.

Frazer's First Thesis

There are many examples of this fetish-body. The Jukun king (Nigeria) is the living source of agriculture, and hence is called 'our millet, our groundnuts, our beans'. He controls the rain and the wind (Meek 1931: 129–30). He possesses a particularly powerful magical charm, which is in fact a part of a former king's body. He is, moreover, supposed to nourish himself periodically by eating the heart of his predecessor. There is nothing banal about this connection with the ancestors. It makes for dynastic continuity and discontinuity at one and the same time: for if the king symbolically devours his predecessor (the full implications of which we will try to elucidate later), the latter is also able to threaten the life of his successor. In fact, the dignitaries in charge of the royal relics need only expose the skull or forearm of a former king to the sun in order to bring about the premature death of the reigning sovereign 'in spite of his divinity' (Meek 1931: 131–2). The fact that a sacred king belongs to a legitimate dynasty is not, therefore, sufficient to establish the sacrality of his power.

The Lovedu queen in southern Africa is the Earth itself, which overheats when she dies. She is able to act on nature's equilibrium through the manipulation of her precious 'rain-medicines'. She also co-operates with a rainmaker (Krige & Krige 1954: 63). She must enjoy robust health, and as she grows old, her mystical power, far from waning, is said to grow in strength.

The Kriges highlight the opposition between the apparent indifference of the Lovedu to the age of their sovereign, and the ideology of more northerly societies (the Karanga) whose dynasties are related to the Lovedu. Sovereigns among the Karanga must avoid all physical decay, at the risk of inflicting suffering on the entire country. This is undoubtedly an historical transformation. By saying that the body of the queen gains strength with age, surely what is intended is a reassurance that the general fertility of the kingdom, which depends upon her health, will not be threatened as she grows old. Remarkable too is the fact that she is not allowed to live out her days: she must commit suicide during the fourth session of the circumcision school, counting from the beginning of her reign (Krige & Krige 1954: 64).

Before examining the Frazerian thesis of regicide, let us be clear that the symbolism of sacred kingship does indeed provide a structurally ordered, coherent system, whatever its contingent manifestations. That the Lovedu sovereignty has a purely symbolic orientation can be ascertained by reading the Kriges' analysis. The 'queen of the rain' is neither a political leader nor a military chief. Regarded as masculine, she is the nucleus of a vast network of exchanges of women managed by her close relatives who rule in her name (de Heusch 1983). She herself is confined to the environs of her capital (Krige & Krige 1954: 64). Her function is essentially ritualistic.

It is difficult to defend the thesis, whether functionalist or Marxist, according to which such institutions are viewed as the superstructure of a hierarchized socio-economic order. The ritual function of the sacred king is sometimes radically divorced from the political order. This is certainly the case among the Nyakyusa of Tanzania. Wilson, who studied them, does not hesitate to refer to the Lwembe, that supreme moral authority and ritualist, as a 'divine king' (1959: 17–48). This eminent figure, who lived as a recluse, was said to guarantee the prosperity of the country because he was the seat of the power of growth: 'The Lwembe in his own person, and to a lesser degree his "sons" who are ordinary chiefs, are identified with the power of growth' (1959: 23). In his very body lay 'the power of making rain, food, milk and children'. This is why he was ritually strangled or buried alive when he fell gravely ill. Before being killed, fingernails and locks of hair were torn from the Lwembe's body. These precious relics were then buried in the mud of a river to maintain the prosperity of the country.

Here, then, the continuity of the sacred body was more important than the continuity of the dynasty as such: as among the Jukun, the ritual chief was chosen alternately from the two lineages descended from the eponymous ancestor Lwembe. The holder of this position was a genuine incarnation of Lwembe and the question of his divinity is worth considering. It is well known that Frazer insisted at length on a similar institution among the Shilluk of the Upper Nile, where the king was identified with the ancestor Nyikang. There are, then, several examples of the fetish-body revealing itself to us as a body that is 'ancestralized', if not deified.

The king's fetish-body is also capable of operating through his sexual life. The sexual activity of the Bemba king distributed his beneficence across the country, which he helps to 'reheat' (Richards 1968: 29). Richards argues prudently that this unique mystical property of the royal body compels us to look upon the function of the king as different from that of a high priest. Other aspects of Bemba kingship lead me to the same conclusion. Richards tells us that illnesses that afflicted the king bring equal harm to the country, as did his sufferings, pains, dreams, or lapses of behaviour (1968: 26). When the sovereign was in good health, he communicated 'life' (*bumi*) to the kingdom, and was responsible for rain, milk and children, as was the case among the Nyakyusa (1968: 31). To reduce the function of a sacred king to that of rainmaker would clearly be a distortion of Frazer's thesis and would prevent any new interpretation of the symbolic complex it portrays.

The relationship between the Bemba king and his ancestors hardly differs, it seems, from the relationship between his subjects and their ancestors. As is the case in every rite of succession, during his investiture he assumed the place of the dead ancestor he was supposed to replace (1968: 27). However, this link is so vital for the nation that the king was ritually strangled just before his natural death in order to prevent his spirits, whose beneficent influence extends to the whole country, from escaping his body with his final breath. Is this particular ideology incompatible with the Frazerian interpretation of regicide as Richards affirms? Nothing could be further from the truth. In the end, it is the power of giving life (*bumi*), inherent in the very body of the king that is recovered at the point of death. If the king's ancestors appear at times to be the ultimate source of the sacrality of power, the connection to them does not, of itself, explain this sacral quality.

In all the examples discussed so far, it has been necessary to avoid the natural death of the king and to impose on him a cultural end, as if the society sought to reappropriate control over the cosmic forces incarnated in him. Whatever the extent of his power, more often than not his freedom of movement is carefully controlled; the sacred king is always, in one way or another, the prisoner of the group, and his regime is one of curtailed liberty. The Jukun strangled their sovereign when he was gravely ill, but they justified this practice on very different grounds than the Bemba: to wit, that the dying king's groans should not be allowed to sow discord in the spirit of the people (Meek 1931: 127). Does this new interpretation run counter to the proposition at hand? I would argue, on the contrary, that the Jukun put the emphasis here on the social function of sacred kingship (the maintenance of group unity), while insisting strongly on the identification of the king with the power of growth (see above). Africanists know full well that the body of the royal personage is precisely the place where the natural order and the cultural order interconnect, safeguarding the equilibrium of the former and the harmony of the latter. It would be absurd to disassociate them.

In a remarkable book devoted to the sacred kingship of the Moundang of Chad, Adler forcefully demonstrates that the Frazerian thesis of regicide must be taken seriously in Africa. He has no doubts that the Moundang put their king, the master of the rain, to death at the end of a reign that could not exceed ten years. Adler regrets that the dominantly functionalist Anglo-Saxon perspective neglects the study of the sacralization of authority, 'reducing it to a means among others of imposing and consolidating a power essentially dependent on more constraining factors: ecology, demography, social morphology, the economy and structures of lineage and family' (Adler 1982: 262). The Shilluk sovereign, who was the guarantor of fertility, was ritually strangled by one of his sons once he began to show signs of impotence. Evans-Pritchard (1962) explained this on purely sociological grounds, regarding it as a variety of political assassination. He thus utterly rejected Frazer's interpretation, leaving unanswered 'the question of the royalty's symbolic efficacy' (Adler 1982: 266). Young had already shown that the Oxford don's interpretation was not applicable to Jukun kingship (1966). Muller (1980) forcefully countered Evans-Pritchard's thesis in his turn by examining the theme of the king as scapegoat in small Rukuba societies lacking any centralized political apparatus.

Frazer's Second Thesis

In a work dated 1919, and pertinently entitled 'The Scapegoat', Frazer begins by recalling that the king–god is sacrificed to prevent his physical decay from endangering nature's life force, of which he is the guardian. He then adds that the same personage, charged with the 'sins' and sufferings of the people, is sometimes entrusted with the mission of taking them away in the manner of a scapegoat. From then on, the interpretation becomes more complex and Frazer is unable to explain why these two different aspects of sacred kingship come to be fused in the same institution. I will show that this new paradigm is not so far removed from the earlier one.

While describing the small chiefdom of Rukuba (Nigeria), Muller recalls that the chief in every village is held responsible for major natural or social catastrophes. On these occasions, the chief runs the risk of being deposed 'for mystical incompetence' (1980: 160). In a later article, Muller holds that as a general rule the king or chief only acquires his sacred status at the cost of a transgression that radically transforms his very being. Only then does he become 'responsible both for the prosperity and for the major catastrophes that affect his people' (1990: 49). I myself have drawn attention on several occasions to the symbolic functions of royal incest which, in many Bantu kingdoms, cuts the sovereign off from the ordinary framework of kinship at the time of his investiture, and places him in an ambiguous zone where he is viewed as either a sacred monster or a dangerous sorcerer (see, for example, de Heusch 1997). Muller states that while this theme is absent from the ritual investiture of the Rukuba chiefs, one finds it in a surrogate form of 'dietary incest': cannibalism. In great secrecy, and without his being aware of it, the heir apparent eats the flesh of a newborn child of his clan (i.e. his own flesh). If he is strong enough, the newly installed chief will reign for a probationary period of seven years before being assured of a long life. But in three villages that enjoy a privileged status, a special ritual is staged every fourteen years. An old man representing the person of the chief is charged with impurity and expelled from the community. He is to die, at the latest, by the end of the seventh year to follow. Muller boldly compares this rite with the Jukun ethnography referred to above. He demonstrates brilliantly that the Rukuba and Jukun representations constitute a system and that each throws light upon the other, both being aspects of a system of transformations centring on the number seven. While they are not neighbours, the Rukuba and Jukun do live in the same geographical area and it is entirely possible that their histories overlap.

In theory the Jukun limited the reign of their sovereign to seven years. But at the end of this period, they submitted him to a ritual of regeneration, the *ando ku*, in the course of which the king was invited to kill a slave with his own hands. He was then symbolically reborn and authorized to rule for a further seven years. Muller makes a connection between this surrogate human victim and the old man who is expelled in Rukuba society. For seven years the latter takes upon himself the inauspicious aspects of kingship: he becomes, in other words, a scapegoat. In a sense, the living body of the leader becomes divided in two. For seven years, 'the good king reigns while the bad king haunts the environs of the village where he accumulates dirt and impurity' (Muller 1990: 60).

Ritual regicide clearly appears to be one of the symbolic foundations of sacred kingship. But as Frazer himself suggested, this central theme evolves on two levels. Sometimes the king is put to death because his physical enfeeblement threatens the universe and society; sometimes he is killed as a scapegoat. The Rukuba seem to have preferred the second option, the Jukun the first. It is noteworthy that the sacred leaders of the Rukuba, who are held responsible for catastrophes and for order of every kind, are not considered masters of nature in any sense. They do not even perform agricultural rites, which, significantly enough, are considered in this society to be the least 'weighty, the least profound' (Muller 1981: 193). Nor are they responsible for the rain. One of the clan leaders intervenes when there is a drought or flood, but he is considered a ritualist of secondary importance. The Jukun, on the other hand, stress the primary function of kingship, the one that corresponds to Frazer's first thesis. They identify their king with the crops they cultivate. But he is also treated as a scapegoat when necessary. In spite of the *ando ku*, he was secretly put to death in the event of a succession of bad harvests or droughts (Meek 1931: 130). These disasters were attributed to the sovereign's negligence or to a weakening of his mystical force. In this case, the first function of sacred kingship prevails while the second is latent. The reverse is true of the Rukuba, who only invoke the responsibility of the sacred chief when there is a natural disaster. Here I rejoin Muller's conclusion, but by another route.

Muller's analyses of the king as scapegoat appear all the more apposite in that they take into account little village chiefdoms (such as those of the Rukuba in Nigeria), and put them on the same footing as those greater political entities we call 'kingdoms' – which would be the category applicable to the Jukun. One must recall here that Frazer did not associate his 'divine king' with centralized forms of government as others have done on numerous occasions.

It is remarkable that the sacralization of power as I have defined it is found elsewhere in western and central Africa, in small societies lacking any state structure.

Frazer's first thesis as concerning the 'divine king' is most salient to the Samo of Burkina Faso. They entrust to a 'rain chief' the task of mastering the heavenly waters vital to the fertility of their arable fields on the one hand, and that of ensuring village and inter-village peace on the other. According to Héritier-Izard,

> The common good is essentially rain, harmony, and the absence of misfortune. It is embodied in a figure – the *lamutyiri* or *tyiri* – whose responsibility is burdensome and costly ... he 'gathers together' or 'upholds' the village in the sense of maintaining the cohesion of juxtaposed elements ... everything rests with him, everything is expected of him; it is upon his 'head', be it good or bad, that depends the coming of the rains. (Héritier-Izard 1973: 127)

The *tyiri* belongs to a specific lineage, from which he is literally uprooted during his early childhood. Ideally they choose a child yet to be born, although this rule is not always adhered to in practice. For seven years his responsibilities are assumed by a relative of the defunct *tyiri*. At the end of this period, 'the child is immobilized, dressed in the emblematic clothes of his charge, his head is shaved for the first time' (Héritier-Izard 1973: 128). Until he is able to assume his functions, they will be exercised by his father, who will observe many of the numerous interdictions that come with them. These interdictions, which vary from village to village, 'have in common that they make apparent the individual's exceptional, solitary and dangerous status, and the fact that he is cut off from everyday life' (Héritier-Izard 1973: 128). The sacred chief here is literally the prisoner of the group that invests him with power; he is supposed to have been 'caught, and tied', he is treated as 'garbage'. He exercises no authority, it is the group that inflicts its violence upon him: 'one makes of him, and his unwilling body, a sacred figure' (Héritier-Izard 1973: 128). The socioreligious order is assured by the complementarity of the rain chief and the earth chief.

The Samo have neither state nor chiefdom properly speaking. And yet the institution of *tyiri* presents the most important ritual characteristics of sacred kingship, as Adler (1977: 56) observed. That this function is primordial – and even primal – is clearly attested in the little Lovedu kingdom in southern Africa (Krige & Krige 1943). The state machine here, as we have seen, is in the hands of the close relations of the queen. Her only function is to control the rain, just like the *tyiri* of the Samo. She must be without physical infirmities, and her emotions can influence the rain, just as the good or bad mood of the *tyiri* can.

Sacred kingship cannot, therefore, be considered as the superstructure of a centralized society serving to express the symbolic unity of a state composed of different populations. It is true none the less that this institution is generally linked to the existence of a state and acts to reinforce its cohesion. I would even go so far as to suggest that the sacralization of power is one of the important constituent elements in the birth of the state.

The Samo *tyiri* is surrounded with interdictions, just as a king is. But more often than not, kings are at least partially freed from the hindrances that the Samo seem to enjoy heaping upon the *tyiri*, who is in the service of those who have chosen him. When a state forms around this ritual nucleus of sacralized power that is the monarchy – in short, when a king becomes sovereign – men become its (i.e. the state's) subjects. This in no way eliminates the burden of the interdictions that remain the price of the assumption of power. Royal sacrality may even veer into sorcery.

Kingship and Sorcery

Among the Bolia in the Democratic Republic of the Congo, the royal genealogy included no fewer than thirty-eight sovereigns (Sulzman 1959, Gilliard 1925, van Everbroeck 1961). Four dynastic lineages were at the head of one province. They assumed the functions of kingship by turn. In each one of these groups, several pretenders to the throne would come forward. At night, they were supposed to undergo a series of magical tests in order to be invested. Ancestors appeared to them in dreams, and took them before the master of the spirits of nature, Mbomb'Ipoku. To reach his subterranean dwelling, candidates had to walk on a long slippery tree trunk with the risk of falling into an abyss. The pact entered into with this great genie was the essential factor in their sacred power. The candidate had to deliver to the master of the supernatural world a certain number of human victims, chosen from among his relations. This master of the spirits of nature mixed only with the big chiefs, who themselves only came into contact with him once in their lives: at the moment of their initiation. They then maintained more familiar relations with lower ranking spirits, who were their 'wives'.

Bolia royalty is therefore built upon a massive incursion into the shadowy world of sorcery – not an unusual phenomenon in central Africa. Several times throughout my investigations, I had occasion to observe the singular links between the royal function and sorcery – that negative and destructive side of magic. In the words of Vansina, the Teke royalty in Congo-Brazzaville was 'the epitome of sorcery' (Vansina 1973: 378). The king of the Kuba (Democratic Republic of the Congo), who is supposed to exercise his mystical powers for the greatest good of his kingdom, also has the power to turn himself into a leopard to wreak vengeance on his enemies. The leopard is at once the symbol of royalty and of sorcery (Vansina 1964: 98–116). The Bolia king, whose initiation is an act that qualifies as sorcery (*iloki*), is no less mystically responsible for the general prosperity than his Kuba and Tyo counterparts.

Conclusion

The sacralization of power can be considered as an ideological revolution of a magico-religious order if one observes that it implies that the person who is its object symbolically denies the order of family and lineage, or finds himself a stranger to it. Throughout my first studies in this domain, I was struck by the violation of the laws of exogamy that is fundamental to this order. A Kuba king loses all ties to his clan at the moment of his enthronement. He may have sexual relations with a sister and marry a niece – i.e. women of his own clan – in defiance of exogamous practice. There are other forms of transgression: I have mentioned one in passing – murder by sorcery (Bolia). Muller raises another form of transgression, which he calls 'dietary incest' – the cannibalistic ritual of transgression that the Rukuba chief performs when he acquires his sacred status (Muller 1990).

Sacred kingship, then, appears to require a symbolic rupture with the domestic order. It designates a person who is out of the ordinary, out of place, potentially dangerous, whose power over nature is appropriated by the group, even as it condemns him to a quasi-sacrificial death. To say, as does René Girard, that this institution is 'a mechanism for converting sterile and contagious violence into culturally positive values' is an utter misapprehension of the role of scapegoat that the king is often made to assume (Girard 1972: 155). It is to forget too readily that the primary function of this symbolic machination is to 'gear down' the vital forces by means of an artifice that can only be understood as a sort of cultural and supernatural gearing system for promoting fecundity and fertility. In every case I examined, the king was forbidden to see the spilling of blood. This is why his personal participation in war is often forbidden, even when engaging in warfare would be to his profit. If the sacred king is an ambiguous, ambivalent, creature, divorced from culture and placed, paradoxically, at the centre of the social order, it is because he bears a crushing responsibility for the natural order, as Frazer understood so well. In a certain number of cases, the royal body can be used to this end, as long as it is perfect, intact or in full possession of its genetic powers. In other cases, this mechanism must be replaced by another after an arbitrarily fixed period unless a surrogate sacrifice provides the indispensable regeneration.

The Swazi conception of royalty in southern Africa is of this second type. Every year, at the time of the austral summer solstice, the naked king, proclaimed the 'bull of the nation', sits on the head bull of the herd, which has been thrown to the ground, after another animal, stolen from an ordinary man, has been hammered with blows and sacrificed (Kuper 1947). The sun king takes charge of the 'stain' that has accumulated in the kingdom during the past year and which threatens its very existence. Various ritual accessories, notably the remains of the sacrificed bullock, will be burnt on a great pyre lit by the sovereign in person on the last day of the ritual. A violent and beneficial rain will soon come and extinguish it. To conclude, as does René Girard, that the entire institution of sacred royalty was 'devised' solely in order to enable the Swazi nation to discharge upon the king its constitutive violence is an arbitrary and unverifiable affirmation. It would seem to miss the main point: the function of cosmic regeneration inherent in this annual ritual, where the king 'outstrips the sun in a race', as the Swazi themselves affirm.

Even if a king reigns thanks to the violence of war, the symbolic system of the kingship is fundamentally oriented towards the conservation of life. Hocart was not mistaken when he affirmed the ritual nature of the royalty in this 'life-giving' way (1927). Our studies have been directed solely at the vast African continent. But Toffin (1990:133) has underlined that the analyses of Hocart 'are still of great pertinence today and throw light on a number of ethnographic phenomena in South Asia'. And Quigley's work (2000) points in the same direction. Hocart was mistaken only in that he, like Frazer, adopted the evolutionist perspective. We may also pay tribute to Le Goff, who, in his preface to a new edition of *Les rois thaumaturges*, congratulated Marc Bloch for inaugurating 'a history of power that is not cut off from its ritual base ... a renewed political history: an historical political anthropology' (Le Goff 1983: XXXVIII).

The power of a state apparatus gives a new face to the sacred chief once he becomes the sovereign of a stratified society. It is doubtless in this perspective that we should consider the true deification of the sovereign as it occurred in ancient unified Egypt. The divine king deserves to be considered as a new structural transformation of the sacred king figure. Whereas this last acquires his status only through a transgression that sometimes projects him to the frontier between magic and sorcery, the pharaoh was equal to a god. However, every thirty years he had to perform a grand ritual, the *sed*, that 'mimicked a veritable rebirth of the king, his rejuvenation, his renewal' (Derchain 1962: 71). It was repeated at progressively shorter intervals for Ramses II during the last years of his life, 'for the injection of vitality became ever more necessary as the king grew older' (Derchain 1962). I would even venture to compare the Egyptian *sed* to the *ando ku* ritual, through which the vital force of the Jukun king was regenerated every seven years by virtue of the substitute sacrifice of a slave (Muller 1990). Obviously I intend to draw no historical connection. The Jukun king was the centre of all germination; the pharaoh was responsible for the cosmic order. But unlike the pharaoh, the Jukun king was not a god. 'One designated [the king of Egypt] by the same name *nir* [god], as Thot, Atoum, Amoun or Osiris, denoting ... that the pharaoh could deal with the other gods as one among equals, and cause them to act in a manner favourable to the nation' (Derchain 1962: 69). One may thus better understand why it seems to me an error to classify the African royal figures we have been considering as 'divine' in the Anglo-Saxon sense inherited from Frazer.

Divine kingship seems to characterize only a certain number of civilizations that, like the Egyptian, associated the spectacular development of the state with the religious reinforcing of the sovereign's autocratic power, backed by a sacerdotal class possessing literacy. The importance of this in Egyptian society is well known. In the small Sumerian city-states, at the dawn of their entry into written history, the king was simply the 'great man', that is the priest, he who 'has possession, in the name of and on behalf of the divinity, not only of the land, but of all sorts of goods' (Finet 1962:75). Finet demonstrates well how this situation underwent radical change during the Assyrian conquest in the middle of the third millennium. Sargon of Akkad, who consolidated his power over all Mesopotamia from the Persian Gulf to the Mediterranean, proclaimed that he was himself a god. 'It is under the Akkad dynasty that, for the first time in the history of the Near East, we find in inscriptions the divine determinative before the names of sovereigns' (Finet 1962: 75). The Akkadian concept of the king–god takes root and spreads throughout the Sumerian cities at the time of the decline of the first Assyrian empire. 'It was then, under the third dynasty of Ur, that one of the favourite themes of glyptic art is born: tributes to the deified king' (Finet 1962: 76). We know that the successors of Alexander would borrow the same concept from the Middle East, and that Rome would adopt it in its turn at the time of the emperors.

Of course Christian and Muslim monotheism was opposed to the deification of emperors or caliphs, who had to content themselves with being God's lieutenants on earth. And, faced with the papacy, the kings of France could resort only to the quasi-ecclesiastic unction that confers upon the sovereign a dignity comparable to a bishop. The kings of France were the earthly auxiliaries of a divinity that was guarantor of their absolute power. A remarkable fact from an anthropological perspective is that this function conferred upon them the magical power to heal scrofula after coronation. We owe our understanding of this phenomenon to Marc Bloch's stunning book on the thaumaturgical kings (Bloch 1924).

Charles X was the last monarch to be anointed in Reims. One could not say with any certainty that the French Revolution completely abolished the sacrality of power by secularizing it; rather, its status was changed. After the quasi-sacrificial execution of citizen Louis Capet (formerly Louis XVI), the Convention decreed on 21 September 1792 that the Seal of State should represent France 'with the traits of a woman in antique dress, her right hand holding a pike surmounted by a Phrygian cap, or cap of Liberty, her left leaning on a pile of arms' (Levêque 1989: 374). A new female divinity is born: Patrie-Liberté. It is she, slightly dishevelled, that Delacroix paints in 1831; she would lead a new generation of revolutionaries to the Paris barricades. When, after the intervention of Napoleon III, who re-established a parody of empire, she reappears on the public scene, she takes on the traits of an appealing young woman, Marianne, whose smile brings French kingship to an end once and for all. In a few neighbouring countries, most of them Protestant, a king or queen is ritually exhibited at great ceremonies to an adoring public, who are enthralled and strangely excited. They no longer expect the smile to bring them prosperity, but are pleased to identify themselves with such figures, clad in their illusory fairy tale glitter. Here, the institution of royalty is but an empty shell.

Notes

English translation by A.B. West.

1. This chapter reproduces a part of my (1997) article on sacred kingship. I am grateful to the editors of the *Journal of the Royal Anthropological Institute* for their permission to include these passages in the present chapter, which considerably expands the argument.

References

Adler, A. 1977. 'Faiseurs de pluie, faiseurs d'ordre', *Libre* 2: 45–68.

—— 1982. *La mort et le masque du roi: la royauté des Moundang du Tchad*. Paris: Payoy.

Bazin, J. 1986. 'Retour aux choses-dieux', *Le temps de la réflexion* 7: 253–85.

Bloch, M. 1924. *Les Rois thaumaturges*. Strasbourg: Publications de la Faculté des Lettres de l'Université.

Cissé, Y. 1985. 'Les Nains et l'origine des boli de chasse chez les Malinké', in A. de Surgy (ed.) *Systèmes de pensée en Afrique noire*, vol. 8, *Fétiches, objets enchantés: mots réalisés*. Paris: CNRS.

Derchain, P. 1962. 'Le Rôle du roi d'Egypte dans le maintien de l'ordre cosmique', in L. de Heusch (ed.) *Le Pouvoir et le sacré*. Brussels: Université Libre.

Evans-Pritchard, E. E. 1962. 'The Divine Kingship of the Shilluk of the Nilotic Sudan', Frazer Lecture 1946, in *Essays in Social Anthropology*. New York: Faber

Everbroeck, N., van 1961. *Mbomb'Ipoku, le seigneur de l'abîme*, Tervuren: Annales du Musée.

Finet, A. 1962. 'Le Pouvoir et les dieux en Mésopotamie', in L. de Heusch (ed.) *Le Pouvoir et le sacré*. Brussels: Université Libre.

Frazer, J. 1911. 'The magic art and the evolution of kings', in *The Golden Bough*. London: Macmillan.

—— 1919. 'The scapegoat', in *The Golden Bough*. London: Macmillan.

Gilliard, L. 1925. 'Au lac Léopold II. Les Bolia. Mort et intronisation d'un grand chef', *Congo*, II: 223–39.

Girard, R. 1972. *La Violence et le sacré*. Paris: Grasset.

Héritier-Izard, F. 1973. 'La Paix et la pluie. Rapports d'autorité et rapport au sacré chez les Samo', *L'Homme* XIII(3): 121–38.

Heusch, L. de 1983. 'Du bon usage des femmes et des boeufs. Les transformations du mariage en Afrique australe', *L'Homme* XXIII(4): 5–32.

—— 1997. 'The Symbolic Mechanisms of Sacred Kingship: Rediscovering Frazer', *Journal of the Royal Anthropological Institute* 3(2): 213–32.

Hocart, A. M. 1927. *Kingship*. Oxford: Oxford University Press.

Krige, E. J. & Krige, J. D. 1943. *The Realm of a Rain Queen: A Study of the Pattern of the Lovedu Society*. Oxford: Oxford University Press.

—— 1954. 'The Lovedu of the Transvaal', in D. Forde (ed.) *African Worlds: Studies in the Cosmological Ideas and Social Values of African Peoples*. Oxford: Oxford University Press.

Kuper, H. 1947. *An African Aristocracy. Rank Among the Swazi*. Oxford: Oxford University Press.

Le Goff, J. 1983. 'Introduction', in M. Bloch, *Les Rois thaumaturges*, pp. i–xxxviii, Paris: Gallimard.

Levêque, P. 1989. 'Les Français et le pouvoir politique. Institutions et participation (de 1789 à nos jours)', in A. Buguière et J. Revel (eds) *Histoire de la France*. vol. 2 *L'Etat et les pouvoirs*, pp. 361–488. Paris: Le Seuil.

Mauss, M. 1969. *Oeuvres complètes*, vol. 2. Paris: Editions de Minuit.

Meek, C. K. 1931. *A Sudanese Kingdom: An Ethnographical Study of the Jukun Peoples of Nigeria*. London: Kegan Paul.

Muller, J.-C. 1980. *Le Roi bouc émissaire: pouvoirs et rituels chez les Rukuba en Nigeria Central*. Paris: L'Harmattan.

—— 1981. 'Entre le sept et l'indéterminé: rites agraires rukuba', *Anthropology and Society* 5: 191–214.

—— 1990. 'Transgression, rites de rejeunisssement et mort culturelle chez les Jukun (Nigeria Central), in L. de Heusch (ed.) *Systèmes de pensée en Afrique noire*, vol. 10, *Chefs et rois sacrés*. Paris: CNRS.

Quigley, D. 2000. 'Scapegoats: The Killing of Kings and Ordinary People, *Journal of the Royal Anthropological Institute* 6(2): 237–54.

Richards, A. I. 1968. 'Keeping the King Divine', *Proceedings of the Royal Anthropological Institute*, 1966.

Sulzman, E. 1959. 'Die bikopo-Herrchaft de Bolia', *Archiv für Rechts-und Sozialphilosophie* 55: 389–417.

Toffin, G. 1990. 'Hiérarchie et ideologie du don dans le monde indien', *L'Homme* 114: 130–40.

Vansina, J. 1964. *Le Royaume Kuba*. Tervuren: Musée Royal de l'Afrique Centrale.

—— 1973. *The Tio Kingdom of the Middle Congo*. Oxford: Oxford University Press.

Wilson, M. 1959. *Communal Rituals of the Nyakyusa*. Oxford: Oxford University Press.

Young, M. W. 1966. 'The Divine Kingship of the Jukun: A Reevaluation of Some Theories', *Africa* xxxvi, 2, 135–53.

Sacred King, Sacrificial Victim, Surrogate Victim *or* Frazer, Hocart, Girard

Lucien Scubla

Introduction

Erudition is not the same thing as science. As A. M. Hocart used to say, science does not consist in accumulating facts, but in finding ways of sifting through the mass of facts. The following chapter in theoretical anthropology is faithful to this idea. It does not add either to the ethnography of kingship or to the history of ideas on the subject. No new facts are presented. What I present is an attempt to understand the institution better. There is no survey of theories of kingship here. Instead I set out a selection of convergent and complementary hypotheses. I do not offer empirical proof of these hypotheses and their implications, but rather certain unifying principles from which they can be derived.[1]

In the field of kingship we risk being overcome by the weight of facts already gathered by ethnographers and historians. But the means whereby we might make sense of this material is already available. This is all I wish to demonstrate in this chapter. It is possible to produce a more general and complete theory, but this would demand more elaboration than I have space for here.

In the Beginning there was Frazer: Sacred Kingship and Regicide

Sir James Frazer constructed his theory of sacred kingship around two fundamental ideas. The first is a matter of fact. Kingship is not a discretionary power, but a heavy responsibility which almost always leads to the killing of the incumbent. The second idea is a brilliant intuition. The strange kingship of the grove of Nemi is not an isolated phenomenon. It is a condensation of the entire system of monarchy and the key to its interpretation.

These two themes of *The Golden Bough* are well known but still merit our close attention. Let us briefly recall, for each of them, some essential points. First, the 'burden' of royalty. The accumulated ethnographic and historical facts show that kingship is not, in principle, political power. It is an onerous ritual duty which results, more often than not, in the killing of the king. To reign does not mean to govern or to give orders, but to guarantee the order of the world and of the society by observing ritual prescriptions. The king is a sacred figure, but for this very reason he is 'bound' by the ritual. Under house arrest and a recluse in his palace, he submits to the same type of restrictions as those who are in a state of impurity: menstruating women, warriors who are tainted by death and criminals. He is like someone condemned to death who is awaiting execution. Regicide is not accidental: it is an integral element of the institution of kingship.

This is how Frazer summarized his findings:

> The idea that early kingdoms are despotisms in which the people exist only for the sovereign, is wholly inapplicable to the monarchies we are considering. On the contrary, the sovereign in them exists only for his subjects; his life is only valuable so long as he discharges the duties of his position by ordering the course of nature for his people's benefit. So soon as he fails to do so, the care, the devotion, the religious homage which they had hitherto lavished on him cease and are changed into hatred and contempt; he is dismissed ignominiously, and may be thankful if he escapes with his life. Worshipped as a god one day, he is killed as a criminal the next. But in this changed behaviour of the people there is nothing capricious or inconsistent. On the contrary, their conduct is entirely of a piece. If their king is their god, he is or should be also their preserver; and if he will not preserve them, he must make room for another who will. So long, however, as he answers their expectations, there is no limit to the care which they take of him, and which they compel him to take of himself. A king of this sort lives hedged in by a ceremonious etiquette, a network of prohibitions and observances, of which the intention is not to contribute to his dignity, much less to his comfort, but to restrain him from conduct which, by disturbing the harmony of nature, might involve himself, his people, and the universe in one common catastrophe. Far from adding to his comfort, these observances, by trammelling his every act, annihilate his freedom and often render the very life, which it is their object to preserve, a burden and sorrow to him. (Frazer 1994 [1890]: 138–9)

All of the research on kingship since the appearance of *The Golden Bough* corroborates this picture, and complements it with some additional features.[2] The king is not the master of the institution but its captive. Even if he is not always killed, he is nevertheless touched by death. For example, during the festival of the guinea fowl, the Moundang king is stripped and surrounded by his people, who are armed.[3] Sometimes a ritual substitute must die in the king's place, often in violent and ignominious circumstances – such as the Mossi king's horse which is beaten unconscious by court slaves.[4]

On the other hand, the explanation of these royal customs has hardly advanced since *The Golden Bough* appeared. The only notable 'progress' during recent decades has been the rehabilitation of Frazer in certain quarters after a long period in purgatory. Specialists in the understanding of royal ritual agree with his presentation of facts and with his ideas about the coherence of the institution of royalty. This coherence is not obvious. If the king is a sacred, or even divine, figure, it is not at all clear why his subjects should judge him and put him to death. In the passage from *The Golden Bough* above, Frazer writes of regicide as being a necessary, and almost commonplace, consequence of a sensible rule: '[i]f their king is their god, he is or should be also their preserver; and if he will not preserve them, he must make room for another who will' (1994 [1890]: 139). But in claiming to explain men's actions by their representations, he simply shifts the focus of the question. The sacred and the divine are not primitive facts from which one could deduce institutions. One must simultaneously make sense of actions and representations. I will return to this after completing the review of Frazer's principal ideas.

Let us turn now to 'the king of the grove'. Frazer is not the only person to have been intrigued by the strange ritual of Nemi, but he is the first to argue that by explaining it, we would be able to make sense of most myths and rituals. If *The Golden Bough* appears to be a huge detective novel whose aim is to resolve a tiny enigma, it is because the expected solution is supposed to illuminate all of the 'elementary forms of the religious life'. The peculiar monarchy of the sacred grove is not simply a 'reference rite' in the manner of the 'reference myth' of the bird spotter in Claude Lévi-Strauss's *Mythologiques*. It is not an arbitrary point of departure,[5] or just another term in a series whose members are structuralist transformations of each other. Here we are concerned with an archetypal model of all monarchical institutions, one which generates the entire royal system and its transformational avatars.

Frazer describes it in this way:

> In the sacred grove there grew a certain tree round which at any time of the day, and probably far into the night, a grim figure might be seen to prowl. In his hand he carried a drawn sword, and he kept peering warily about him as if at every instant he expected to be set upon by an enemy. Here was a priest and a murderer; and the man for whom he looked was sooner or later to murder him and hold the priesthood in his stead. Such was the rule of his sanctuary. A candidate for the priesthood could only succeed to office by slaying the priest, and having slain him, he retained office till he was himself slain by a stronger or craftier [sic].
>
> The post which he held by this precarious tenure carried with it the title of king; but surely no crowned head ever lay uneasier, or was visited by more evil dreams, than his. For year in year out, in summer and winter, in fair weather and in foul, he had to keep his lonely watch ... (Frazer 1994 [1890]: 11–12)

As can be seen, the king of the grove is truly a singular figure. He brings together traits and functions which are normally kept apart: those of the murderer and the king; of the king and the priest; of the sacrificer and the sacrificial victim – since the putting to death of the king is a ritual act; and finally, of king and slave – since the incumbent was a fugitive slave who owed his new status to robbing his predecessor of his position (Frazer 1981 [1911]: 20).

The ritual itself achieves maximum compactness by uniting in a single act the regicide which ends one reign and the installation ceremony which inaugurates a new reign. The king is dead, long live the king. One could not have found a better way to mark the continuity of the institution of royalty despite death, and indeed because of it.

The kingship of Nemi may appear to be a marginal rite in relation to Roman religion, but it is the most stable of the institutions of the Latin world, having only disappeared, it seems, with the fall of the Empire (Frazer 1981 [1911]: 19, note 2). Like mathematical singularities, it concentrates properties that are generally disjoined and in this way constitutes the germ of many variations on the same theme that are deployed in a multitude of institutions. This is the reason that resolving the enigma of Nemi and constructing a general theory of kingship are really one and the same thing.

Within the framework he set himself, Frazer appears to fail to elucidate fully either the mystery of Nemi or the institutions surrounding it (1981–84 [1911]: 5). As is known, he proposed two theories regarding the enigma of the condemned king, but did not manage to combine them in any satisfactory manner. According to the first theory, the king represents the forces of nature and is the guarantor of general prosperity. He must be killed because, once his health begins to decline, he risks harming those around him. According to the second theory, the king is a scapegoat who takes upon himself all the evils which might afflict the group. In this case, he must be put to death in order to purify the people whenever their safety requires it. Frazer believes that these two explanations of regicide are complementary rather than alternatives, and that the former was more crucial than the latter. Hence the order in which the two hypotheses appear in *The Golden Bough*, the respective space that they occupy (at least on a first reading), and the efforts made by Frazer to graft the second hypothesis on to the first. But his demonstration is far from perfect and has not convinced the majority of his readers. Neither the respective weight of the hypotheses nor their compatibility are clearly established by Frazer.

Things have not progressed much since Frazer's death. However, the descriptions of sacred kingship accumulated by specialists have clarified one point which would only have been seen if one had read *The Golden Bough* very attentively. They show that the king is primarily, and not secondarily, a scapegoat. This is shown particularly clearly in the recent work of de Heusch and Quigley.[6] Here I would like to take this idea further and make its theoretical consequences more explicit.

Let us examine Frazer's two theories from the point of view of their respective coherence. The first theory has an unfortunate characteristic which is little remarked upon, but which is a fatal drawback: it does not explain regicide. The decline in the king's health risks affecting his surroundings, indeed the whole world. It is therefore imperative to get rid of him. But the king derives this contagious power, which is sometimes beneficial and sometimes destructive, either from nature or from ritual. If it comes from nature, its deleterious influence will undoubtedly extend, step by step, to everything that surrounds it. But the death of the king could only precipitate problems. Far from halting the evil, regicide would aggravate it and would even bring about the destruction of the universe. But it is much more likely that the king holds his power as a result of the installation ritual. This is true even if the incumbent had been chosen for his youthful vitality, and it is all the more obvious if he is an old man. In this case, it would be enough to depose him and replace him with someone else. What good would come of killing him? In short, Frazer's first theory is implausible since, in either possible eventuality, regicide does not appear to be a necessary element of the institution of monarchy, but to be a superfluous or counterproductive addition.

On the other hand, the second theory is immediately satisfactory. If the king is a scapegoat, it makes sense that the most radical way to get rid of the evil which he incarnates is to kill him. From this perspective, regicide is meaningful and virtually necessary.

If the ritual of the grove of Nemi serves as a touchstone, it leads us to the second theory. If the king must be, above all, a guarantor of prosperity, it is not clear why he should begin his career with a transgression as is found, not only in Roman ritual, but in the majority of installation rituals. However, if he is a potential scapegoat, the murder that he commits in the sacred copse makes him responsible for an original crime which turns him, from the very beginning of his reign, into a potential receptacle of all the evils of his people. The effect is the same as that of the incest and ritual cannibalism found elsewhere. The king becomes the 'pile of filth' of the community, as he is called in certain installation chants of the Mossi (Girard 1977: 107; de Heusch 1990: 26n) and the Samo (Héritier 1973: 121; de Heusch 1990: 26).[7] This justifies his execution in due course. The regicide that takes place in the grove of Nemi eliminates one scapegoat and in doing so simultaneously creates another.

With this established, we must return to the question of the compatibility of Frazer's two theories, or, more precisely, his two *theses*.[8] Even if Frazer's first thesis – according to which the king guarantees fertility – does not explain regicide, it is not a gratuitous invention on his part. *The Golden Bough* assembles much supporting evidence and since it first appeared this thesis has been corroborated by other ethnographic facts. It would appear, therefore, to contain some truth, but the exact nature of this truth remains to be specified. It is possible, for example, that some forms of royal institutions are not explained by the theory of the scape-goat. Or perhaps the fertility theory constitutes a complement to, or a natural pro-gression of, the scapegoat theory.

In a synthesis of recent monographs, de Heusch (1990, 1997) seems to lean ini-tially towards the first hypothesis. On this view, there is no unique model of monarchy (de Heusch 1990: 18) but Frazer's two 'theses' – or 'theories' in my ter-minology – correspond to two possible forms of the institution that societies could choose between. However, the facts show that the two royal functions are almost always joined and that societies tend to limit themselves to emphasizing either one or the other. We are not therefore concerned with forms which are essentially dif-ferent and mutually exclusive, but with a single institution which combines the same characteristics in different ways.

For this reason, de Heusch is ultimately led to conclude with a straightforward endorsement of the standard Frazerian doctrine: i.e. that the king guarantees pros-perity and becomes a scapegoat when the occasion calls for it.[9] But this is not the only possible conclusion. There is another, simpler, way of uniting Frazer's two 'theses' into a single doctrine. We have already seen that the scapegoat theory imme-diately explains regicide. We can therefore begin with this thesis and see if it is pos-sible to deduce from it – not simply add on – the thesis of the king as a guarantor of prosperity. This way of proceeding has the advantages of being more elegant, of ren-dering the institution of monarchy more coherent, and of fitting the corpus of mate-rial studied by de Heusch much better. Indeed, on close inspection de Heusch's analysis contains all the pieces of evidence required to arrive at this conclusion.

At first the general postulates of structuralist method and a rapid survey of the facts suggest that each of the theories of regicide corresponds to one variant of the institution of monarchy, and only partly explains it:

> Sometimes the king is put to death because his physical weakness menaces the universe and the society; sometimes he is killed as a scapegoat. The Rukuba seem to have opted for the latter solution, the Jukun for the former. It is striking that the sacred chiefs of the Rukuba, while being responsible for catastrophes of all kinds, are not at all regarded as masters of nature. They do not even preside over agrarian rites ... They do not control rainfall either. The Jukun, on the other hand, stress the first function of sacred kingship, that which corresponds to Frazer's first thesis. They identify their king with the plants they cultivate. (de Heusch 1990: 16)

This structuralist conjecture is, however, immediately contradicted because the Jukun king, de Heusch notes, 'is *also* treated as a scapegoat when required [emphasis added]' (1990). In spite of a ritual called the *ando ku*, during which he is said to regenerate himself by killing a slave with his own hands, thereby enjoying a new seven-year lease (de Heusch 1990: 15), 'he is secretly put to death following successive bad harvests or droughts' (de Heusch 1990: 16).

Frazer's two theses are not, therefore, mutually exclusive. They do not refer to two different forms of kingship, but to two aspects of the same institution, which are given more or less emphasis according to the circumstances. What is more, comparison of the Rukuba and Jukun kingships shows us another feature of the institution. The two kings have a common trait and one which differentiates them: they are both scapegoats, but the Jukun king is *also* responsible for cultivation. To put it the other way and say that the Jukun king is *also* a scapegoat is to turn things the wrong way round. It is to put forward an order of precedence which comparison of the two forms of kingship does not justify. On the contrary, it tends to call it into question.

This is not all. The Jukun ritual of regeneration shows that certain functions can be delegated. When the king kills a slave at the end of his first seven-year reign, in some way he makes this slave die in his place. This suggests that the different royal functions are not necessarily devolved to one and the same person, but may be distributed among several figures who have distinct but complementary remits.

Two further examples that are also compared by de Heusch – the Samo chiefship and the Mossi kingship – lend weight to this hypothesis. De Heusch looks at these two cases when he examines the emergence of the state, that is to say, when a new royal function emerges. This function – political power – is additional to the king's traditional ritual functions. This issue is important because, in Africa as in Europe, pre-state institutions and the modern state itself were forged (or born) from kingship. Every historian is agreed on this point. It is therefore crucial to understand how the king, who was originally a prisoner of his people and destined to undergo a violent death, can metamorphose into a head of state, that is the individual who has a monopoly on legitimate violence.

The two examples cited above show that the central functions of sacred chiefship can be assumed by one person or shared by several ritual figures. They also demonstrate that political power emerges when these sacred functions are split. But above all, these cases confirm that the first function is indeed that of the scapegoat. This function constitutes the keystone of the system of kingship and all its variations.

Among the Samo, the *tyiri* 'brings together ... the two Frazerian functions' (de Heusch 1990: 26). He is the rainmaker and the peacemaker, but he is also, above all, a scapegoat. As a ceremonial chant documented by Héritier (1973: 121) puts it, he is 'the pile of filth, the person who picks up everything and takes it upon himself'. Among the Mossi, royalty is associated with '*naam*, legitimate authority which is used in moderation, and *panga*, predatory violence' (de Heusch 1990: 19). These two opposed properties are split between a king of peace and a king of war. But what is remarkable is the way these two figures are linked. The 'king of peace' can only prolong his reign every seven years by killing his double, the 'king of war'. This latter embodies the predatory violence of the king, just as the king's youngest son (the *kurita*) does during an interregnum. Both the warrior chief and the *kurita* play the role of the king's scapegoats, the former during his entire reign, the latter following his natural death (de Heusch 1990: 22). De Heusch himself highlights this relation between the two kings since he first believed that it had escaped the attention of Izard, the ethnographer of the Mossi (compare de Heusch 1990: 22 and 1997: 221). The pre-eminence of the scapegoat function is clearly established. It is not merely the invariant characteristic of the institution of kingship; it is what makes the other functions possible.

In all the cases I have considered, what we see are variations on the same scheme. Kingship is always double, with a good face and a bad face, a positive aspect and a negative aspect, and in such a way (as de Heusch rightly emphasizes) that the positive is subordinated to the negative. This proves that the two theses of Frazer are not only compatible but, by reversing the order of precedence, one is able to deduce the former from the latter. If the elimination of the scapegoat is a remedy for all the evils which beset the group, one can see that, by extension, the royal personage can be the source of all that is good. If it is this figure that assures the permanence of the kingship and stabilizes the social order, one can understand that he can be seen as the guarantor of the order of the natural world.

However, so that this should be perfectly clear, one needs to be able to explain the scapegoat mechanism itself, and also its effects. In particular one needs to explain the fundamental duality of the royal person which is illustrated by the Samo case, and the splitting of the two functions which is illustrated by the Mossi case. In short, it is necessary to bring to light kingship's generative principles and the dynamic which underpins its transformations.

Before coming to this, it is necessary to make some additional remarks about Samo chiefship and Mossi kingship. One might object that these two examples do not really corroborate the reworked Frazerian theory that I have just sketched out. According to this theory, kingship has a double function: first the scapegoat function, then the function of guaranteeing fertility. The two functions may be joined in one person, or separated. But one should point out that neither the Samo nor the Mossi provide perfect illustrations of the two cases. Among the Samo, the *tyiri* is both a scapegoat and the master of the rains, but he is connected to a 'master of the earth', the *tudana*, who has the important function of selecting the *tyiri* (Héritier 1973: 127; de Heusch 1990: 126). Therefore they already have a double leadership. As for the Mossi, they have a king of war who takes on the function of scapegoat and is coupled with a king of peace. But the latter does not guarantee fertility (de Heusch 1990: 22).

In reality, these objections are not critical. Or rather, they confirm that Frazer's first function, which is apparently absent among the Mossi, is decidedly not the most important one. For the Mossi king, *naam* is a political power which is specifically the attribute of the king of peace. However, among the Tallensi, who come from the same linguistic group, it designates the power to ensure well-being and fertility by performing certain rites (de Heusch 1990: 24; 1997: 225). We are not, then, very far from my amended version of the Frazerian model. What is more, among the Samo, the *tyiri* is, in principle, the only one to take upon himself the burden of the kingship. This is not only because he is both scapegoat and rainmaker, but because he also performs the functions of the *tudana* which are not always separated from his own. According to Héritier (1973: 123), 'in certain villages, these responsibilities are assumed by a single person'.

This is not all. The Samo case suggests that it is difficult for kingship to remain a monarchy in the strict sense of the term, that is to say, an undivided function which is the prerogative of a single individual. Kingship is an unstable compound which tends to break apart into its component elements in order to stabilize. The Mossi case, which illustrates the bifurcated kingship, suggests that, from being the master of nature, the king can become the effective master of men and society when the scapegoat functions are completely taken over by one or more of his doubles. Everything happens as if political power emerges thanks to an internal dynamic in the system of kingship, which leads it towards a more stable state through the separation and balanced deployment of its constituent elements. The Samo chief, the scapegoat prisoner of his people, is already a peacemaker, but only in the same way that he is a rainmaker. That is to say, he is held responsible for conflict, as he is for drought. The Mossi king of peace, unburdened of his scapegoat functions, is genuinely the master of peace and conflict which he can respectively guarantee or suppress by force without having to remain the master of nature.

The pages which de Heusch devotes to the appearance and development of political power are simultaneously stimulating and ambiguous. In spite of the many accounts which describe the king as a foreign conqueror or captive, he suggests that, at bottom, coercive power comes from an endogenous process. It emerges from 'an internal division of the group which is not in any way due to military conquest' (1990: 26). It results from a separation of the sacred centre from the rest of the society which is equally present 'in the vast kingdoms as in the small village societies' (1990: 29). This separation thus precedes the state (1990: 30) while serving it as an anchor point. However, when de Heusch describes the Mossi kingdom, he does not present its state organization as the spontaneous transformation of an underlying ritual structure, but as the 'political hijacking of a truth of a different order' (1990: 24). That is to say, it is the effect of a power endowed with its own causality which has come parasitically from outside the original ritual system. This comes down to recognising the sudden emergence of the state without in any way explaining it.

The following lines, which conclude de Heusch's comparison between Samo chiefship and Mossi kingship, illustrate well the limits of an explanation which attempts to be faithful to Frazerian orthodoxy and a static structuralism:

The example of the Samo obliges us not to restrict the problem of sacred power to the dialectic of conquerors and autochthonous people. It is from the very interior of the undivided society that one forcibly extracts the figure responsible for rain and peace who has all the characteristics of a sacred chief. But far from imposing any authority, he remains the prisoner of the group which has elected him to bear the ritual burden of power. From the sacred Samo chief to the powerful Mossi king, a spectacular reversal takes place: the new association of violence and the sacred. This phenomenon, which is not at all original as René Girard arbitrarily supposes, is tied to the birth of the state, in the form of a coercive power, with its division into socio-economic statuses, perhaps even classes. (de Heusch 1990: 29)

To link the structural reversal which propels the sacred king from scapegoat to head of state with the birth of the state is simply to observe that centralized political power is present in the state and not earlier. To conceal this tautology by reproaching Girard for not seeing that the state structure associates violence with the sacred for the first time is strange to say the least.[10] This downplays the importance of regicide which, even within the framework of Frazer's 'standard' theory, is the most striking feature of sacred kingship.

It is all the more regrettable that Girard is so peremptorily rejected when his hypotheses allow one to clarify the institution of monarchy and its potential developments. His approach allows us to see all of the features of sacred kingship and to glimpse how the king's elevation from scapegoat to sacred king and head of state comes about not through a spectacular and mysterious upheaval, but through an intelligible morphogenetic process.[11]

However, before recalling the key ideas of Girard, it is necessary to examine the contribution of a theorist of kingship whose posthumous work, *Social Origins*, serves as a turning point between *The Golden Bough* and *Violence and the Sacred*. This theorist is Arthur Maurice Hocart who is curiously absent from the writing of de Heusch and from the work of all those Africanist colleagues on whom he comments.[12]

The Hocartian Reversal: Regicide Precedes Kingship

In defence of those anthropologists who neglect Hocart it should be said that reading his work can be disconcerting. In his history of British anthropology, Stocking (1995: 220–28) presents Hocart with the help of a nice little formula: 'the Boasian ethnographer as Frazerian diffusionist'. I would prefer to say that Hocart combines attention to ethnographic detail with the requirement of intelligibility, and the meticulous transcription of facts with the search for universal explanatory principles. While admiring his genius, Lévi-Strauss (1954: 134) once described him as a 'Sunday painter' kind of ethnologist. It would be more appropriate to describe him as an old master who has left only his sketch books behind, or a mathematician, such as Fermat, who can provide theorems without any proof. It is necessary to do some work in order to retrace Hocart's steps, re-enact his reasoning, and verify or complete his conjectures. I have taken up these tasks elsewhere.[13] Here I will restrict myself to a few essential points.

The first point is the unity of all rites. The installation and consecration rites of the king are all built on the same model and composed of the same elements (Hocart 1927), and all the other rites and sacraments derive from royal ceremonies of which they retain only some characteristics (Hocart 1927, 1954). Marriage, for example, is first and foremost an important element of the installation ceremony. In this respect, it is initially reserved for the king. Later it is extended to the dignitaries of the court and it finishes by reaching, little by little, into every corner of society. Numerous marriage rituals retain traces of their royal origins, such as the crowning of the bride and groom during the ceremony.

One can undoubtedly improve on the list of items given by Hocart in his enumeration of royal rituals (Hocart 1927: 70–1). One does not find ritual transgression (incest, murder or cannibalism) there, and it is an essential element of the installation ceremony. In its basic approach, however, Hocart's work remains an excellent base for further research (as Fortes 1967 pointed out). The African material brought together by de Heusch confirms its importance. Amongst the Mossi, for example, the marriage of the king is above all a succession rite. His principal spouse, who has the title of queen, is one of his predecessor's young widows. He passes one night with her but will never again have sexual relations with her nor children (de Heusch 1990: 20). In this group one also finds the Hocartian idea that the coronation ceremony is associated with a cosmic sacred marriage: the royal lineage is born from the union of the sky and the earth (cf. de Heusch 1990: 23 and Hocart 1970 [1936]: ch. 20).

The second point is that culture has its origins in ritual. Numerous techniques and the majority of institutions spring from the demands of the cult (Hocart 1935). The division of labour is not, in principle, an economic necessity but a ritual requirement (Hocart 1970 [1936]: 108–110). The caste system allows us to understand how the division of labour can lead to professional specialization (1938: 261–2). The same is true for political institutions. In contrast to religious institutions, they are no more necessary for societies than the nervous system is necessary for single cell organisms. The first function of the king is not to rule but to reign, i.e. to be the main figure in great ceremonies. It is only because of the doubling of the ritual functions of the king that political power and state organization emerge and develop. Hocart devoted an entire book to this question (1970 [1936]). One may also see that war, before being a matter of foreign affairs, is a ritual activity the aim of which is to procure sacrificial victims (Hocart 1954: 143–4).

If one were to employ a Marxist vocabulary, one might say that ritual is not the ideological or symbolic superstructure of human societies, but their infrastructure.

It is the source of social bonds and of the institutional means and materials which allow society to be consolidated. De Heusch rediscovers this idea in the African ethnography where it is demonstrated clearly. The ritual functions of the king are a primitive feature of the institution and not the reflection, or disguise, of a 'hierarchical socio-economic order composed of diverse elements' (de Heusch 1990: 10). In the Voltaic region at least, a 'more fundamental structural dualism' derives from these ritual functions, and imprints itself on society. Onto this may then be grafted the internal and external relations which come with political and military domination (de Heusch 1990: 25). And yet, while recognising that sacred kingship has shaped social life and played a crucial role in the history of humanity (de Heusch 1997: 231), de Heusch argues as if this outcome was, when all is said and done, accidental. Or he gives the impression that it is enough to characterize the ritual power of the king as 'symbolic' in order to make sense of it.[14]

As with Frazer, at the basis of this idea is the notion that the king is first and foremost a magician. His 'fetish-body' (de Heusch 1997: 231) is endowed with imaginary powers which only ever give him an illusory mastery over nature and society. Hocart, however, and Durkheim before him, saw that if ritual did not control the forces of nature, it did allow men to master themselves through the organization which it required, and to then present a united front against the vagaries of fate (Hocart 1927: 56–7). Put differently, ritual constitutes a kind of self-domestication[15] of man and self-regulation of social life. From these can come all the other means of controlling nature and governing society – some less effective, some more so.

Hocart's third point is that the first kings were dead kings. Let me return to the unity of all rites which comparative study demonstrates. The kinship of the different sacraments leads one to construct their genealogical tree and to search for a common source (Hocart 1954: 76 and summary table, p. 85). Since they all derive from the king's installation ritual, one is led to the original form of this royal ceremony. This amounts to searching for the most important and characteristic element of this ceremony and then returning to its source.[16] Comparison of sacraments brings out two possible solutions – marriage and funerals – during which a large part of ritual is brought into play. Of these, the latter is the better solution because every sacrament (birth, initiation, marriage etc) elevates its beneficiary to a higher status, and the ultimate promotion takes place at the time of the funeral ceremony.

But this presents a difficulty: how could royalty begin with funerary ritual? How, asks Hocart, could this be royal in nature if monarchy did not yet exist? The only way in which this could have been possible, he answers, is if the first kings were dead kings (1954: 77). This hypothesis would be absurd if the first function of the king was to be a political leader. But it is entirely plausible if the first function is to be the central figure in all the great rituals. It is just this position that the dead person – not the principal officiant – occupies in any funeral service. That said, everyone dies but not everyone becomes a king. Natural death is not enough to make a king. One must surmise, then, that the person who becomes king does not die naturally but is put to death ritually. This is all the more plausible because the installation ceremony as we know it always includes a fictive killing followed by a rebirth. As Hocart claims, 'it is an invariable rule that a fiction is a substitute for reality' (Hocart 1954: 76). The pretend killing of the king takes place because in earlier times he was really killed. One becomes a king by being sacrificed. The original sacrament, the ritual source to which all other rites are joined, is thus human sacrifice (Hocart 1954: 78, 117).[17]

This conclusion simultaneously confirms and reverses the central thesis in Frazer's theory. Regicide is not just about killing; it is at the very basis of the principle of kingship. For Frazer, the king is killed. For Hocart, a man is killed so that he can become king. In *The Golden Bough* the reign ends with an execution. In *Social Origins* it commences with one. From one perspective the killing, even when ritualized, is negative. Its sole function is to expel evil. This may come from the fading strength of the king who may thus bring about a general decline in the society. Or it may come from the inauspicious qualities which pervade the society and which the scapegoat king carries away. From another perspective, the killing of the king is the source of life and even the generating force of the sacred and the divine. These are the characteristic properties of the king once he has been invested with his functions.

Hocart's thesis may seem audacious, but the African material provides revealing illustrations. Among the Evhé of southern Togo, the period of seven years between the installation of the king–priest and his ritual execution 'can be considered as a period of initiation to the kingship and the effective reign begins when the king moves to the next world' (de Heusch 1990: 17). In other words, the real king is a dead king. Besides, we have seen that human sacrifice can be a source of life. The Mossi king prolongs his reign by seven years thanks to the execution of his double. Similarly, the Jukun king enjoys a new seven-year reign by killing a slave with his own hands. In each case it is the killing which confers kingship, but it can be displaced onto a scapegoat or simply symbolically enacted, without any actual execution, as in the majority of installation rites.

The facts thus support Hocart, but nevertheless leave us with an enigma. If human sacrifice is indeed the original sacrament; if it is the source of kingship and all the institutions which spring from it; and if it is, as its etymology suggests, responsible for generating the sacred and, consequently, not only kings but the gods themselves, from where does it derive such power? Many myths tell how all cultural things, and even the entire universe, issue forth from the body of a sacrificial victim. Hocart's thesis tends to lend weight to this idea. We need to be sure that we are not dealing here with some collective delusion. To do this it is necessary to explain how the execution of a man is far from being a negative act or even – the scapegoat idea

– the lesser of two evils. We need to explain how this killing could not only be the fount of civilization, but could be the very basis of social life and all the institutions and representations which support and maintain it.

Unfortunately Hocart himself did not broach this problem. While his examination of the facts leads him to make human sacrifice the matrix of all culture, there is no trace in his writings of even a sketch of a theory of this violent rite whose origins, he simply says, remain very obscure (Hocart 1954: 143). It was obviously with extreme reluctance that, in his posthumously published *Social Origins*, he acknowledged that sacrifice should take centre stage.[18] In *Kingship* sacrifice is merely one of twenty-six rites that constitute the installation ceremony (Hocart 1927: 70–1). In *Social Origins* it does not figure at all in the list of fundamental rites (1954: 39) even though it is mentioned in virtually every chapter. Where it appears, it is as an ingredient, and it is in the shadow of other rites. See, for example, the way in which it is drowned, so to speak, in the ritual bath of Fijian ceremonies (Hocart 1927: 45).

There is a significant detail here. Hocart uses the term 'sacrifice' as little as possible, preferring instead 'sacrament'. While the two words have adjacent senses, he says, 'sacrifice' used to have a broad meaning but has now annoyingly become associated with cutting the throat of a victim. In other words, one associates it with one particular episode in the ritual, an episode that is far from being the most important (Hocart 1933: 145; 1951: 501; 1954: 48). Yet, very strikingly, at the end of his life he was obliged to conclude that this episode enjoyed the pre-eminent place of being the original sacrament.

Hocart did not wait until his last years to integrate sacrifice into his general theory of ritual and even to accord it, in a certain sense, a central place. His definition of ritual – as 'an organisation to promote life, fertility, prosperity by transferring life from objects which are abounding in it to objects deficient in it' (Hocart 1970 [1936]: 3) – is nothing other than a description of ritual killing and the beneficial effects which flow from it. However, this implicit definition of sacrifice converts it into a simple transfer of life. Without infinite regress, it supposes, like Frazer's first theory, that certain beings are naturally endowed with certain properties which can be transferred to others. This sits uneasily with a fundamental principle of ritual according to which: 'no authentic instance has ever been recorded of a thing or person having virtue inherent in it. Whenever the *full* history of an object endowed with power is known, it is found to have acquired it after consecration, that is after being endowed with "life"' (Hocart 1933: 187). If human sacrifice really is the original sacrament, this principle invites us to consider the ritual killing not as a *transfer* of life, but as the *source* of life.

However, Hocart does not manage to reach this last step, either before or after his discovery that the first kings were dead kings, and that sacrifice generates sacred kingship and all the institutions which come from it. To be sure, in *The*

Progress of Man, he writes that ' [t]he whole point of the ritual is that virtue is not inherent, but has to be transferred from one carrier to another' (Hocart 1933). This opens the door to an interminable regression which becomes explicit in Ch 10 of *Social Origins*. While this chapter is entitled 'The Origin of the Sacraments', in reality, it is a study of their transformations which goes back as far as possible into the past and even reconstructs a hypothetical form of primitive royal ceremony. But Hocart never manages to reach a true starting point. For if one is not a king naturally, but only because one is a sacrificial victim, how does one first acquire the status of a victim who is worthy of being sacrificed? Since no-one is sacred by himself, there must be a rite whereby the victim is consecrated (Hocart 1954: 81). But if this is the case, then human sacrifice properly speaking, that is the killing, is not the primordial rite, and so on. That is not all. If every rite supposes another rite which, in turn, supposes an already established society, one can no longer hold to the thesis of the ritual origin of society.

In order to escape from this problem, one has to be able to go back to a pre-ritual matrix of society. In other words, it is necessary to discover a spontaneous process which is capable of giving rise to the rites – beginning with human sacrifice – which, as we know, form the infrastructure of social life. The merit of the authors I am about to discuss is that they have confronted this problem. They have not so much looked for the original form of the prototypical ritual and its transformations as for its genesis in universal conditions and recurrent situations.

Girard's Contribution: From the Sacrificial Victim to the Surrogate Victim

It was just before his death in 1939 that Hocart discovered that the king is in principle a sacrificial victim. In so doing, he gave new life to Frazer's theory of sacred kingship. According to Hocart, it is the ritual killing that elevates an individual to the status of king and makes him the central figure in all the collective ceremonies, the pivot or the cornerstone of the social group. Freud, who read Frazer and Robertson-Smith avidly, also died in 1939. Paralleling Hocart, in *Moses and Monotheism* he re-examined and strengthened the theory he had first presented in *Totem and Taboo* – that social life is based on the murder of the father.

For both of these authors, then, society is formed and organized around a dead person, and, more precisely, a victim. For Hocart the victim is ritually killed by a sacrificer.[19] For Freud, in contrast, the victim is murdered in a spontaneous collective action. Hocart, the anthropologist, returns to the beginnings of social life by describing the first sacramental forms. Freud, the psychoanalyst, returns to the origins of social life in another sense, by looking at their psychological and historical roots. Their approaches are simultaneously close and different, one being more cautious, the other more ambitious.

In his search for the ritual foundations of social life, Hocart sees the necessity of deriving all the sacraments found in ethnography and history from a common source that is external to all of them rather than from any particular one. But, in his mind, this source is yet another sacrament, more ancient and prototypical. It has the same status as a hypothetical dead language whose existence is postulated in order to understand the properties of living languages – without, for all that, explaining the origin of language.

Freud, on the other hand, looks for the very origin of social organization and its ritual forms. He sees that in order to find it one must situate oneself upstream from rites and institutions; that is to say, establish a pre-cultural state that allows one to determine how rites and institutions are generated. His ambition is legitimate and is to his credit. But his method has two serious defects. The first is his attempt to extrapolate, from a unique and exceptional event, the entire family, religious and political history of humanity. The second is to presuppose the principal structure which this event is supposed to bring about – i.e. the Oedipus relation, which is already implicitly present in the primitive horde.

However, in spite of its weaknesses, Freud's work remains an important contribution to science. It is less about the haunting traces of an unpardonable crime than it is about how societies are made and unmade by general and recurrent causes, and how they periodically return to a fixed point when they ritually commemorate, or even spontaneously reproduce, the primitive scenario. Without saying it expressly, *Moses and Monotheism* suggests the possibility that the founding murder is not an event that has no conceivable precedent or that could not be repeated. On the contrary, it could happen every time that the generic conditions recur.

Unfortunately Freud did not have the time to develop this late discovery or even to see it clearly. And his successors neglected to take it up and develop it. On the contrary, psychoanalysts and anthropologists would conspire to throw a veil of modesty over this part of his work. One would have to wait until 1972 for an independently-minded thinker, who was studying Greek tragedy, to re-open a dossier that had been abandoned since 1939, to rediscover the most important intuitions of Freud and Hocart, and to find the means to use them to build the first plausible theory of the violent origins of human society. I am speaking of René Girard who lays down the bases of a general theory of the elementary forms of religious and social life in *Violence and the Sacred*.[20] He does so without invoking an improbable primordial rite from which all others are supposed to derive. Nor does he invoke a prehistoric event which allegedly left its imprint on all societies past and present. Instead he brings to light a mechanism which is universal and timeless, which can be reactivated endlessly, and which constitutes a permanent matrix, pre-ritual and pre-institutional, of rites and institutions.

For Girard, humans are the most mimetic of the animals. Starting with this unique, distinguishing property, from which he systematically draws the consequences, he believes it is possible to deduce all of the other traits which characterize humanity. This applies particularly to culture. His work very naturally extends the results of those who had already established the ritual origin of civilization, for it shows that a growth in mimesis brings a growth of intra-species aggressivity in its train and in order to regulate this, new ritual forms are required.

As the principal factor in the diffusion of customs, as Hocart noted (1952, ch. 13), mimesis favours the reproduction and stability of cultures. But as a force which promotes homogeneity, it risks erasing differences. And differences are, for Girard just as much as for Lévi-Strauss, the very essence of culture. The loss of difference is responsible for bringing about the 'sacrificial crisis' of which the paradigm is the confusion of sacrifice and murder in Greek tragedy (Girard 1977: ch. 2, Burkert 1966). As the agent of convergence of desires and actions, mimesis may alternatively promote division or union. By directing individuals' desires towards the same indivisible objects, and by sweeping them along in a game of mirrors of negative reciprocity, it divides the group into brothers who are enemies, and whose rivalries it stirs up. Mimesis triggers the sacrificial crisis. It ends up causing all external anchor points to disappear, every other object of conflict except conflict itself. By using simple mimetic contagion to channel all violence onto a single individual – the 'surrogate victim' – it spontaneously re-establishes the unity of the group in a renewed unanimity, the all-against-one convergence of collective violence. Mimesis thus ends the crisis by re-establishing a third external object among society's members: the victim, the god who has triggered panic and then resolved the crisis by bringing peace, the sacred king, the totem or any other transcendent mediator.

Girard's theory does not privilege any particular rite. It shows the common origin of all rites. It does not presuppose the existence of society, but describes a mechanism capable of bringing it about or renewing it. Girard avoids the problem of Hocart's endless regress with his theory of double substitution (1977: 101–3) and the very clear distinction it implies between the founding murder and the ritual killing (sacrifice, regicide etc.). The founding murder, as we have just seen, is the product of a *spontaneous mechanism* which, at the paroxysm of a crisis, substitutes a single member of the group, the 'surrogate victim', for the group as a whole. In the case of sacrifice, or any other sacred killing, this spontaneous process is replaced by a *ritual procedure* which consists of substituting for the original surrogate victim a sacrificeable victim who comes from outside the group or from its margins: an animal, a prisoner of war, a criminal, and so on. This substitute is sacrificed after being integrated into the group (the Aïnous' bear is fed at a woman's breast; the Tupinamba prisoner marries a woman of the group which has captured him, and so on).

Other kinds of substitutions, with other rites, are possible, but there are also permanent features. In most Melanesian chiefdoms and African kingdoms, the king, whether put to death or not, is often a foreigner, like the sacrificial victim. On the one hand he is from outside the group; on the other, he is the revitalising centre of the group. Among the Mundurucu head hunters, the great collective ritual is celebrated around the head of an enemy which has been decorated with the tattoo marks of the capturing group. And the person who has captured the head is subject to the same prohibitions as a sacred king (Menget 1996). All these rites are from the same matrix and are related to each other, yet are quite different.

When it is not confused with the sacrificial rite or the scapegoat ritual, Girard's founding murder is often assimilated to Freud's murder of the father of the primitive horde. Far from explaining society scientifically, Girard is sometimes seen as making society derive from rites which already presuppose it, or simply coming up with a new variant of the Freudian myth. This complaint is surprising because *Violence and the Sacred* carefully avoids falling into either trap. It pioneers an alternative approach to those found in *Social Origins* and *Totem and Taboo*. For Girard the sacrificial crisis and its violent resolution are not archaic institutions or events. They are canonical forms of destructuring and restructuring the social fabric which can emerge at any moment in history in any human group because they are due to general and permanent causes which underpin all institutions.

Girard's explanatory model has a classical form which brings out its distinctive content and should help to make it clear. Indeed, from many perspectives, Girard's work resembles that of Hobbes. Both try to understand how the social bond is formed and maintained. If we compare the first chapters of *Violence and the Sacred* with chapters 13 to 17 of *Leviathan*, we see that Girard's sacrificial crisis has the same status as Hobbes' state of nature. They come more or less from the same sources and have roughly the same effect: the emergence of a transcendent other who is simultaneously situated at the centre of society and outside it.

In either case, it is not a matter of describing a particular moment in human history, but the permanent nature of the interactions between individuals and groups.[21] If, as Hobbes says, the state of nature is necessarily a state of war, it is not because men are inherently vicious, but because they are all rational and dread death. Brother will turn upon brother because the desires of men converge on things which cannot be shared and, in the absence of any institutional mediation, no-one can be expected to behave differently from his fellow man. Everyone anticipates conflict and renders it inevitable by making the first move for fear of being the first victim. If man is a mimetic animal, as Girard believes, the convergence of desires goes from being possible, as Hobbes has it, to necessary. And the war of all against all takes off simply because of contagious conflict: one does not have to appeal to the postulate of rationality.

Girard's hypothesis appears ever more elegant and powerful when it comes to explaining the resolution of the crisis. Because men are rational, says Hobbes, they try to escape from the state of war. They therefore all agree to give their allegiance to, and invest supreme power in, one among their number: the Sovereign. Although he is not a party to the contract, he safeguards the peace simply by existing, like 'a mortal god beneath the immortal God'. Girard shows that simply because of mimesis conflicts mechanically converge on a single victim and result in Hocart's dead king, Frazer's sacred king, and Hobbes' absolute monarch, all of whom are successive incarnations of the scapegoat.

There is a better demonstration. In contrast to Girard's theory, Hobbes' theory shows that men need to provide themselves with a king, but does not explain how this king is chosen. Dumouchel has succeeded in filling this gap by establishing from Hobbes' premises that the Sovereign must be the enemy of the people. In the state of nature he must have been at odds with all other individuals (Dumouchel 1986). The surprising consequence is that the only person who is still able to kill everyone – the definition of the Sovereign – is the same person that everyone would like to kill. This reversal would be paradoxical if we did not already know how close the king and the scapegoat are. This is not all. Commenting on the ethnographic work of Drucker-Brown (1991), Devictor (1993), in a fine study of oath-taking among the Mamprusi, shows that the social group is organized around an ambiguous figure who begins his reign with an act of perjury that places him simultaneously in the position of chief and public enemy.

The way in which these results accord with each other is all the more remarkable because they are, for the most part, independent of each other. Dumouchel's reasoning is purely axiomatic and ignores ethnography. Devictor depends entirely on legal anthropology and the ethnography of the Mamprusi. The only common point of these two authors is that they have read *Violence and the Sacred* and have extended its arguments beyond the original framework. Girard himself says nothing about the political theory of Hobbes or about oath-taking. Girard's theory does, however, explicitly broach the theme of kingship (1977: 103–18, 299–306; 1978: 59–66; 1985: 128–41), and along with the works of Frazer and Hocart seems to provide us with a means of understanding the institution in its totality. If the king is a kind of scapegoat, one sees immediately what his function is, the rites he must undergo, the transformations and possible variations in his status, and how political power emerges.

Two principal reasons explain how the scapegoat can contain all the potential recensions of the institution of kingship, and many other things too. These two reasons are tied to the time dimension of the founding murder and its ritual repetition. The first reason concerns the superimposition of two opposed representations of the surrogate victim. Just before his death he appears as a monster and a troublemaker. Just after his death he appears as a tutelary deity who has re-established order and peace by converting an ignominious death into an apotheosis. All the ambiguity of the sacred person of the king derives from this fundamental contrast. One sees an oscillation between impurity and holiness, which all of the ritual precautions respectively defend against or protect. One sees too the ritual doubling of this unstable compound: Mossi kingship provides a particularly good illustration of this.

The second reason is that a delay – sometimes longer, sometimes shorter – takes place between the moment the ritual victim, the substitute for the spontaneous surrogate victim, is selected and the moment he is sacrificed. If this delay is very short, we witness sacrifice and divinity. The latter appears later as the being to whom the sacrifice is addressed but he is first created by the rite and kept at a good distance by it.[22] If the delay becomes longer, we witness sacred kingship and regicide. Girard says that it is due to this delay that the king can transform his ritual responsibility into political power – thanks to the principle of substitution that is the heart of the surrogate victim mechanism, and permits a ritual double to assume the sombre face of the institution. And there are also intermediary forms such as Tupinamba cannibalism. Besides, the god and the king are never completely separated. Just as the king is a kind of living god, the divinity is 'a kind of dead king, or at least an "absent" king' (Girard 1978: 66).

All this confirms that the king is first a scapegoat, as the finer details of Frazer's standard theory already allowed us to see. However Girard's theory shows us that this function is not magical or symbolic. On the contrary, the victimary mechanism reveals that long before he becomes the champion of political power, the king, as substitute for the surrogate victim, is *ipso facto* someone who regulates social life. This is not trivial. When he presents ritual as a means of uniting against adversity, Hocart is thinking above all of external dangers – drought, bad weather, sickness etc. But the more formidable forces, as Hobbes saw, are inherent in human nature. It is precisely to hold these forces in check that people need royal or sacrificial rites. As the Samo say with every justification, the *tyiri*, the scapegoat king, is the one who ' "brings together" or "holds" the village in the sense of keeping the different elements together' (Héritier 1973: 127). While he is 'bound' by his people, and by the ritual, he is in his own way, and in spite of himself, the maker of the social bond. Like the sacrificial victim, and for the same reason, he is a stranger to his own people. And like the surrogate victim from whom both king and sacrificial victim come, he is the *vinculum substantiale* ('great bond') of the community.

Such facts are well known and there are many more examples of them. But Girard's theory is the only one to make these facts completely comprehensible.[23] It can easily be shown that the structure of the great royal rites can be deduced from it, beginning with the installation ceremonies and numerous related rites which are found in the most diverse societies. But my purpose here has simply been to put forward the principles. Once these are established, the rest falls into place.

Notes

1. I am grateful to Mark Anspach for a number of suggestions, to Declan Quigley for his translation, and to the latter and Anne McLaren for their editorial work.
2. See, for example, two publications from the Paris team studying 'Systems of thought in Black Africa': de Heusch (ed.) (1990) and Cartry and Detienne (eds) (1996).
3. See Adler (1982: 364–5).
4. Izard (1990: 85), and personal communication.
5. On this point I disagree with Izard and Belmont in their introduction to the 1981–4 French translation of *The Golden Bough*, though many of their other comments are very useful.
6. See de Heusch (1990; 1997) and Quigley (2000). De Heusch (1997) is an English translation (by Quigley) of an edited version of de Heusch (1990).
7. In the English translation of *Violence and the Sacred*, the original French expression 'tas d'ordures' is translated as 'heap of refuse' – Girard (1977: 107).
8. Following the practice of logicians, I mean by 'thesis' a proposition, and by 'theory' an explanation, i.e. a relation of inference between propositions. This distinction is useful for clarifying my argument: Frazer's first 'theory' does not stand up: it does not explain regicide. However, it contains a valid thesis: the king guarantees prosperity. One might note that de Heusch (1990, 1997), who does not pick up on the weaknesses of the first theory, uses the expression 'Frazer's theses' for what I call here 'Frazer's theories'.
9. 'Though it appears in diverse historical forms, sacred kingship always has a common theme: the body-fetish of the chief or king articulates the natural and social orders. It is a body condemned to be sacrificed before its natural end, and which, in the event of calamity, will be society's scapegoat. It is just as Frazer envisaged it' (de Heusch 1997: 231).
10. It seems that by 'new association of violence and the sacred' de Heusch does not mean a new instance of such an association, but an association which would bring about a novel situation.
11. In the English version of his argument, de Heusch comments on an article by Emmanuel Terray. Here he sees clearly that sacred kingship is an institution which transforms brute violence into a legitimate violence that the head of state will inherit. But he leaves it at that (de Heusch 1997: 229). In *Violence and the Sacred*, Girard brings to light the mechanism which makes this transformation possible and explains the 'formidable ritual power' (1977) which will serve as the source of political power.
12. This is, at least, the case for all those whose work appears in volume 10 of *Systèmes de pensée en Afrique noire* (de Heusch ed. 1990).

13. I have given a more complete presentation of Hocart's principal theses in Scubla (1985, 2002).
14. As Descombes (1980: 93) has shown, recourse to the term 'symbolic' has been judged by some to be more elegant than 'sacred', but has not improved the comprehension of religious phenomena.
15. The term 'self-domestication' was used by Girard at a public seminar.
16. Here I reconstruct Hocart's (1954: ch. 10) reasoning rather freely while trying to do so as fully, coherently and faithfully as possible.
17. While Hocart presents human sacrifice as 'the original sacrament' (1954: 117), he also speaks of it as a rite which precedes sacraments properly speaking when he writes that 'the king's death has been commuted to a sacrament' (154: 82).
18. It is possible that Hocart's study of caste, which he explicitly defined as a sacrificial organization (1938: 29), played a role in this discovery. But the reasoning he developed in chapter 10 of *Social Origins* does not depend on particular empirical material.
19. *Translator's note*: the author's original French here is *sacrificateur*.
20. One should add that 1972 is also the year of publication of another book which marked the renaissance of a grand anthropology of religion: Walter Burkert's *Homo Necans* (1983 [1972]). Like Girard, Burkert (1966) has written beautifully on the relation between Greek tragedy and sacrifice. For a brief presentation of their respective theses, see Scubla (1999), and for a debate between the two authors see Hamerton-Kelly (1987).
21. The only important difference between Hobbes and Girard is at the level of epistemology. Hobbes is a constructivist: he believes that the objects and theories of political science can be constructed and established *a priori* like the subject-matter and theories of mathematics, while the objects of the physical world may only be reconstructed *a posteriori* (*De Homine* 10: 5). Girard is more modest: he is simply attempting to reconstruct the spontaneous morphogenesis of the social order.
22. For an analysis of an African example that clearly shows that the gods of the sacrifice are none other than human violence reified and externalized by the founding murder and the rites which repeat it, see Scubla (1999: 157–9).
23. For an excellent presentation of Girard's theory and some original developments of it, see Simonse (1991).

References

Adler, A. 1982. *La Mort est le masque du roi. La royauté sacrée des Moundang du Tchad*. Paris, Payot.
Burkert, W. 1966. 'Greek Tragedy and Sacrificial Ritual', *Greek, Roman, and Byzantine Studies* 7: 87–121.

—— 1983 [1972]. *Homo Necans. The Anthropology of Ancient Greek Sacrificial Ritual and Myth*, translated by P. Bing. Berkeley and Los Angeles: University of California Press.

Cartry, M. & Detienne, M. (eds) 1996. *Systèmes de pensée en Afrique noire*, vol. 14. *Destins de meurtriers*. Paris: CNRS.

Descombes, V. 1980. 'L'Équivoque du symbolique', *Cahiers confrontation* III: 77–95.

Devictor, X. 1993. 'Sacramentum: une étude du serment', *Cahiers du CREA* (Paris, Ecole polytechnique) 16: 161–200.

Drucker-Brown, S. 1991. 'Mamprusi Oaths of Office', in R. Verdier (ed.) *Le Serment*, vol. 1: 315–28. Paris: Editions du CNRS.

Dumouchel, P. 1986. 'Hobbes: la course à la souveraineté', *Stanford French Review* x: 153–76.

Fortes, M. 1967. 'Of Installation Ceremonies', *Proceedings of the Royal Anthropological Institute*: 5–20.

Frazer, J. G. (1981–1984 [1911]) *Le Rameau d'or* [*The Golden Bough*, French translation by P. Sayn and H. Peyre], 4 vol. Paris: Robert Laffont.

—— (1994 [1890]) *The Golden Bough*. Oxford: Oxford University Press.

Freud, S. 1913. *Totem and Taboo* in *The Standard Edition of the Complete Psychological Works of Sigmund Freud*, vol. 13. London: Hogarth Press.

—— 1939. *Moses and Monotheism* in *The Standard Edition of the Complete Psychological Works of Sigmund Freud*, vol. 23. London: Hogarth Press.

Girard, R. 1977 [1972]. *Violence and the Sacred*, trans. Patrick Gregory. Baltimore: John Hopkins University Press.

—— 1978. *Des choses cachées depuis la fondation du monde*. Paris: Grasset.

—— 1985. *La Route antique des hommes pervers*. Paris: Grasset.

Hamerton-Kelly, R. G. (ed.) 1987. *Violent Origins, Walter Burkert, René Girard, and Jonathan Z. Smith on Ritual Killing and Cultural Formation*. Stanford: Stanford University Press.

Héritier-Izard, F. 1973. 'La Paix et la pluie. Rapports d'autorité et rapport au sacré chez les Samo', *L'Homme* XIII(3): 121–38.

Heusch, L., de 1990. 'Introduction', in de Heusch (ed.) *Systèmes de pensée en Afrique noire*, vol. 10, *Chefs et rois sacrés*: 1990, 7–33. Paris: CNRS.

—— (ed.) 1990. *Systèmes de pensée en Afrique noire*, vol. 10, *Chefs et rois sacrés*. Paris: CNRS.

—— 1997. 'The Symbolic Mechanisms of Sacred Kingship: Rediscovering Frazer', *Journal of the Royal Anthropological Institute* (NS) 3: 213–32.

Hobbes, T. 1651. *Leviathan*.

—— 1658. *De Homine*.

Hocart, A. M. 1927. *Kingship*. London: Oxford University Press.

—— 1933. *The Progress of Man: A Short Survey of His Evolution, His Customs and His Works*. London: Methuen.

—— 1935. *Les Progrès de L'homme*. Translated from the English by G. Montandon. Paris: Payot.

—— 1938. *Les Castes*. Paris: Annales du Musée Guimet.

—— 1951. 'Sacrifice'. *Encyclopædia of the Social Sciences* XIII: 501–3.

—— 1954. *Social Origins*. London: Watts.

—— 1952. *The Life-Giving Myth and Other Essays*. Edited, and with an introduction, by Lord Raglan. London: Methuen.

—— 1970 [1936]. *Kings and Councillors*. Edited and with an introduction by Rodney Needham, Chicago: University of Chicago Press.

Izard, M. 1990. 'De quelques paramètres de la souveraineté', in de Heusch (ed.) *Systèmes de pensée en Afrique noire*, vol. 10, *Chefs et rois sacrés*. Paris: CNRS.

Lévi-Strauss, C. 1954. 'L'Art de déchiffrer les symboles', *Diogène* 5: 128–35.

Menget, P. 1996. 'De l'usage des trophées en amérique du Sud. Esquisse d'une comparaison entre les pratiques nivacle (Paraguay) et mundurucu (Brésil)', in Cartry, M. & Detienne, M. (eds) 1996: 127–43.

Quigley, D. 2000. 'Scapegoats: The Killing of Kings and Ordinary People', *Journal of the Royal Anthropological Institute* (NS) 6: 237–54.

Scubla, L. 1985. 'Logiques de la réciprocité', *Cahiers du CREA* no. 6. Paris: Ecole Polytechnique.

—— 1999. ' "Ceci n'est pas un meurtre" ou comment le sacrifice contient la violence', in *Séminaire de Françoise Héritier, De la violence,* II: 135–70. Paris: Editions Odile Jacob.

—— 2002. 'Hocart and the Royal Road to Anthropological Understanding', *Social Anthropology* 10(3): 359–76.

Simonse, S. 1991. *Kings of Disaster. Dualism, Centralism and the Scapegoat King in Southeastern Sudan*. Leiden: E. J. Brill.

Stocking, G. W. Jr. 1995. *After Tylor: British Social Anthropology, 1888–1951*. Madison: The University of Wisconsin Press.

—4—

A Reply to Lucien Scubla

Luc de Heusch

Lucien Scubla provides a sustained and knowledgeable discussion of the neo-Frazerian thesis that I have defended in the first chapter of this book.[1] We are agreed on one essential point: the reality of ritual regicide, which Frazer insisted upon but which was denied by his successors for a long time. I am delighted by our agreement on this point. Let me come, then, to our amicable differences.

Essentially we part company on the question of the interpretation of the phenomenon of ritual regicide. The reader will have to choose between the two options we present. Scubla's hypothesis is that ritual regicide is explained solely with reference to the scapegoat function, which the king assumes, and that this function is primordial. My contention is that the positive function of kingship is to ensure prosperity and fertility, and that ritual regicide provides the corresponding negative aspect of this.

The only theory of regicide that satisfies Scubla is that of the scapegoat. This theory is fundamentally dependent on unqualified adhesion to the conjectural theses of René Girard. These have always seemed very debatable to me. Scubla reproaches me for impugning Girard without giving due consideration to his work, so I will take this opportunity to explain my position carefully. In my view Girard obstinately defends a reductionist theory of cultural order, asserting that every aspect of culture can be explained by mimetic behaviour and the repression of violence through sacrifice.

In particular I am critical of Girard's poor understanding of many of the aspects of sacrificial ritual that he places at the centre of his theory. In *Violence and the Sacred* he begins by re-writing *Totem and Taboo*, Freud's intriguing imaginary story of the origins of human society. Girard deletes the Oedipus complex from this story but preserves the primordial murder. He credits Freud with 'a formidable discovery: he has been the first to affirm that every ritual practice, every mythic significance, has its origin in a *real* murder' (Girard 1972: 276). It is 'a theory of myths and rituals, that is to say, of ritual in its entirety', a theory that Girard is ambitious to construct using scapegoats as his foundation (1972: 149). The last chapter of *Violence and the Sacred* is entitled: 'The Unity of all Rites'. In 1978 it was followed by *Des choses cachées depuis la fondation du monde* ('Of things hidden since the beginning of the world') where Girard professes his Catholicism by proclaiming the thesis that Christ came on earth to abolish sacrifice once and for all.

One can agree that Girard has the merit of seeing clearly that in Africa the sacred king is: 'a man who is condemned to a sacrificial death' (1972: 154). But he spurns Frazer's views and presents this sacrificial victim to us arbitrarily as: 'a machine for converting sterile and contagious violence into positive cultural values' (Girard 1972: 155). As with every ritual killing, the victim plays the purificatory and regenerative role of scapegoat. In constructing his theory, Girard offhandedly attributes one particular aspect of ritual killings to all of the great diversity of sacrifices that are practised in human societies. He takes the Oedipus myth and the rite of the *pharmakon*, where one sees an entire community turn violently on a scapegoat who is held responsible for all the evil of the city, to be paradigmatic of all Greek practices and beliefs. By adopting this selective stance, Girard ignores the Greek practice of sacrificing to the gods as Detienne and Vernant (1979) described it. I will not go into the details of the analysis of this animal sacrifice as a 'cuisine' that unites the immortal citizens with the immortal Olympians while simultaneously strongly marking the difference between them by the fact that the former eat meat while the latter delight in the smoke from the long bones.

Butchering is thus closely associated with cosmogony in this particular case. Let us also be clear that there is a resolute avoidance of violence or any desire to transform the animal into a scapegoat in this sacrificial practice. The animal can move freely and is watched discreetly in the sanctuary. Describing this, Détienne says: 'the sacrificial ritual simulates a silent renunciation – by inviting the victim to lower its head as if it was submitting of its own accord'. It is only when the animal has given its permission that it is felled, 'always by surprise, and so as to avoid as far as possible the violence done to the victim from showing through' (Détienne and Vernant 1979: 19). No doubt Girard will object that 'the faithful do not know, and do not need to know, the role played by violence' (Girard 1972: 21). But from where does he derive this certainty other than his own premises which state that: 'it is violence that constitutes the true heart and secret soul of the sacred' (Girard 1972: 52), and that the function of ritual is to 'purify' this violence (Girard 1972: 59)?

Let us move on to a more careful examination of some of the objections made by Scubla in his careful analysis of my material. Scubla looks at the structure of the Mossi kingship in Burkina Faso as I have described it on the basis of Izard's reports. He says that I was right to have insisted on the bifurcation of the kingship into a king of peace – the holder of legitimate authority (*naam*), and a figure whose responsibility was predatory violence – a war leader, who took upon himself the role of scapegoat. Scubla concludes that the scapegoat function is the pre-eminent element even though this 'king of war' was only the king's double. He was condemned to die in place of the king after having commanded the army for seven years (de Heusch 1990: 22). The fact that the king did not take part in war, and could neither see nor shed blood, strengthened my conviction that the ritual function (the maintenance of peace and abundance) was 'the essence of royal power' in the Mossi case as in many other societies.

Izard comments that, 'the royal rites refer to a system of representations of power whose inspiration is solar' (Izard 1985: 303). The mystical function of the sovereign is no less present even though he is not the master of the fertility rituals which, in this case, take the form of lunar rituals performed by the people of the earth. One cannot conclude from this, as Scubla does, that Frazer's first function (the positive function) is 'apparently absent among the Mossi'. Scubla is convinced that the scapegoat function, the remedy for all evil, is pre-eminent. Without offering any proof, he states that, 'by extension, the royal personage can be the source of all that is good'. He is satisfied with a functionalist explanation of this: '[i]f it is this figure [the royal personage] that assures the permanence of the kingship and stabilizes the social order, one can understand that he can be seen as the guarantor of the order of the natural world'. The function of scapegoat, tied to ritual killing, would thus be performed by one or more doubles.

As for the Hocartian thesis according to which regicide precedes kingship, this appears to me to be completely untenable. Scubla is correct to state that Hocart, who maintained the ritual nature of kingship, is an author who is unjustly forgotten in France. But how can one take seriously Hocart's hypothesis that the first kings were dead kings, the idea that once upon a time one became a king by dying? In order to defend this idea, Scubla relies on research on the Evhé, a population from southern Togo, documented by de Surgy, that I drew attention to in earlier publications. The priest of the Evhé blacksmith god undergoes a seven-year initiation after which he is put to death. It is in the next world that his real reign commences (de Surgy 1990). However, this formula is avowedly exceptional in Africa, and it is a singular reversal of the ideology of the Bemba of Zaire. While the Evhé 'king' is obliged to abstain from all sexual activity during his long initiation, the sexual life of the Bemba king, who gets to become a protecting ancestor, is said to reheat the country (Richards 1968).

Elsewhere I have indicated other examples of sacred chiefs who were condemned to abstinence, total seclusion, or symbolic death (de Heusch 1982). I would suggest that these kings who are encumbered with a particularly rigorous prohibition take upon themselves, and channel, the evil, dangerous aspect of sacredness. In any case, nothing permits us to see the primitive form of kingship in these somewhat aberrant cases, or to believe, as Scubla says here, that, in a general way, 'it is the killing which confers kingship'. More often it signifies the contrary: the end of a reign, or, more exactly, its regeneration by the accession of a successor to the throne.

It is equally perilous to follow Hocart's belief that the origin of all rituals is the royal installation rite. Not only does this thesis smack of evolutionism; it ignores the fact that there are societies which have rituals but which know nothing of the sacralization of power. The sacred chief emerges from a society based on lineages or clans as the result of a breakdown of the domestic order. This is the significance of royal incest in the Bantu world which I have drawn attention to elsewhere. The phoneme that separates the English words 'kinship' and 'kingship' deserves to be known as the 'g' factor in history. The phenomenon of royalty is the principal motor of this development, not its origin. Whatever the reason for the sacrifice of the king, it cannot therefore be considered as 'the original sacrament' with any justification.

Notes

English translation by Declan Quigley.

1. Unfortunately Lucien Scubla was not able to attend the conference in St Andrews that led to this book. I am grateful to him for giving me the opportunity to comment on the text he submitted for publication.

References

Detienne, M. & Vernant, J-P. 1979. *La Cuisine du sacrifice en pays grec*. Paris: Gallimard.

Girard, R. 1972. *La Violence et le sacré*. Paris: Grasset.

—— 1978. *Des choses cachées depuis la fondation du monde*. Paris: Grasset.

Heusch, L. de 1982. *Rois nés d'un coeur de vache*. Paris. Gallimard.

—— 1986. *Le Sacrifice dans les religions africaines*. Paris: Gallimard.

—— 1990. 'Introduction', in L. de Heusch (ed.) *Systèmes de pensée en Afrique noire*, vol. 10, *Chefs et rois sacrés*. Paris: CNRS.

Izard, M. 1985. *Gens du pouvoir, gens de la terre. Les institutions politiques de l'ancien royaume du Yatenga (Bassin de la Volta Blanche)*. Paris & Cambridge: Maison des Sciences de l'Homme & Cambridge University Press.

Richards, A. I. 1968. 'Keeping the King Divine' *Proceedings of the Royal Anthropological Institute*, 1966.

Surgy, A. de 1990. 'Le Prêtre-roi du Sud-Togo', in L. de Heusch (ed.) *Systèmes de pensée en Afrique noire*, vol. 10, *Chefs et rois sacrés*. Paris: CNRS.

–5–

Tragedy, Ritual and Power in Nilotic Regicide: The Regicidal Dramas of the Eastern Nilotes of Sudan in Comparative Perspective

Simon Simonse

Introduction

Regicide as an aspect of early kingship is a central issue in the anthropological debate on the origin of the state and the symbolism of kingship. By a historical coincidence the kingship of the Nilotic Shilluk has played a key role in this debate which was dominated by the ideas of Frazer as set out in *The Dying God*, the third part of *The Golden Bough* (1913). His symbolic interpretation of kingship has been opposed by a post-war generation of empirical anthropologists who analyse symbolism in terms of underlying political interests. With respect to Shilluk king-ship it was Evans-Pritchard (1948) who proposed an interpretation from this new perspective by bringing in his first-hand knowledge of kingship among the Anuak.

Since the 1980s we have witnessed a reappraisal of Frazer's emphasis on the symbolism of the death of the king. During this same period I have carried out research in a string of Sudanese communities which still practise regicide – some distance to the South of the Shilluk, in Eastern Equatoria. My work takes a new view of the interface between ritual and power in early kingship, the stumbling block in anthropological analyses of kingship. This chapter is a recapitulation and update of the central point of my study *Kings of Disaster* (1992). I owe my theo-retical inspiration largely to the work of René Girard, especially his suggestion that the mechanism of consensual scapegoating is at the bottom of the confusing com-plexity of sacred kingship. But it was the uniqueness of the political arrangements that I had the privilege of studying in the field that forced me to develop a more comprehensive perspective. I will begin my argument with the presentation of a fictive ancient Sudanese kingdom called Kasch as it is painted with a rough brush by the Italian novelist Calasso. I have chosen to begin with literary Kasch because it reflects the dominant stereotyped way African stories of regicide are perceived by the West, by novelists as well as contemporary anthropologists, including

Girard: as a ritual permeated with deep symbolism, and controlled by a priestly caste.

Kasch

The main theme of Calasso's *La Rovina di Kasch* ('The downfall of Kasch') concerns the deeper implications of the transition from the *ancien régime* to modern forms of political power and legitimation. Episodes from the biography of Talleyrand – the French diplomat who survived the French Revolution and the Empire and who was one of the architects of the Restoration – provide the narrative context where the forces of the old and the new order meet. The tale of the fall of Kasch provides an understanding of the nature of the *ancien régime* as rooted in sacrifice.

The legend of Kasch, a slight corruption of the biblical name of Ham's second son Kush who founded the kingdoms in the Upper Nile Valley, was collected in bits and pieces during a field trip in Sudan by the famous German ethnologist Frobenius. It is the story of the destruction of the glorious sacrificial order that preceded the historical kingdoms based on the religions of the book. The heroes of the legend are king Akaf and his prime minister, Far-li-Mas, who was an immigrant storyteller from the Middle East. In the sacred order of Kasch the king is killed at a time fixed by the position of the stars. It was the principal duty of a caste of priests to monitor the stars. In case of occasional failure of duty, sacrifice could correct the mistake. The king was accompanied at his death by his prime minister. A sacred fire was kept burning by a boy and girl who had to be pure and who were killed at the enthronement of the new king when a new fire was lit.

This sacrificial order is undermined by the stories of Far-li-Mas who has an interest in this subversion, not least because of his love for the girl guarding the fire. The stories are so enticing that the priests forget their astrological duties. They lose track of the timing of the king's death, such that it can not be corrected by sacrifice. A final showdown between Far-li-Mas and the priests leaves the priests dead. With this, the new order without regicide commences. The king takes off his veil, the fire is extinguished, and all ritual killing is stopped. The kingdom enters a period of unprecedented prosperity which makes it the envy of its neighbours. After the death of Akaf and Far-li-Mas, however, barbaric people destroy everything. Evaluating the historic revolution, Calasso's narrator concludes that the sacrificial, astrological order of Kasch is superior to the order that is established as a result of the *word* of Far-li-Mas. From an order built on a purposeful but limited human sacrifice in the real world, we move to a 'story' that will justify the elimination of non-believers on an unprecedented scale. From the limited violence of myth we have stepped into the bloodbaths of history.

Calasso then applies this conclusion to the social transition in revolutionary France, inviting comments from a wide range of thinkers including René Girard 'the hedgehog who knows one big thing: "scapegoat"' (Calasso 1994: 157–8). The message that Calasso invites us to take home is that we should not trust our modern order to be less sacrificial than the pre-revolution one. While we are expelling sacrifice through the front door it is already entering through the back door. Never before were the killing fields so vast.

The legend of Kasch serves as a point of reference and contrast for this brief study of Nilotic regicide. It encapsulates the dominant view of the evolution of kingship in anthropology. According to this view, kingship, in its primitive stages, is an institution steeped in myth and ritual. The royal person is a mere puppet in a ritual drama and the only initiative belongs to dignitaries operating from backstage – like the priests in the story. As time passes, evolutionary pressures lead to a gradual differentiation of political and religious roles. When the king's political and military roles begin to crystallize, the first contours of the early state become visible. This view is implicit in recent work on African sacred kingship written from a neo-Frazerian inspiration: the study of Rukuba kingship by Jean Claude Muller (1980), of Moundang kingship by Alfred Adler (1982), and the monumental work of Luc de Heusch on Bantu kingship (1984, 1982*a*, 1982*b*, 1987, 2000). I am not playing down the wealth of ethnographic data presented by these scholars. I do not deny the importance of symbolism. Yet, I cannot make full sense of my own data if I limit my understanding to the study of royal myth and ritual.

The methodologically innovative step I choose to take is to approach kingship as a *drama* without prejudging the content – symbolic or political – of the drama. Watching the drama unfold will enable us to distinguish political, ritual or economic moves by the actors. It will also be possible to describe and analyse changes in the overall composition of the drama, including shifts from ritualization to politicization and vice versa. Finally, this approach yields an unexpectedly simple answer to the classical anthropological question: *under what conditions does a kingdom become a state?* By investigating kingship as drama, it is possible to model the evolutionary transition from early kingdom to state as a process that may have been tried, successfully or unsuccessfully, in many places and over a long period of time.

Kingdoms of the East Bank of the Upper Nile

The ethnography of the Southern Sudan presents us with a rare variety of political forms, not only of acephalous polities, but also of monarchical structures. There is tremendous diversity: from sizeable kingdoms covering areas as large as Belgium and incorporating over 100,000 individuals to polities limited to a single agglomeration. Some of the acephalous structures – such as that of the Nuer – have the capacity for massive political mobilization that far exceeds that of the largest kingdoms. We noted already that the Shilluk of South Sudan became the classical anthropological case of 'divine kingship' and of 'ritual regicide'. The Nuer, on the other hand, became the textbook example of an egalitarian society that renounced central authority, generating political unity from the systematic polarization of its constituent segments.

The societies from which I draw my ethnographic material live in Equatoria, the southernmost region of Sudan, on the East Bank of the Nile, east of Juba. They include the Bari, the Lotuho, Lulubo, Lokoya, Ohoriok, Lango, Lopit, Dongotono, Logir, Imatong, the Pari, the Tenet and the northeastern Acholi. Except for the Pari and Acholi who are Western Nilotic Lwoo speakers, the Lulubo, who are Central Sudanic Madi speakers, and the Tenet who are Surma speaking, all of the groups mentioned are Eastern Nilotic. According to an outdated but still popular classification they are known as Northern Nilo-Hamites (Huntingford 1953). These societies are unique in the open, confrontational style that characterizes the dealings between king and people. The men are organized in quasi-generational age grades. The core responsibility of the age grade in power is to monitor the security of the polity in all its aspects. This includes policing the king's movements. When there is reason to believe that the king is not acting in the community's best interests, especially where food security is concerned, women convene their own assembly issuing resolutions that usually outdo the men in radicalness.

The aspect of kingship that has struck early travellers and colonial administrators most is the fact that kings are answerable to their subjects on the state of the weather. In the literature these kings have therefore come to be known as 'rainmakers', a title that connived to bolster the nineteenth-century stereotype of magic, cunning and superstition as the source of power in 'primitive' polities. Frazer adopted this characterization and put the kings of the Bari, Lotuho, Lokoya and Lulubo in a different, lower, class from the 'divine kings' of the Shilluk.[1] According to him, the kings we are discussing here represented an older evolutionary stage, that of 'magical kingship' (1913, part 1, vol. 1: 345). Placing the sovereigns of the East Bank in a different category from the rulers of the Shilluk is not helpful, however. It obscures the continuity between the different political systems and discourages an approach in which different specific formations are studied as transformations of the same underlying structures. Nor is size a good reason for treating the kingdoms of the Equatorian East Bank differently. It is true that most are smaller than the Shilluk kingdom, but the pre-1850 Bari kingdom was probably larger. Moreover, size was variable, depending in large measure on the perceived rain-giving capability of a given ruler. The reach of a polity under a king who was successful in rain matters could extend as far as his fame spread, comparable to the size of the following of an evangelist in the modern West. As Hocart (1970: 86) remarked, 'it is not the size of the civil list or the extent of square mile ruled' that concerns the anthropologist but the structure of kingship.

The polities I studied all had a notion of ultimate sovereignty. All communities recognized one person as having the highest authority. In practically all cases he or she was the Master of Rain and Drought. If there were two claimants to this role, they would have to fight it out till one of them won lest the kingdom split. Next to the king, most communities had a variety of other offices: for fertility and health of humans and cattle and freedom from pests (birds, worms, insects) and predators (leopards, lions, crocodiles). While in some languages the holders of these offices could be addressed by the same honorific title as the king, there was usually a special term of address. I am using the term Master (Master of the Land, Master of Birds etc.) for the incumbents of these offices. Since they were ultimate authorities in their own domain, I do not use the term 'priest'. This word is better reserved for elders of descent groups, territorial groups or age-groups who perform sacrificial duties on behalf of these groups and for the ritual assistants of the various 'masters'.[2] The assistants of the sovereign are more appropriately termed 'ministers' in English as their role is likely to have significant political content.

During successive episodes between 1981 and 1986 I carried out field research on local institutions of kingship – or what remained of it. I worked intensively among the Lulubo and Lokoya and later, when it was unsafe to spend long periods in the field, I collected material on Lotuho, Bari and the Pari during short visits and from people displaced in town. This fieldwork was complemented with archival work in Khartoum, Entebbe and Rome.[3]

The Scenario of a Rain Drama

By the end of my fieldwork period I had collected twenty-four case histories of regicide covering a period of 130 years. Since 1986 I have received information about five more cases that had occurred. It would seem that the ongoing war in the region and the resulting generalized insecurity raised the frequency with which community leaders were accused of collective misfortune. I will begin by presenting the general scenario of a rain drama, before analysing two rain crises that occurred in the early 1980s. Both resulted in the killing of the rainmaker by his or her community. Drama here is defined as a sequence of interactions between actors holding expectations of each other for which they demand compliance, if necessary on pain of death. The justification for such a violent definition of 'drama' will become apparent.

In the dramas of kingship studied here there are two principal protagonists:

- *the king*: an individual designated as the incumbent of a set of expectations concerning security in the widest sense by a community believing itself dependent on the powers attributed to him;
- *the people*: a collective body from which the king expects submission, in recognition of his status as the upholder of orderly and lawful behaviour in the widest sense.

The security expected from the king includes protection from violence by enemies, but also from epidemics, earthquakes, droughts, pests and plagues. It embraces health (of man and cattle, including procreative health), economic and social security. The king is the community's protective cosmic shield. He is perceived as exercising an heroic kind of brinkmanship, facing, annihilating or redirecting the many dangers impinging on the community from outside. But he is also believed to have the capacity to turn into a diabolic destroyer of the community. The orderliness expected by the king from his people includes abstention from violence, either by the use of arms or witchcraft, respect for the taboos underpinning orderly relations between groups (incest), looking after the weak (widows) and appropriate and timely displays of gratitude for his cosmic patronage. The terms used by a former generation of anthropologists to describe the relationship of king and subjects have sometimes been unnecessarily exotic – for instance Seligman's formulation of the king as 'the dynamical centre of the universe' (1934: 4), or the term 'rainmaker' itself. What the Nilotic subject expects from his king is, in fact, very similar to what modern citizens expect from their welfare states: protection from violence in a wide sense – enemies, a wide range of factors influencing the security of livelihood, epidemics and diseases.

Considering the fact that the relationship between king and subject has been the favourite stuff of playwrights for many centuries, it is remarkable that anthropologists have not made more use of a theatrical model in their studies of kingship. Frazer's description of the Nilotic rainmaker as a performer persuading a sceptical public of his power is apt. It is true that the king seeks to accumulate credit so that he can withstand the accusations of his subjects. In this respect he is like a magician who cannot afford to be transparent about his performance. But this is where the parallel stops. The drama played by king and people is intensely interactive, with ups and downs, angry confrontations, mediation efforts leading either to the settlement of the dispute and a new start, or to a showdown between king and people – in which the king's life is at stake.

Common security from drought, enemy attack, epidemics, and so on are the central issues that define the public sphere in these societies, as opposed to the sphere of private family interests. Any development requiring a community response prompts a meeting. The ruling age grade (*monyomiji*) is responsible for calling these public meetings. The same drum is beaten for war and in response to a threat of drought, plague or cattle epidemic. Women have their own public meetings, separate from the men. The weather is an ongoing public concern offering very rich material for dramatic interaction: prompting accusations, arrests, payment of fines, sacrifices and reconciliation rituals. Rainfall is very erratic in the area. One village may benefit from timely rains while its neighbour's fields are left parched, or destroyed by floods. The changes in the weather are monitored and interpreted on a day-to-day basis causing a great deal of worry and suspense.

Recently deceased members of the community may also be agents of rain and drought. If identified as the cause of drought, they need to be placated or exhumed or have the remains of their body completely removed from the community, for instance by throwing it in the Nile.

In the process of identifying the cause of disaster, king and subjects stand face-to-face. The understanding between king and people stipulates that if no other agents are left to be identified, it is the king who carries the blame. It is this ultimate responsibility that motivates the king to do everything in his powers to mend the situation: by directing the blame onto others, by performing sacrifices and by praying to his fathers for assistance. Normally rain will fall while this process is still running. If no rain falls, his subjects' accusing fingers end up pointing at him. He will be faced with an ultimatum, or a succession of ultimatums, to relent and allow the rain to fall. If he does not, the only course of action left to his subjects is to seek his death. If disaster persists even then, people have to accept that God is responsible, as the king claimed in his defence during his last days.

Two Case Studies of Regicide

I collected twenty-four more or less detailed cases of regicide that occurred between 1850 and 1985 in the stretch of Equatoria that is located between the Nile and the Kidepo river. I have selected the ethnographically most complete cases for analysis. The first, the burial alive of the Lowe rainmaker, came to my knowledge more than a year after the event. I visited the community and interviewed the people who had been immediately involved in the event, including the brother of the murdered rainmaker and his son who had played a leading role in the killing.[4] The material for the other case, the killing of the Queen of the Pari in 1984, was collected by my friend, the Japanese anthropologist Eisei Kurimoto. He has carried out research among the Pari since 1978 and visited the community within a month of the tragedy.[5]

The ethnographic background information in Table 5.1 and Table 5.2 concerns the main actors in the drama is necessary to be able to follow the case studies:

The Regicidal Polities: Lafon and Lowe

These two communities, 75 kilometres apart, are both located at the foot of hills. The Pari call their agglomeration Lafon. It consists of six sections surrounding the small hill of Lipul. Starting with the largest these are, in clockwise order: Wiatuo – the king's section (and the largest), Bura, Pucwa, Pugeri, Kor and Angulumere. The total population at the time of the event was about 10,000.

The population of Lowe, located around a much higher hill, may have been slightly larger. Lowe had seven sections located in a semi-circle at the bottom of

Table 5.1 The Killing of the Queen of the Pari

Period	Weather	Action by the People	Action Taken by the Queen and Rainmaker
May 1982	poor rains	Wiatuo Bura section accused of having caused the drought; Wiatuo takes revenge in a stick fight killing two men of Bura. Queen and Kor rainmaker king submitted to an ordeal: jumping over sacred stick.	Rainmaker of Kor flees to District Headquarters.
June 1982	poor rains	Assembly of *monyomiji* in which the queen is summoned to make rain on pain of death.	Queen flees to a location across the Nile, crossing the desert east of Lafon on foot.
August 1982	floods	*Monyomiji* install an interim king from Acholi, a friend of the former king, the late husband of the queen.	
	measles epidemic killing 30 children weaver bird plague		
September 1982	floods spoiling harvest	*Monyomiji* ask the interim king to stop the rain and leave Lafon.	Exit interim-king.
Dry season 1982–1983			
April–May 1983	poor rains	Delegation of elders invite the queen and rainmaker of Kor back from exile.	Queen and Rainmaker return
June 1983	drought and famine	Assembly of *monyomiji* decide to exhume the corpse of the previous king to remove his posthumous curse.	
	brief spell of rains	Corpse exhumed and thrown into the river.	

Period	Weather	Action by the People	Action Taken by the Queen and Rainmaker
July 1983	drought	*Monyomiji* consult diviner to verify the interpretation according to which the late king was responsible for the drought; the diviner says the cause was different.	Queen and rainmaker of Kor accompanied by two elders consult diviner who, as comes out later, puts the blame on the rainmaker of Kor; however at their return to Lafon they do not reveal this information.
August–October 1983	good rains resulting in good harvest	General Assembly of *monyomiji* of all six sections; the truth of the oracle of the diviner consulted by the queen, the rainmaker of Kor, and the two elders of Kilang generation is now revealed; the elders are fined one ox each; the oxen are sacrificed to restore the trust between the *monyomiji* and the elders. Queen and rainmaker of Kor are put under house arrest.	Rainmaker of Kor escapes through a hole he has dug in the wall of his house: second period of exile.
Dry season of 1983–1984			
April 1983	promising start of rainy season		
May 1983	faltering rain	Assembly of *monyomiji* of Wiatuo section; the posthumous curse of an elder of Kilang is identified as the cause of the irregular rain; his corpse is exhumed and thrown into the river,	

Period	Weather	Action by the People	Action Taken by the Queen and Rainmaker
June 1983	no rain	Second Assembly of *monyomiji* of Wiatuo; the Queen is accused of dishonesty, alcoholism and hiding medicines. *Monyomiji* contribute fifteen Sudanese pounds and one tin of sorghum flour per section to make beer for the queen.	Queen attributes the drought to God and denies possessing rain medicines. Aware of and resigned to the fact that she will be killed the queen goes on drinking.
7 July 1983	no rain	General Assembly with compulsory attendance of all adult members of the communities of all six sections location: place of trial and execution of grave offenders. Queen is accused of drought, forcing the community to migrate to another place, and so destroying it; members of the generation of aspiring rulers start beating the queen but are stopped by retired elders. Renewed attempts at beating her; and an offer that she will not be killed if she hands over the rain medicines or if she makes rain.	Apparently as a delaying tactic, the queen now admits to possessing rain medicines; at her house she only has the official rain stones to hand to the delegated of the *monyomiji*.
8 July 1983	no rain	Assembly of *monyomiji* only of all six sections; location: bush. Queen put in front of fire and told that she will die in the flames. A cripple, a leper and a blind man, in turn, accuse the queen of being responsible for their deaths that will inevitably result from the destruction of the community. The lame man is the first to push the queen into the flames using his stick; the crowd joins in using whips and sticks. The Queen's corpse is carried some distance into the bush and stretched on the ground. Her stomach is slit open and treated	Queen accepts the sentence and promises that she will take no posthumous revenge on her community. Queen tries to run away on several occasions. Queen dies as a result of burns and beating.

Period	Weather	Action by the People	Action Taken by the Queen and Rainmaker
		with a particular kind of melon and her tongue is immobilized by thorns, both being done in order to prevent her curse. Queen's body is left in the bush as is the practice with the bodies of warriors slain in battle.	
	7 mm of rain registered on the rain-gauge of the Rural Development Centre	Before returning to the village the *monyomiji* perform a purificatory sacrifice and treat their bodies with protective substances.	
9 July 1983	10 mm of rain		
11 July 1983	10 mm of rain		
13 July 1983	15 mm of rain		
18 July 1983	60 mm of rain		

Table 5.2 The Killing of the Rainmaker of Lowe

Date	Weather	Actions Undertaken by the People	Actions Undertaken by the Rainmaker
1959–1974 rule of Thimomonye	years with relatively good rains	Rainmaker inherits the rain powers as priest of his section; he is successful and gains recognition from a neighbouring section; people start to call him *ohobu* (king); he becomes a *de facto* king of his moiety, formally under the overall King of Lowe.	Rainmaker steps up his demands from the *monyomiji* of the moiety demanding a day of cultivation, a privilege reserved for the king.
c. 1966		*Monyomiji* refuse to perform the services demanded by the Rainmaker.	Rainmaker demonstratively sells his rain medicines off to the king of neighbouring Liria.
	drought	*Monyomiji* give in, buy the medicines back from the King of Liria, perform cultivation service for the rainmaker and request him to make rain.	Rainmaker continues to put high demands on the community repeatedly getting into conflict with the Anyanya rebel army.
c. 1978	drought	New *monyomiji* accuse the rainmaker of being responsible for the drought.	Rainmaker accuses the *monyomiji* of having cursed his last surviving full son and designate-successor to death.
April–June 1981	poor rains	Renewed accusations by *monyomiji* against the Rainmaker; tension mounts; when the rainmaker calls his son, there are immediate rumours that the rainmaker knows he will soon die and that he has no intention to relent; the crisis is felt to have run out of hand.	Rainmaker calls his half-son home; this is a son he has fathered in the name of his late elder brother with the wife he inherited from the same brother; the half-son works in a forestry project; the issue is the responsibility for the children of the full-son; the half-son who is unmarried expects to inherit at least one of his late half-brother's wives; he blames his father for not having taken steps to get him a wife.

Date	Weather	Actions Undertaken by the People	Actions Undertaken by the Rainmaker
Day 1, June 1981 (true date not known)	no rain	Meeting between rainmaker and his half-son turns violent, the father shooting the son with an arrow, the son hitting the father's head with a club; members of the *monyomiji* of the the location come to the scene of the violence, interrogate the rainmaker and lash him. Spokesman of the *monyomiji* replies that the rainmaker will be the one to die first. Same afternoon members of the *monyomiji* led by the half-son of the rainmaker start digging the rainmaker's grave; members of the *monyomiji* try to stop him but he retorts 'Don't you want to eat food?' and he is left to dig.	Rainmaker curses the *monyomiji* of the four sections controlled by him announcing that for seven years they will lack rain.
Day 2, June 1981	no rain	Assembly of the *monyomiji* of the village; the rainmaker is put on a chair in the middle to be interrogated.	Rainmaker admits having hidden rain medicines in a tree four hours distance from the village, in Acholiland.
Day 3, June 1981	no rain	Rainmaker and delegation of the *monyomiji* inspect the tree, do not find the medicine and sacrifice a goat to normalize the tree.	
Day 4, June 1981	no rain	Assembly of the *monyomiji* of the sections receiving rain from the rainmaker decides that rainmaker should die; there is general consensus; the brother–catechist and village headmen later claim to have opposed the decision but say they were afraid to speak out. Grave dug and rainmaker is made to measure the grave before he is put down in it.	

Date	Weather	Actions Undertaken by the People	Actions Undertaken by the Rainmaker
		Rainmaker's half-son lists his father's crimes while the *monyomiji* cover his body with soil. Sacrifice of a goat made on the grave to prevent the rainmakers' posthumous revenge.	Father orders his son to stay at home observing the customary mourning period of seven days.
Day 5, June 1981		Police arrest twenty-two men who participated in the killing; the rainmaker's half-son who has returned to his place of work is arrested there.	
June 1981, four days after day 4	heavy rain	*Monyomiji* conclude that they took the right course of action.	
End June 1981		All men arrested have been released or have escaped except the Rainmaker's parricidal son.	Parricidal son stays in prison till it closes as a result of the spreading hostilities of the civil war in the area. He is waiting for the day the *monyomiji* will carry him home on their shoulders to install him as the rainmaker.
July–August 1981	drought conditions	Posthumous revenge of rainmaker identified as the cause of the drought; sacrifice of apology is made on the grave; the skull is removed and set to rest in a rock vault as an act of respect and reconciliation.	
1982–1984	poor rains	*Monyomiji* reinvestigate the cause of the drought and conclude that the swallowing of rain medicines by the rainmaker is the cause.	

Date	Weather	Actions Undertaken by the People	Actions Undertaken by the Rainmaker
1985	poor rains	*Monyomiji* led by the rainmaker's brother refuse the demand for payment of blood-wealth, thus continuing the cycle of hatred in the family.	Parricidal son of the rainmaker returns from prison; he demands payment of blood-wealth by the *monyomiji* for killing his father claiming that this was the cause of the current drought: rain crisis continues.

the hill. Clockwise from north to south we have Lobugi, Losok, Pura, Lohera (the section of the King) Logilo, Omirai and Hojofi.

The killing in Lowe happened when the police of Torit District were still functioning. Twenty-two *monyomiji* were arrested; some were released within a week, others escaped. The killing in Lafon happened at a moment when the area was already affected by the spreading civil war. A development project in the village had already been stopped. There was no response to the killing from the government.

Moieties   Most communities in the area are polarized in halves, or 'moieties' as they are conventionally termed in anthropology. Lafon and Lowe are no exception. Lafon is divided between the Boi, comprising all the sections except Kor, and the Kor, a moiety consisting of a single section. Lowe is divided into the Lotuho, comprizing the four northern sections, and the Omirai, comprizing the three southern ones.

Kings, Priests and Rainmakers   Apart from the king who is the sovereign, politically as well as in rain matters, both communities have hereditary officers with rain-powers. Kor, the smaller moiety, has its own rain maker. He plays a role of some importance in the events related here.

In Lowe we find, besides the king, two rainmakers residing at both extremities of the crescent-shaped string of villages. The case related here concerns the rainmaker at the southern tip. He is the descendant in a line of priests assisting the king. The rainmaker who was killed in 1981 had a great deal of success in the early 1960s and extended his power to include the neighbouring section. He was recognized as the rainmaker of the southern moiety and assumed the title of 'king'.

Monyomiji, Elders and Young Extremists   The men in Lafon and Lowe are organized in 'quasi-generations' based on age which succeed one another every twelve to sixteen years. The generation carrying responsibility for the security of the community is called *monyomiji* meaning the 'owners' or 'fathers' (*monye*) of the community (*amiji*). The young age at which these societies allocate public responsibility is in stark contrast to the gerontocratic set up of most of the societies of the Karimojong cluster to the east. A newly completed generation – consisting of four age sets – will push the sitting *monyomiji* out when they see their numbers equal those of their seniors. Included in the new generation-set are males from about 16 years onwards. Power is handed over after a contest, often in the form of a stick fight. The retired *monyomiji*, as elders, will continue to play a role as political moderators. Some of these 'elders' are still in their early forties when they retire. Before acceding to public responsibility, the younger generation act as radicals and extremists. In the case of the killing of the queen these stereotyped roles and behaviours of the different generations are clearly apparent.

In the Lowe case the rainmaker managed quite well as long as he was dealing with his own generation mates, the *Thimomonye* ('those who ignore their fathers'), the generation that took over after independence, at the onset of the civil war in which Lowe played an important role. But when faced with a new generation of radicals, after the conclusion of the war, he ran into great problems and was killed. The rainmaker was one of the first primary school leavers of the village. During the civil war he ran the bush school in Lowe. Second son of the sectional rain-priests of Hojofi, he succeeded to his father's responsibilities, his elder brother becoming a catechist. His only surviving full son, who was foreordained to succeed him, was killed when a lorry hit him while he was riding a bicycle. The rainmaker was reluctant to hand the responsibility to the son he had fathered in the name of another brother. This son had grudges *vis-à-vis* his biological father. An employee with a modest income at a nearby forestry project, he was still unmarried at thirty. He blamed his father for not having passed the wives of his dead half-brother to him.

The Lokoya rainmaker in Lowe had exercised his responsibility for twenty-three years when he was killed in 1980. He was replaced as rainmaker by his wife, the Pari Queen of Lafon who was herself killed after only four years in office. She had been installed by the *monyomiji* as a caretaker until her son was old enough to take over. In contrast to the rainmaker of Lowe, she took little interest in rain-matters. From the beginning they had been a source of problems for her. In the short period she was queen she only experienced the scapegoating dimension of her role. Even before the crisis related here she had been blamed by the *monyomiji*. Typically, in 1981, when I tried to pay her a visit, she went into hiding, fearing only trouble from the white man. In rain issues she relied heavily on the advice of her fellow rainmaker and fellow scapegoat from Kor.

Comparing Regicide in Lowe and Lafon to the Story of Kasch

If we keep Calasso's story of Kasch in mind as we read these accounts, we immediately notice the following differences:

1. *The killing of the king is not a ritual.* It is the unintended, yet inevitable, consequence of a process that should have resulted in rain but has failed to do so. It is the culmination of an escalating conflict; the killing would have been avoided if rain had fallen before the crucial moment.
2. *The king is not a passive victim.* He has a whole range of tactics that he uses to influence the course of events. He:
   (a) takes risks to obtain maximum benefit from the expectations raised about

his power. He may raise the stakes by demanding services, tribute or a wife when the *monyomiji* have already started accusing him of sabotaging the rain.

If this game of bluff fails,

(b) influences the public interpretation of weather-events through friendly diviners, through investigations into abuses and broken taboos in the community;

(c) he can propose sacrifices to win time;

(d) to win time he can confess to having tied up the rain using rain medicines, thus affirming his power and upping the ante in order to win time. Both rainmakers resort to this tactic;

(e) he can flee if the situation becomes too risky (as the queen and the rainmaker of Kor actually did);

(f) he can fight back and defend himself. When kings were the only gun owners in the community this was sometimes a successful tactic. King Nyiggilo of the Bari, the first native owner of a gun, used his gun on three successive occasions to prevent the crowd from fetching him to be killed. He managed to survive for over two years more (see Lejean 1865: 75).

3. *The killing of the king cannot be considered as the outcome of purely political processes.* It is not the assassination of an oppressive ruler who does not deliver what he has promised. It is not the death of the king that is desired by the community, but his blessings. In its last stages of escalation, regicide is a necessity imposed on the community – not so different from the obligation to revenge a killed relative. As the son of the Lowe rainmaker said to me about his father: 'He is killing us, so why should we not kill him?' In its origins kingship may have depended on the very possibility of an all-out confrontation with the community just as a system of complementary segmentary opposition depended on the possibility of revenge. Instead of going through the disruption of regicide – which includes the possibility of conflict with supporters of the king, of posthumous curses on the community and potential rivalry about the succession – the community would rather have the rain.

4. *Regicide is the outcome of a reactive process to protracted drought in which the king, considered guilty of the situation, gradually becomes the sole target of a slowly intensifying, condemning consensus of ever larger sections of the population affected by the drought.* The process is reactive, because the build-up of consensus stalls as soon as rain starts to fall. A timely end to drought may even benefit the power and reputation of a rainmaker: if he can come up with a good justification for temporarily withholding the rain, his power and reputation may benefit from the drought. This is a striking example of the scapegoating process as it has been analysed by Girard. Initially unfocused discontent in the community in crisis gradually converges on a single person

who is identified as an agent of evil. It is believed that the expulsion of this person resolves the crisis.

The gradual build up of consensus is clearly demonstrated in the case of the Pari queen. From the six sections of the Pari, only two brought up charges against the queen in 1982. Before that they had blamed one another. In 1983 three sections were involved in the accusations. In the course of 1984 as many as four meetings took place. The first was a meeting of the largest section, which is also the royal section. The second comprised the adult men of all sections, the third all the people including women, children and old people. In the final showdown only the warriors participated. The venue was a location far enough away from the village that it could have been a battlefield. It was an act of violence comparable to war. The elders who could have given some protection to the queen were absent.

Sacrifice as a Buffer

While in Calasso's Kasch the performance of sacrifices according to an eternal astrological order is presented as the fundamental guarantee for prosperity, the Eastern Nilotic communities expect deliverance from imminent disaster by raising the suspense of their relationship with their king to a pitch of deady intensity. There is a general belief that the greater the pressure that is brought to bear, the more likely the king will be to give in and deliver. This explains the use of torture and threats. In this context sacrifice has a moderating influence on the progression of the build-up of suspense. It is an action that king and people carry out jointly. Sacrifice, varying from the crushing of a wild cucumber to the immolation of one or more human beings, has its own repertoire of alternatives of varying degrees of violence and effectiveness. It is the most important buffer in the escalation of a regicidal crisis. The following brief note by a District Administrator working among the Bari catches this relationship between suspense and sacrifice:

> There comes a time when the need is too great, and he [the rainmaker] is given a last chance. Then an ox, if they can afford it, is slaughtered, and a great feast prepared, and some of the blood with some round pebbles [the rainstones] is put in one of the hollowed stones used by the women for grinding corn.[6] This is left on one side, I presume as an offering to some higher power. The feast is held with much drumming; at its conclusion, on a given signal, amid dead silence, all retire to their huts, and not a sound is made till morning. If no rain comes in three weeks from that day the Rainmaker is killed and his son rules, his cattle being divided among the villagers. (Jennings-Bramly, 1906: 102)

Sacrifice has its own build-up of suspense. Long-term suspense is generated by the escalating seriousness of the stages of the crisis and a short-term suspense generated by the sacrificial events. In popular belief, the rain is released by the suspense. If other conditions are fulfilled, only the deliberate undoing of the suspense can stop the rain. This belief is dramatized by the speed with which the participants leave the scene of the sacrifice. They run to get home before the rains – without looking back. Ignoring the suspense is a subsersive act of disbelief, like that of the wife of the patriarch Lot, looking back at her native city.

The importance of the event is marked in various ways:

1. by the venue selected:
    (a) at the meeting place of the *monyomiji* opposite the king's palace (the location for discussing day-to-day issues);
    (b) in front of the gate of the village (a liminal position where issues of war and peace are discussed);
    (c) in a location in the bush. Apparently in Lafon there are at least two locations for meeting, respectively associated with different levels of the violence that issues from execution and war.
2. by the degree of inclusiveness of the participants, varying from:
    (a) a solo performance by the king;
    (b) a sacrifice performed at the request of a delegation from a particular area by the priest (or king) and the delegation;
    (c) a ritual performed by the king with participation of a selected group of elders or big men elders only;
    (d) a meeting or ritual with participation of the *monyomiji* in varying degrees of territorial inclusiveness;
    (e) a meeting with compulsory presence of all members of the community.
3. by the value of the victim immolated, ranging from:
    (a) a wild cucumber, a minimal substitute victim in the Nilotic world;
    (b) one or more goats or sheep (usually a black he-goat for rain);
    (c) one or more bulls;
    (d) one or more human beings.

Only one community in the area of study is known to have sacrificed young men for rain. Note that the scenario of human sacrifice is very different from that of regicide. The young men who are selected as victims are only made aware of their destiny at the end of the process. They are pure. They have not yet killed or had sexual intercourse. They have no association with violence and evil. In contrast, the king is killed in revenge – for killing his subjects with drought – and as an incarnation of evil. Table 5.3 shows how sacrifices are part of the build-up of a rain crisis. Sacrifice mitigates the antagonism and the suspense. It provides a domain of joint action between the king and the people. By using the sacrificial repertoire parsimoniously regicide can be avoided.

Beyond Tragedy

How should we relate the ritual kingship of imaginary Kasch, as our stereotype of an African kingdom, to these observations? How does the ritual model of Kasch relate to the 'tragic' model presented here? Can they be related as exemplars of different steps in a process of political and social differentiation? Can they be construed as transformations of a single underlying structure? Are there historical factors that can account for the transformation from one system into another?

The last question has an obvious answer: the inherent instability of a political system based on confrontation that could result in regicide must have been a powerful argument to look for change, to make the system more amenable to control. Ritualizing the regicidal drama, having the king killed without the mess of a concrete murder, would be an attractive option for community leaders with a stake in stability and maintenance of the status quo. The targets of regicidal aggression, the kings, should also be expected to have looked for ways to deter their subjects from killing them.

I will show that both suspected responses to 'tragic regicide' were indeed operative in the political constellation of the East Bank of the Nile. First I look at various ways in which regicide has been ritualized. Then I will show that much of the observed political action of kings corresponds to strategies that improve their security and, eventually, reverse the balance of victimhood. From being at the mercy of their subjects, kings pro-actively sought to establish a situation where their subjects would be at their mercy.

Ritualizing the Scapegoating of the King

We found a tremendous proliferation of ritual forms relating to the violent dimension of kingship in the communities that have occasional recourse to the scapegoating of their king. This variety of ritual forms testifies to the fact that we are dealing with fresh ritual creativity by communities that are still in direct touch with the practical purpose of the ritual: the need to transfer undirected, subliminal discontent to the well structured, polarized relationship of the community with its king. The forms can be divided into three categories: (1) rituals in which the king is designated as a victim of his community, usually at his installation; (2) ritual procedures mitigating or controlling the violence of regicide; (3) ritual elaborations of the king's natural death as an event where evil is expelled.

Table 5.3 Typical Sequence of Escalation in a Rain Crisis

Demands by People	Alternative Courses of Follow-up Action on Demands by People	Public Action/sacrifice	Alternative Courses of Follow-up Action by the King	Demands by King
Customary humble request for rain at the start of the season carried out by the women.	Customary reminder by women at start of season.		Customary washing of rain stones.	Demand for respectful recognition of his sovereignty and for respect of order and abstention from violence.
Demand for the truth concerning the cause of the drought: In emergency meeting of the *monyomiji*; Or in emergency meeting of women. Emergency meetings have different degrees of seriousness (reflected in the location of the meeting and different scopes of participation.	Purificatory sacrifices in case of breach of taboo, of violence, adultery, for social exclusion, with special attention for grievances of member of the royal (=rain) clan. Settlement of debts and disputes.	Collective prayer accompanied by the sprinkling of water heavenwards celebration of communal unity (for instance by spitting in the water that is sent to the sky; quasi-sacrifice by crushing wild cucumbers to represent oxen.	Circulate interpretations of drought that link it to particular shortcomings, insults and other mistakes (non-attendance of funerals) by community-members with respect to the king. Pray to ancestors, overhaul the rain stones by first drying them and then thoroughly washing them.	Demand for tribute settlement of debts and settlement of disputes.
Repeated demand for rain: villages, territorial section request the King to make rain in their area, bringing him animals in payment and for sacrifice.	Delegation sent to the King with payment of tribute and/or sacrificial animal. Accusations that the rainmaker or his close collaborators are sabotaging the rain.	Sacrifices of small livestock or cattle for rain, at increasingly potent locations and at graves, or on the skulls or bones of increasingly powerful royal ancestors.	King meets special requests from various locations in his kingdom by washing the rain stones.	Demand for livestock, cattle or even a wife from the *monyomiji*.
Renewed demand for truth: specialized investigations into the causes of drought	Accusations may be alternated with mollification of the King ('cooling	Public invocation of supreme god blaming god for the drought and begging him	Accusations directed at particular individuals (witches), neighbouring	Much now depends on the King's taste and the community's taste in risk

Demands by People	Alternative Courses of Follow-up Action on Demands by People	Public Action/sacrifice	Alternative Courses of Follow-up Action by the King	Demands by King
by diviners. According to the seriousness of the situation increasingly famous diviners can be selected and increasingly drastic divination techniques used from the cucumber oracles to reading the intestines of an ox.	his heart'), by the gift of a wife, cattle, delicacies, alcohol (the alcohol given to the Queen of Pari).	to relent, accompanied by sacrifice and communal with relevant elders. Perform a human sacrifice; only practised in one community in the research area.	communities, enemies and territorial sections or age sets in the community.	taking; he can win a lot if the rain comes. The King has the choice to step up his demands or, in a theatrical move, he may opt out, refusing gifts, selling off his rain medicines (as in the Lowe case) or secretly fleeing (as in the Lafon case).
Demand rain using increasing amounts of physical force on the king to release the rain.	Face the king with an ultimatum to make rain or be killed. Women perform the ritual of symbolically killing the king by killing (if it is an animal) or burning (if its is a plant or tree) the totem of the royal clan.	In response to the ultimatum have the King perform a sacrifice with the most sacred of paraphenalia at which the king solemnly declares that it will rain within a specified period of time.	The interpretations of the drought promoted by the King will put the blame with the god or with actors that can safely be accused without raising the tension.	The King will do all he can to save his life; he may flee, defend himself from the aggression of his community now turned into lynching mob.
	Torture the king.			
	Kill the king.			
	Take precautions against posthumous revenge.			The King's successor to demand compensation from the community for having killed their man.

Rituals in Which the King is Designated as a Victim of his Community at his Installation

A preliminary step in ritualizing the scapegoat role of the king is the separation of the royal office from the pre-existing person of the king. In our area of study this differentiation of 'the two bodies of the king' is achieved either by designating the undifferentiated body as 'wild' or 'predator-like' and extracting the royal body by a process of purification – as among the Lokoya – or by adding sacral powers to the pre-existing, supposedly innocent body of the designate king – as among the Bari.[7]

The Lokoya and Lotuho stage the installation of the king as the capture of a dangerous animal. In Liria the *monyomiji* beat the war-drum for an emergency meeting and pass the message around that a leopard or lion has been spotted near the village. The *monyomiji* collect in front of one of the gates of the village. Their number includes the prince to be installed as king: he is not supposed to be aware of his selection. One of the senior *monyomiji* will come forward to congratulate the king with his selection. This will lead to a fight between his brothers and the rest of the *monyomiji*. The *monyomiji* will win and carry the king into the village where he will undergo a long series of purification rituals that will make him fit to be the king. The Lotuho have a similar procedure. Among them the king is an aquatic monster (crocodile), captured from the river through the power of the instant performance of a quadruple sacrifice carried out by the four clans of the Lotuho.

While the Lokoya and Lotuho humanize a monster from the wild to become their king, the Bari and Lulubo deliberately turn their king-elect into a kind of monster: a receptacle of evil. This making of the king is a curse, and the word used for the 'cursing of the king' is the same as the one used for cursing the enemy. The Bari thus transfer all diseases to the king elect:

> Let measles be with you!
> Let syphilis be with you!
> Let smallpox be with you!
> Let scabies be with you!
> Let conjunctivitis be with you!, etc.

AIDS would have been added to this list had the curse not been recorded before the mid 1980s. The Lulubo have several expressions that betray their understanding that the king elect is designated as a victim: the king is 'going to be cut' (as a victim in a sacrifice), and 'he is put in the eye of evil' (as the target of evil).

Ritual Procedures Mitigating or Controlling the Violence of Regicide

These procedures are found outside the immediate area of my research. Instead of allowing the relationship between the king and the people to escalate and degenerate to the point that the community has no other alternative than to kill its king, the Dinka and Shilluk prevent all kings from dying a natural death. The obligatory killing of the king is postponed till the time that the king is sick or about to die of old age. If a king would die a natural death, the community would lose the essential power of kingship.

The Masters of the Fishing Spear, who are the Dinka rainmakers and sacrificers, decide themselves when they should be killed. When they think the right moment has come they make their wish known. Among the Dinka of Bahr-el-Ghazal they would be buried alive. A grave is dug and the spearmaster seats himself on a roofed platform, singing solemn songs while the grave is filled by the crowd. The mood of the crowd is festive and aggressive. The men are armed. When the grave is filled they throw themselves on a calf – which had been treated with reverence until then – and kill it by trampling and suffocating it under their joint weight (Lienhardt 1961: 298–319).[8]

Among the Donjol Dinka of Northern Upper Nile, the spearmaster would be walled in a hut together with his first wife and favourite ox and left to die of starvation and thirst (Bedri 1939: 131). The Padang Dinka used to suffocate their spearmaster. The suffocation was carried out by the members of the age sets he had initiated (Bedri 1948: 50). The Bor Dinka had their spearmasters suffocated by dancers raising dust around them. The spearmaster was put in the middle of a closed stable and died as a result of the dust raised by the feet of his people from the loose soil consisting of burnt and dried dung.

From the middle of the nineteenth century onwards, the Shilluk changed from immuring their kings to suffocating them. The reason for the change was concern for a king who, while still alive, was exposed to the stench of the corpse of his female companion (Seligman & Seligman, 1932:92). This shift can count as evidence of a tendency to mitigate the violence of regicide. The killing of the king was the duty of a particular caste who also buried him. For the Shilluk, I have found only one mention of a fixed period of reign after which the king would have outlived his royal potency and should be killed. The period mentioned is ten years (Hofmayr, 1925: 179).

Frazer's famous image of the Shilluk king spending the night waiting for his rival 'as a sentinel on duty prowling round his huts fully armed, peering into the blackest shadows' (Frazer 1913, part 3: 22) is confusing. It is presented to underpin his vision of the king as the incarnation of the 'dying god'. The attacks that must have been the primary concern of the king were political assassinations by rivals – not the ritual death that occurred when his term was considered to have ended. Early travellers' reports indicate intense dynastic rivalry. The king's palace was built as a true labyrinth and the king changed his sleeping hut every night (Beltrame 1881: 79). The position defended by Evans-Pritchard in the Frazer lecture of 1948 maintains this confusion. Against Frazer, Evans-Pritchard argues that all the historic cases of Shilluk regicide were political and that their representation as having a deeper meaning was just a part of the mystifying ideology surrounding kingship. The evidence does not support Evans-Pritchard's position. Riad's detailed review of the reported causes of death shows that out of thirty-one rulers, the first four mythical rulers vanished mysteriously, nine kings were killed in dynastic rivalry, six were killed in war, and six others were ritually killed. The six remaining kings either died of other causes or information is lacking on their death (1959: 52–163).

The Ritual Construction of the King's Natural Death as a Salutary Event

Regicide carried out in response to drought or to another disaster has two closely linked aspects – the expulsion of evil and the collection of the blessings:

Averting the Evil of the King   The royal funerary rituals of the communities under study are extraordinarily complex. After the king has died, the greatest precautions are needed to defend against the evil powers that are believed to be incarnate in him. These powers must be contained or channelled to safe locations lest disorder should follow. It was a general practice in the area to plug the orifices of deceased kings with leaves or sesame paste. Before laying the king in his grave, the leaves were taken out. They were carried in a solemn procession to the river or to a cave away from the village by old women who advanced on their knees. While moving in this way they waved their arms, as if they were harvesting sorghum. The Bari dispose of the royal hair – which has not been cut since the king's installation – in a similar way.

During the period immediately following the king's death wailing and strict non-violence are prohibited lest evil powers be unchained. The king might turn into a leopard. Sacrifices at the funeral should be by suffocation – bloodless and noiseless. The practice of burying the prime minister (Lotuho), a slave (Bari), a nubile maiden (Shilluk), the king's favourite ox (Dinka, Shilluk) with the king should probably be interpreted as attempts to avert the posthumous anger of the king. These performances on the body of the king who has died a natural death have the same objective as the piercing of the tongue of the Queen of the Pari and the mixing of a crushed melon with her blood and stomach contents.

Collecting the Blessings of the King   There is a widespread belief that the death of a king is bound to cause rain. (If rain falls out of season there is immediate speculation about which rainmaker's death might have triggered it.) The death of the king must therefore be exploited to the maximum. The Bari prolong the king's dying. In fact the Bari king is made to die three times. After his 'medical' death, which is bound to cause some showers, people wait for his 'effective death' when the bloated stomach of the plugged corpse, placed on a platform, bursts. The dripping of the body liquids on the land below, and on the slave positioned under the platform, is the most potent manifestation of his power. This slave, if not buried with his master, thus receives the most powerful blessing as the assistant of the future king. The grave of the king will continue to produce miracles for one rainy season. After that the tumulus on top of the grave will be levelled: his third and final death.

The power of the king is considered most effective in the period after his death. The rains following his death are attributed to him. The dead king will remain 'in power' for at least one cultivation season before a successor can take over. After this reign of the deceased king, his bones are exhumed, placed in pots and transferred to the royal shrine in stages. This ritual is even more elaborate and sophisticated than the burial itself. The process of reaping the benefits of the king's death, from the time of the burial to exhumation, is surrounded by a variety of purification sacrifices. These range from the crushing of cucumbers to the killing of a big black bull. The ritual surrounding the king's funeral aims at purification, at separating the beneficial powers of the king from his evil. The funeral process among the Lotuho, which culminates in the exhumation, can be interpreted as a long extended purification process. At each stage some evil is removed; simultaneously the blessing deriving from the king becoming purer, but also less virulent. The fact that no flesh was left on the bones of the king of Tirangore at his exhumation in 1986 was a posthumous confirmation of his good-naturedness, of the purity of his soul.

There is a striking parallel with the dual rule of the dead king and the live king in ancient Egypt. Dismembered Osiris, the dead king, comes to life each year with the flooding of the Nile. I believe the parallel should be explained by the universal origins of kingship in the scapegoat mechanism, rather than in cultural borrowing or diffusion. Moreover, the kind of sacrificial order that characterized these kingdoms has developed as a very specific response to preliminary disorders. The ethnographic material presented here gives us a glimpse of the nature of that disorder. In comparison to the spontaneous regicidal dramas I have recorded, the sacrificial killing of the king is a step in the direction of greater priestly control, greater mystification, and reduced popular participation in the drama of kingship.

What requires more consideration is the epistemological incapacity of researchers to capture kingship as the multi-dimensional drama it is. Once embarked on the fascinating wealth of royal symbolism and ritual, too many lose sight of the realpolitik of kingship. And when the point of departure is the political economy of kingship, it would seem that ritual and symbolism are only allowed to appear as false consciousness.

The Revolution of the Scapegoat Kings

Even when the drama of kingship is staged on a level playing field, where the expectations of the people are matched by the blessings of the king and the expectations of the king by the obedience and tribute of his people, the king is under permanent pressure to strengthen his position. When it comes to the use of physical force, the king, his kinsmen and clients will just form a minority in the wider community. It is not only his interest in his own survival but also his duty to his clansmen that forces the king to try to consolidate and strengthen his power. If he enjoys taking risks he may use the changes in the weather to this effect – by exacting tribute from his subjects. Though profits are sometimes impressive, the risk of being killed in the game are great.

The stability of the king's office is better served by long-term investments in social and economic capital, by obliging his subjects as a 'big man' with generous gifts, by investing in networking through trade, or by engaging in political alliances with neighbouring kings. When we zoom in on these activities we touch the familiar ground of power politics. A brief listing of these political and economic strategies will suffice.

Establishing a Network of Alliances

Matrimonial alliances were the primary means by which the king consolidated his position. The Lotuho king would have a wife, a palace and a household in each of the twenty or so macro-villages that constituted his kingdom. This gave him a *pied-à-terre* in each of the communities of his realm that were frequently in conflict with one another. Government chiefs during and after the colonial period continued to follow the same strategy. To a large extent the tribute in cattle received for the rain must have been used to extend this matrimonial network.

Matrimonial alliances also served as an important political instrument for the conduct of foreign policy. Alliances with neighbouring kings were crucial when the king's position was threatened in a rain crisis. They offered sanctuary to their ally. They also offered military support when their ally was besieged by his own subject *monyomiji*. For example, the powerful town of Imatari came to its end in an attack of the Toposa that was coordinated by its own king against the *monyomiji* of Imatari (Simonse 1992: 173–5). The accounts of the first travellers on the Upper Nile and the first colonial administrators are full of stories of kings eagerly looking for a strong ally to impress their commoners and enemies – categories that sometimes overlapped or coincided. When Samuel Baker came to the Lotuho village of Hiyala, its king 'most coolly proposed that we should plunder one of his villages that was rather too "liberal" in his views' (Baker, 1866:152).

Modifying the Demographic Balance

As a result of the multiple marriages of the kings, royal families and clans grew more rapidly than those of the commoners. The section that was home to the royal family was normally the largest of the community. As a result of networking by the kings, the society on the east bank developed two clearly marked trans-ethnic classes: the royals and the commoners. The lack of restraint with which allied royals of different communities joined hands in punishing and plundering their subjects could be interpreted in terms of an emerging class contradiction.

Establishing Monopolies of Trade

Intertwined with these political and matrimonial networks were trade relations. In the middle of the nineteenth century political and trade networks on the East Bank overlapped, the two Lotuho dynasties dealing with competing northern traders of slaves and other commodities. After 1840 the demand for ivory allowed the kings of the Upper Nile to increase their wealth rapidly. Cotton textiles, which had reached the Bari from the Indian Ocean well before the arrival of the first traders from Khartoum, were a trade monopoly of the king. Trade became the most important asset of power in the latter half of the nineteenth century, especially among the Bari who were strategically located on the Nile. The power of the Egyptian governors (Baker, Gordon and Emin) was to a large extent based on their brokerage of the trade from the north.

Establishing Monopolies of Production

Kings sought to control all specialized branches of production. Blacksmiths, who were the weapons producers, were attached to the royal courts as slaves (as in Bari) or as close allies of the king (Lulubo). The power of the Bekat kings of Bari was closely associated with their control of the extraction of iron ore found in large quantities on Bilinyan mountain. The disintegration of Bekat power in the middle of the nineteenth century may be largely due to the import of cheap scrap iron and copper from the north in 1841, the year that the first expedition from Khartoum reached Bariland. Control of metalworking was also a feature of the Lotuho kingdoms. Up to the twentieth century the Lotuho king was the owner of all the copper helmets made from re-processed bullet cartridges. When the bearer of a helmet died the helmet was returned to the king, who would distribute it to another follower. Among the Bari, hunters and fishermen were dependants (clients or slaves) of the king.

Tribute

The king's fields were cultivated by his subjects. Each year the *monyomiji* of each community were expected to spend one day of clearing and digging on the king's fields, while the women had to spend one or two days weeding. In the larger kingdoms such cultivation was done in all the local communities, supervised by the resident queen. As a result of this labour the king had significant surplus resources at his disposal. We have seen how, on the smaller scale of the sections for which the Lowe rainmaker was responsible, this prestation of labour was a major issue between the *monyomiji* and the rainmaker.

Armies and the Monopoly of the Use of Physical Force

Despite their control of blacksmithing, and their role as military commanders of the *monyomiji* – at least among the Lotuho – kings had limited control of the use of physical force of their subjects. *Ex officio* the king's only instrument of power was his curse to bring drought. When two clans or villages had fought, and the king had settled the case, the threat of drought had a restraining influence. His position was really determined by the balance of power between his own clan, usually one of the bigger ones, his internal and external allies, and whatever coalition chose to oppose him.

The introduction of firearms offered an opportunity to tilt the balance of power in the kings' favour. Kings started to establish armies equipped with firearms from the 1880s. By the end of the Mahdist period (1898) King Lomoro of Tirangore was reported to have 200 men under arms organized as his royal army. Bariland, along the Nile, was divided into a number of zones controlled by warlords, each with his own army. Many, but not all, were rain kings who had succeeded in using the opportunities offered by the new times to consolidate their position.

The Centralization of Ritual

A last strategy in consolidating power is the centralization of ritual powers under the king. The societies studied here show a graded scale. At one extreme we have decentralized societies such as the Lulubo and Lokoya where, next to the rain clan and the king, each clan has a specific cosmic responsibility. The title of king is shared by three to six office-holders.[9] In the Bari and Lotuho kingdoms, which are larger in size, many of these minor powers have been incorporated in the power of the king. However, clan traditions still manifest past responsibilities. The seasonal rituals of each community are, in the larger kingdoms, made uniform and subordinate to the kingdom's rituals.

None of the Nilotic scapegoat kings in our area of study was able to tilt the balance of power to his advantage and to the interests of his personal survival irreversibly. The colonial situation spoiled the game. The civil wars that ensued defined a new arena for political competition with completely new stakes. However the evidence that the old kings tried very hard to reverse their social position, put an end to their vulnerability and, in many cases, establish themselves, in turn, as the victimizers of their own communities, is overwhelmingly clear. In doing this they were revolutionary agents in the process of inventing statehood.

The State as Promise of an End to Tragedy

The state is defined by its monopoly of the use of legitimate physical force. None of the scapegoat kings discussed here achieved such a monopoly, despite their best efforts. Their sovereignty remained contested. Some of the kings went a long way toward running their rain kingdoms as states, but they could only succeed at the cost of extreme repression. King Alikori of Lafon, ruling around the turn of the century, is remembered as an absolute despot. His repressive policies caused one complete section of Lafon, Kor, to go into exile in Acholi, only returning after Alikori had died. Lomoro in Tirangore may have been a similar case. As a result of his clever dealings with the Mahdists, and thanks to the army he built up, he attained undisputed local sovereignty and was viewed by the British as the King of all Lotuho. In his case, however, opposition from rivals and *monyomiji* was too strong. In the end he was not assassinated because of drought but, most likely, because of an adulterous affair. Had firearms come earlier to these political entrepreneurs, a belt of small-scale states might have developed between the Zande states in the west and the pastoral gerontocracies of the peoples of the Karimojong cluster to the east.

These effervescent Nilotic polities were characterized by an acute sense of political risk and opportunity. The fusion developed formidable skills in crisis management, skills that may have been the decisive factor that made Nilotic political entrepreneurs such a success in the Bantu kingdoms to the south. In terms of statehood, anthropologists have considered Buganda and Bunyoro among the most advanced kingdoms of Africa. A disconcerting aspect of these kingdoms is the arbitrariness with which their monarchs victimized their subjects. Were these apparently firmly established monarchies still haunted by the spectre of a reversible power balance and the scapegoating of the King?

What is won and what is lost when reversible systems of kingship are transformed into the irreversible system of the state? We win stability, the possibility for sustained accumulation of wealth and power which results in the further expansion of the state at the expense of less effective political systems.[10] What we lose are the regular plunges into political chaos – but also the galvanizing suspense of the stand-offs between king and people. It is this last aspect of kingship that continues to fascinate us, the modern or post-modern citizens of successful and entrenched state systems. It may be the deeper reason why we do not want to give up on our antiquated, non-utilitarian, spendthrift monarchies. Our kings and queens remind us that the state is not an alien straightjacket forced on us, but that it originated as a relationship between social actors, between the people and royalty. The continued presence of royalty among us is an antidote to the bloodless instrumentality of the state. When our contemporary royals rebel against the ruling monarch and compete for the favour of the public we are reminded that, in the end, the workings of the state are embedded in social relationships. When these same royals die as a result of their controversial initiatives we are offered the temporary illusion that the state is still rooted in risk-taking, defiance and suspense.

Notes

1. I will not delve here into the complex issue of the 'divinity' of the powers of the king. I have earlier argued that I see no reason to disallow the claim of 'divinity' for the powers of the Eastern Nilotic kings and rainmakers as Frazer does (Simonse 1992: 277–9).
2. The word 'priest' is derived from the Greek *presbuteros* meaning elder.
3. Between 1898 and 1914 most of the area was administered from Entebbe, Uganda.
4. More details on the case are related in Simonse (1992: 199–204).
5. Kurimoto's account was published in Japanese in the *Bulletin of the National Museum of Ethnology in Osaka*. A translation of the Japanese text, authorized by the author, can be found in Simonse (1992: 366–73).
6. It would seem that Jennings-Bramly was not present at Bari sacrifices. What is used in rain-sacrifice is rumen, never blood.
7. This differentiation was an issue of extensive theological debate in the European Middle Ages, beautifully analysed by Ernst Kantorowicz in *The King's Two Bodies* (1957).
8. This is a manner of killing in which many a rainmaker from the Lulubo and Bari lost his life.
9. Liria, for instance has a King of Heaven (rain), who is considered the most powerful, a King of the Land (fertility of the soil), a King of the Mountain (reproduction of humans), a King of Grain, a King of War , and a King of Winds. Together they are known as the 'Fingers of God' (Simonse 1992: 264ff).
10. Of course this gain is the cause of other larger-scale historical tragedies with ever smaller circles of winners and larger masses of losers.

References

Adler, A. 1982. *La Mort est le masque du roi*. Paris: Payot.

Baker, S. W. 1866. *The Albert N'Yanza: Great Basin of the Nile and Explorations of the Nile Sources*. London: Macmillan.

Bedri, I. 1939. 'Notes on Dinka Religious Beliefs in their Hereditary Chiefs and Rainmakers', *Sudan Notes and Records* 22 (1): 125–31.

—— 1948. 'More notes on the Padang Dinka', *Sudan Notes and Records* 31: 40–57.

Beltrame, G. 1881. *Il Fiume Bianco e i Dénka*. Verona: G.Civelli.

Calasso, R. 1994. *The Ruin of Kasch*. Cambridge, MA: Harvard University Press.

Evans-Pritchard, E. E. 1948. *The Divine Kingship of the Shilluk of the Nilotic Sudan. Frazer Lecture 1948*. Cambridge: Cambridge University Press.

Frazer, J. G. 1913. *The Golden Bough*. Pt I: *The Magic Art and the Evolution of Kings*. Pt III: *The Dying God*. London: Macmillan.

Girard, R. 1972. *La Violence et le sacré*. Paris: Grasset.

Heusch, L. de 1982a. *The Drunken King and the Origin of the State*. Bloomington: Indiana University Press.

—— 1982b. *Rois nés d'un coeur de vache*. Paris: Gallimard.

—— 1984. 'Sacraal koningschap als een Symbolisch-politieke structuur. Frazers interpretatie opnieuw bekeken', *Sociologische Gids* 31(4): 301–26.

—— 1987. *Ecrits sur la royauté sacré*. Bruxelles: Editions de l'Université.

—— 2000. *Le roi de Kongo et les monstres sacrés*. Paris: Gallimard.

Hocart, A. M. 1970. *Kings and Councillors*, Edited and introduced by R. Needham. Chicago: Chicago University Press.

Hofmayr, W. 1925. *Die Schilluk, Geschichte, Religion und Leben eines Niloten-Stammes*. Mödling: Anthropos Verlag.

Huntingford, G. W. B. 1953. *The Northern Nilo-Hamites*. Ethnographic Survey of Africa, Part VI. London: International African Institute.

Jennings-Bramly, A. 1906. 'The Bari Tribe', *Man* 6: 101–3.

Kantorowicz, E. 1957. *The King's Two Bodies. A Study in Medieval Political Theology*. Princeton, NJ: Princeton University Press.

Kurimoto, E. 1986. 'The Rain and Disputes, A Case Study of the Nilotic Pari' (in Japanese), *Bulletin of National Museum of Ethnology* 11(1): 103–61.

Lejean, G. 1865. *Voyage aux deux Nils (Nubie, Kordofan, Soudan Oriental)*. Paris: Hachette.

Lienhardt, G. 1961. *Divinity and Experience: The Religion of the Dinka*. Oxford: Clarendon Press.

Muller, J. -C. 1980. *Le Roi bouc émissaire: pouvoir et rituel chez les Rukuba du Nigéria Central*. Québec: Serge Fleury.

Riad, M. 1959. 'The Divine Kingship of the Shilluk and its Origin', *Archiv für*

Völkerkunde (Vienna), 14: 141–284.

Seligman, C. G. 1934. *Egypt and Negro Africa: A Study in Divine Kingship*. London: Routledge.

Seligman, C. G. & Seligman, B. Z. 1932. *Pagan Tribes of the Nilotic Sudan*. London: Routledge.

Simonse, S. 1992. *Kings of Disaster, Dualism, Centralism and the Scapegoat King in the Southeastern Sudan*. Leiden: Brill.

The Transgressive Nature of Kingship in Caste Organization: Monstrous Royal Doubles in Nepal

Marie Lecomte-Tilouine

Introduction

A great deal of ink has been spilt on the paradoxes inherent in monarchy. Plato and the medieval jurists had already noticed that the king had a unique power to go beyond the law. And one could make a long list of the various clever solutions that have been found worldwide and throughout the ages that allow one person to reach the supreme position of king without acknowledging the potential superiority of the actors who confer the kingship upon him. Kingship poses specific questions in relation to the particular social and cultural contexts where it is found. Within the Hindu caste system both the uniqueness of the king, and his status in terms of purity require particular resolutions. From one perspective, the very idea of Hindu kingship seems anomalous. It transcends the divisions on which caste organization is based, and it appears to challenge the pre-eminence of the *brahman*, a pre-eminence which many commentators take to be one of the hallmarks of caste.[1]

According to an ancient Hindu myth that is very widely known and cited, the universe was created when the body of Purusha, a primordial god–man, was sacrificed. From this sacrifice there emerged, in a hierarchical order paralleling the verticality of the body, the four classes (*varnas*) that form the basis of caste ideology – *brahman* (priest, preceptor), *ksatriya* (king, warrior), *vaishya* (generator of wealth), and *shudra* (servant). The creation of the universe thus demanded that Purusha's oneness be broken. However, during the coronation of a Hindu king, this process is reversed. The installation ritual makes him into a unitary composition of the four *varnas*. The kingship is therefore unique in a manner that is by definition antithetical to the functioning principles of the caste system: distinction and complementarity. While the *varna* of the king's earthly descent group is *ksatriya*, his coronation necessarily renders him apart from, and above, the system he masters. He thus becomes a divine being. At the same time, however, he also possesses a human body, which is inevitably connected with impurity and is therefore incompatible with his divine status. I shall show that, in the Nepalese context, his existence is dependent on the producing of monstrous doubles of himself. These doubles allow him to be detached from the groups to which he belongs and to deal with the impurity inherent in mundane life. It is as if the royal function had the peculiar ability to create a miniature internal caste system, reproducing the principles of distinction and complementarity.

Two Forms of Kingship in Nepal

Nepal was created out of the military unification of about sixty kingdoms during the second half of the eighteenth century during the reign of King Prithvi Narayan Shah. Three stages mark the history of the royal dynasty of the Shahs: its obscure origin in India, its establishment in the hills of central Nepal during the fifteenth century and the rapid conquest of territories lying to the east and west in the eighteenth century. During this time, the Shahs moved their capital from Gorkha in the hills to Kathmandu in the valley of Nepal (now normally referred to as the Kathmandu Valley), where the Malla kings of the indigenous Newars had been reigning since the medieval period. Contrasting Malla kingship with the Shah kingship that succeeded it shows how elements were disjoined and recombined to form a new composite form of kingship, one well suited to the task of maximizing the legitimacy of the newly extended crown in the eyes of all its subjects. This comparison also highlights the specific features of each of the two kingships, showing in passing that Hinduism and caste systems may be associated with very different forms of royalty, even within a similar context in terms of scale, location and period. The distinctive characteristics of Shah kingship and Malla kingship respectively may be examined by looking at three ways in which their principles were (and, in the case of the Shah, still are) conveyed: royal chronicles, the morphology of the royal palace and the main rituals of royalty.

If we first consider the chronicles of the two dynasties, a major difference strikes the reader in relation to their composition and their ultimate subject. The Gorkhali chronicles recall the history of a *line* and follow it in its displacements, while the chronicles of the Malla dynasty provide a (partial) history of a *place*: the Kathmandu Valley. Royalty is thus conceived differently in the two cases.[2] Another related difference is that in the chronicles of the Kathmandu Valley kingship is not primordial, but is preceded by the sacralization of the area by the appearance of gods, the arrival of famous saints and the establishment of great sanctuaries. By contrast, the chronicles of Gorkha take the geographical context into account only when it is connected with the dynasty and its conquests. These differences make it clear that we are dealing with two different types of kingship: a warlike, mobile form and a territorialized form.

If we follow the chronicle accounts, the arrival of these two great medieval dynasties in this area of the Himalayas presents surprising parallels. I will not take into account the opinions of several historians that the mythical founder of the Malla dynasty never reigned in Nepal, or that the Shahs of Gorkha are not Rajputs. I am dealing here with representations, and from this point of view the embellished or modified history contained in the chronicles is particularly important, since it is this that the rulers wanted to retain from their imaginary or real past. In fact, the Mallas and the Shahs shaped their origins in a very similar way, linking them with an escape from India in front of the barbaric Muslims.[3] All the chronicles of the several Himalayan kingdoms included in present-day Nepal claim Indian origins. None relates their coming to Nepal to a military operation. The establishment is either fortuitous, on the way back from a pilgrimage, or is presented as an escape from India at the time of the Muslim invasion.

The Himalayan zone is thus not presented as a natural territory of Hindu conquest, but as a holy zone where Hindu kings settle for devotion or to protect their endangered religion. The ancestors of the Mallas and of the Shahs would have fled towards the wild zone of the mountains, carrying with them their tutelary deity. In both cases, it is this divinity who asked the king to carry her to the mountains in order to protect her from the Muslims. In both cases, the royal families face a very similar episode of confrontation with the wilderness that leads to the degradation of one of their members. Fleeing with his tutelary goddess, the founder of the Malla dynasty, Harasimhadeva, spends the night in a terrifying forest. His deity directs him to a sword concealed under a large stone and tells him to stand on the stone with the sword in his hands, ready to kill the snake that lives there. The king kills the snake and empties the pits that surround the stone of their riches. But the goddess wills that the king designate his own son to sacrifice a buffalo to her. He thus relegates his heir to the low rank of butcher, forming a new caste linked with royal sacrifice.

The founding princes of the Shahs of Gorkha are also said to have fled their Indian kingdom after being attacked by the Muslims, carrying their tutelary goddess with them. On their way, they are obliged to offer to a local goddess another type of impure sacrifice – a pig – in order to cross the river separating them from the mountainous territory where they plan to settle. At the first crest located beyond this limit, one of the princes falls asleep on a large flat stone. While he sleeps, the stone rises from the ground and the tutelary goddess anchors herself in the soil beneath. The princes continue their quest, leaving behind their degraded brother, who performed the pig sacrifice on their behalf, as the priest of this enigmatic shrine. To this day, the goddess is honoured there in the form of a hole in the ground.

The similarity of the events in both stories suggests that this is an archetypical account of the origin of kingship. We are not presented with an origin *ex nihilo*. A royal figure, surrounded by other members of the royal family and carrying his divinity with him, is displaced as a result of some unforeseen trial. In both cases the displacement leads to a transformation or transgression whereby the royal becomes impure, and the new royal and impure element remains forever the mediator between the king and his divinity. In these two myths, the royal transgression is presented as a prerequisite for the advent of a new kingship. The new royal site is not founded as a result of a military conquest, but by the degradation of a potential king. It is significant that in the case of the Shahs it is one of the royal brothers who is degraded, while in the Malla myth, it is the son. Indeed, the history of these two dynasties reveals a major difference concerning the main group of kinsmen in competition for the throne. Among the Shahs many more conflicts are reported among brothers than between fathers and sons. Among the Mallas it is the reverse.[4]

The Anchoring of Kingship in Space

In Shah kingship, the place where the king is established is quite naturally his kingdom. The royal person creates a sacred territory around himself and this is supplemented by the installation of his tutelary goddess. Thus the Shah dynasty, originally settled in Kaski, spread out on two successive occasions when a junior royal brother founded a new neighbouring kingdom. Yasobrahma became king of Lamjung in this way, and then later another junior member of the royal family, Drabyah Shah, was crowned in Gorkha. In both cases, oral traditions and written genealogies tell how the new sovereign was established. He was seated on a large stone, he received a *tika* (a mark placed on the forehead), and was covered with vermilion powder. In the next stage, a part of the family goddess was taken away from the original kingdom and established within the new palace. Kingship is thus attached to the person of the sovereign and the site he occupies, normally a summit or a stone, and is reinforced by the presence of the family goddess.

This schema underlines the extent to which Shah royalty is focused on the person of the king. It is not surprising, then, that the palace of the Shah sovereigns is very modest. It consists of a small building which houses the royal quarters and a temple to the goddess that is constructed as an extension of a natural fortress, i.e. on the top of a steep slope with difficult access. As shown by Inden (1978) and others, the king, his throne and his palace are representations in miniature of the whole kingdom. It is significant that the minimal representation of Shah kingship is a stone for the Shahs of Gorkha: they employed precisely this term, *dhungo* (Nep. 'stone'), to indicate the whole of their kingdom. M. C. Regmi (1978) argues that the use of this term to refer to the kingdom is late (eighteenth century) and underlies the idea of the indivisibility of the royal territory, in contrast to earlier practices. But it seems to me that the indivisibility of the kingdom was not a new idea for the Shahs. What was new, and what this commemorates, was the extension of the concept to a much greater territorial expanse as a result of the conquests inaugurated by Prithvi Narayan Shah during the eighteenth century. Indeed, the history of this dynasty does not reveal any territorial division between brothers or sons, as was so often the case in the Kathmandu Valley and in the neighbouring kingdoms of Western Nepal. On the contrary, from the very start of their history, the eldest son inherited the whole of his father's territory. The younger brother might create a neighbouring new kingdom, but this had to lie outside his brother's territory. As soon as a new kingdom was established, it displayed its independence by entering into war with its kingdom of origin. This occured despite the Hindu rule prohibiting the killing of the members of one's own spiritual clan, or *gotra*. This rule was circumvented by the sovereign by changing his spiritual clan.[5] The uniqueness of the royal person, the kingship and the kingdom is thus a characteristic of the Shah dynasty. The new Shah king may break even one of the most fundamental rules of identity for a Hindu, *gotra* membership, in order to display his independence and uniqueness. A modern example of this fundamental idea of the unit which the kingdom forms can be found in a remark made by Kirtinidhi Bista, former prime minister of Nepal. Bista (1975: 57) reverses the direction of history, writing that before the advent of Prithvi Narayan Shah: 'The kingdom had remained divided into tiny principalities', as if the entity of the 'kingdom' somehow pre-existed its creation.

The unitary conception of Shah kingship, aptly symbolized by the stone, contrasts sharply with the complexity of the Malla kingdoms of the Kathmandu Valley, defined by M. C. Regmi as corporatist. In the Malla kingdoms, the noblemen were able to dismiss a king or even to seize power (as in Patan), and this limited the power of the sovereign.[6] A city within the city, and a fortress within the fortress, the Malla palaces have nothing in common with the modest strengthened dwellings of the Shahs and other Thakuris of central Nepal. This disparity cannot be ascribed simply to differences in topography or wealth between these kingdoms, even if these were significant. The Malla palaces are true cities in the heart of the city. The oldest, that of Bhaktapur, is the most complex. Because each king made additions, it includes ninety-nine courtyards. The Kathmandu palace, which became the royal palace of the modern state of Nepal following the Shah conquest, had a total of thirty-five courtyards before the earthquake of 1933.

Each courtyard has a function and is dedicated to particular divinities. The ensemble does not form a labyrinth but an aggregate of adjacent worlds connected to each other by narrow passages. The most significant courtyard for the Malla kings was without doubt the Mul Chowk or 'main courtyard'. It was built by Ratna Malla shortly after the foundation of the Kathmandu dynasty, and the Malla kings were consecrated there. Though the Malla kings were displaced by the Shahs in the late eighteenth century, Taleju, their tutelary goddess, is still brought down to the Mul Chowk for three days during the festival of Dasai to bestow her blessing on the king. Although we do not possess detailed descriptions of the Malla kings' consecration ritual, we can grasp something of its meaning by combining the two major elements specific to the Mul Chowk where it was performed: the temporal descent of Taleju to the earth from her high temple, and the installation of the king.

The goddess Taleju has a well-known characteristic: no dwelling in the city should reach or exceed the height of her temple.[7] The measurement of the human world was thus given by this mark of devotion by the king towards his goddess. In fact, the Malla kings were careful to confer a monumental character on this temple in order to allow the development of their city. King Pratap Malla, in particular, constructed for her a temple in Kathmandu that exceeded the height of the original temple of the goddess located in Bhaktapur. However this well-known fact becomes much more significant if we consider that the vertical measurement is supplemented by another measurement: the horizontal one, represented by the size of the main courtyard. Hodgson (n.d.: vol. 14) noted that the Mul Chowk corresponds to a *ropani*, the common Nepalese measuring unit of land. This unit differs according to the quality of the land and corresponds to three surfaces associated with four different qualities. The better the quality of the ground, the smaller the unit. The *ropani* unit, with its specific variable geometry, is made concrete in the different contours of the main courtyard. The smallest surfaces are defined by steps while the largest surface is formed by the walls of the buildings that frame this courtyard. In the heart of the palace, located at the heart of the kingdom, the principal courtyard of the Malla kings was a true standard of the kingdom. The vertical measurement of the world – the space between the ground and the sky that was legitimately occupied by the king and his subjects – was fixed by the temple of the goddess. The horizontal standard was defined by the courtyard where she was brought to earth. Created within these two axes of order, the Malla sovereign, who was crowned here, was thus a real geometrician king – a Master of the measuring unit of the Earth and Sky.[8] In contrast, among the Shahs the main idea has been that the territory of the king is unbounded, but organized around a centre, the famous stone.

It seems to me that the Shah sovereigns have sought, at several stages, to reconstitute this idea of the royal stone within the complex Malla palace that they seized. Indeed the Shahs shifted the place of the royal consecration from the main courtyard to another courtyard, the Nasal Chowk, because, according to Vajracarya (2033 VS), this courtyard is much larger than the other. However, one of the characteristics of the Nasal Chowk courtyard is that in its centre there is a platform that was used for sacred dances during the Malla era. The whole courtyard is dedicated to the god of dance, Nasah dyah. At the time of the Malla kings, a golden statue

of Indra, the king of the gods, was placed on this platform during the annual festival in his honour. It may be because of this association that the Shah kings sat
down on this dais. Alternatively, it might be because they found in it a base that
corresponded to their idea of royalty in this building: a focal, elevated and strong
point on which the king stands. This idea was reinforced when King Rajendra
Bikram Shah ordered the Nasal Chowk and its dais, originally made of bricks
according to the Newar fashion, to be covered with black stones (see Ramjham
1975: 12).[9]

Interestingly, during the eighteenth century both dynasties were confronted with
choosing between two possible kings. In Kathmandu, because there was no heir to
the throne, a distant relative who already had sons was crowned in the palace.
When he died, his eldest son, Jayaprakash Malla, was enthroned. However, the
people rapidly replaced him with his own young son and chased him away,
because, report the chronicles, the young prince had been born in the Mohan
Chowk courtyard of the royal palace while his father had not been. Here we come
across the elements I outlined earlier in the Malla kingship: the rivalry between
father and son for the throne and the immanent nature of royal power that seems
to emerge literally from the different courtyards of the royal palace. As for the
Shahs, the chronicles relate that Prithvi Narayan's father had several wives. The
third queen had been pregnant for two months when the second queen started her
pregnancy and dreamed that she had swallowed the sun. As this dream had pre-
dicted, her child was born prematurely, before the child of the third queen. Despite
the rule of primogeniture, the noblemen and the king organized a council to debate
the question of when exactly royalty is transmitted: at the time of conception, or at
the time of birth?[10] The Shah dynasty views the sun as its ancestor and superior
father. When the sun appears, the king and his people experience the monarch's
divinity, and when the king makes public appearances, it is said that the sun shines.
The dream had forecast this link between the heavenly body and the second
queen's child. This was manifested by his early birth, birth being conceived as the
first encounter with the sun. Thus, while the Malla king emerges from the ground
of the palace, the Shah king emanates from the sun.

The Royal Installation Rituals and Royal Funerals

The chronicles do not give details of the installation ceremony of the Malla kings.
They do, however, state that the mark put on the forehead of the new sovereign of
Kathmandu during his installation was given to him in the presence of the other
two Malla kings (of the cities of Bhaktapur and Patan) in the Kathmandu Valley.
Both came from the same dynasty as the king of Kathmandu. The elder of these
two sovereigns used to place the mark on the new monarch's forehead. Seniority
in terms of age, as opposed to seniority in terms of kinship, is specific to the

Newars and is also found in their kinship and political relations. For the Shahs and the hill population of Nepal on the other hand, authority is conferred on whoever has the most senior rank in the line, whatever his age.

The principle of co-consecration of the Malla kings recalls some forms of royalty that existed in the Kathmandu Valley during an earlier era. From the thirteenth through the fifteenth centuries CE the Nepal Valley formed a single kingdom. During this time, two royal dynasties alternated in occupying the throne. When a member of one dynasty held the throne, the crown prince of the other was selected to succeed him, and vice versa. This principle provided for the consecration of the king by an elder of royal status. In contrast to the complexity of their society and administration, the Malla coronation ritual appears as a simple delegation of kingship, if we can judge from the few things we know about it. On the other hand, the Shah king, centre of a much less complex organization, is installed during long rituals in which the whole society is represented. The college of Malla kings appears as an institution that stood apart from the rest of the society and was regulated by the relative criterion of seniority by age. Even if the members of the college of kings were not the only actors in the Malla royal coronation, their importance was such that historical documents have retained only their names. By contrast, even the shortest and earliest descriptions of the installation of the Shah kings provide evidence of its collective and social aspect. In the earliest chronicles, the king is said to be consecrated by a mark put on his forehead by a group of people, among whom Brahmans and noblemen are mentioned.

Currently, the Shah king is initially installed before the cremation of the preceding sovereign. However, the complete coronation ceremony takes place only one year or more after that in order to avoid the paradoxical combination of joy and sorrow, auspiciousness and inauspiciousness. The Nepalese distinguish three principal stages in the complex ceremony of coronation: the *snana*, or royal bath; the *abhisheka*, or sprinkling ceremony; and the *asanarohana*, ascent to the throne. The *snana* consists of the rubbing of the king' s body with twelve different kinds of earth. This earth is not taken from different places of the king's domain, but rather is associated with different qualities. The sanctified king's body is thus not transformed into a precise territory but into an ideal ground, which represents his kingdom. Then the king is anointed by four people representing the four *varnas* of the Hindus: a *brahman*, with clarified butter contained in a gold pot; a *ksatriya*, with milk contained in a silver container; a *vaishya*; with curdled milk contained in a copper vessel; and a *shudra*, with honey from a wooden pot. Then eighteen different kinds of water are sprinkled over the king. Again these do not represent a territory, but rather categories: they are taken 'from a tributary, a stream, a lake, a whirlpool, from a river flowing towards the north, from dew drops, water warmed by the sun … Besides, various … fruits, flowers, leaves and herbs are placed on the head of the sovereign, one by one' (Poudyal 1975: 84). Thus the king is first transformed into an ideal terrestrial body, then he is consecrated by the whole society, represented by its four *varnas*, and finally he is associated with ideal and sanctified waters and plants.

Afterwards the sovereign sits on a throne covered with skins of various predatory animals. There the royal priest, *raj guru*, ties a gold band around the king's forehead and places the crown over it. The Shah king appears as the master of the earth, water, vegetation and animals at the time of his installation, but it is significant that nothing links these elements to a territorialized space. Through this ideal representation of the world, the king is settled as a master of the universe, i.e. of an unbounded kingdom. Clearly this is very different from the Malla depiction of the king as master of a circumscribed kingdom. The whole of the ritual is interpreted as a sacrifice of the person of the king to the sacrificial ceremony, *yagya*, which the nation represents. The platform where the throne is placed is described as the sacrificial surface, *vedi*. The king is said to die to himself and to his family to acquire a collective and cosmic dimension.

> After the completion of snana, the king is considered to be born of a national womb, and as such he belongs to the entire nation, not just to the initial places and family of birth. Soil and water used in the snana are considered to constitute the newly evolved physical system of national magnitude. By requiring the king to accept such inanimates as part and parcel of his system, the king is expected to inject his own consciousness into them so that they can be invigorated with life. With the completion of this part of the ritual, the king belongs to all and all belongs to him. (Sharma 1975: 98)[11]

To this impressive cosmic evocation of the role of the king Sharma adds that, because he is anointed by representatives of the four *varnas*, the king is a symbol of unity and equality. In fact this 'equality' is characteristically Hindu. If there is indeed an equal participation in the building of the king's body by the four *varnas*, the inequality of their nature is attested by the order of the performance and the kinds of substances that are associated with each of them. In fact this aspect is further underlined by the same author when he writes: 'With the king seated on the throne, representatives of all sections of the population profess their loyalty and pledge their support to the king so that the king may have at his command the knowledge of the intellectuals, bravery of the strong, and sweat and toil of those who labour' (Sharma: 99).

This tripartite division recalls the three great functions distinguished by Dumézil. It does in fact correspond to the reality of the Nepalese caste system, which is ternary despite its ideal Hindu quadripartite presentation. It places the king both above and in the centre of the caste system: the system that creates him and that endows him with power. The creation of the king can be seen as a counter-creation – a recombining of the *varnas* – whereas the sacrifice and dismemberment of the primordial Purusha resulted in caste division.

If the Malla coronation ritual appears as a private affair between kings, their death and funerary rituals, by contrast, concerned the whole society. At the time of his death, the Malla king had to impart the *mantra* of Taleju to his son. Then representatives of the 'four *varnas* and the thirty-six castes', as they were called, were obliged to attend the funerals and to take on specific ritual functions, notably by playing different kinds of musical instruments. The surviving sovereigns installed the new king quickly, before the cremation of the previous one. All of them seem to have been present at the cremation. Royal mourning then took place inside the palace, and at the end of the mourning period a more complete form of coronation was held (see D. R. Regmi 1966: 400–4). Thus the society headed by the Malla kings displayed its unity and organization, not at the time of the coronation of the king, but on the occasion of his death, during this second sacrifice of the king's person. Perhaps it was because kingship was not considered as something unique, but shared by different branches of the same dynasty, that the Malla king did not behave in a specified way during the royal mourning period.

This is not the case among the Shahs. The chronicles of Gorkha provide very little information concerning royal funerals. We learn, however, that the great king Ram Shah had a premonition of his death, and then began to educate his son about his new role. He made his way up to the cremation place, followed by all his noblemen, and died there while listening piously to the recitation of a holy text. Alerted by the noblemen, the queen came to the cremation site and placed a *tika* mark on her son's forehead before jumping onto the burning pyre. Immediately the two royal bodies disappeared, astonishing the crowd.

This unique and brief description underlines the essential point of Hindu funerals: the radical manner in which the dead disappear. Ideally, like any good Hindu, the dying king leaves the world before his death, when being taken, or going to, a holy place of cremation (which is considered to be detached from this world), or when leaving the mundane world to become a renouncer.

The dying Malla king used to transmit to his son an essential part of kingship through the *mantra* of Taleju before his kingship was later confirmed by the neighbouring and related kings. Shah kingship does not possess such mechanisms of continuity. In the current rituals of the Shah kings, the break is avoided by a negation of the interval between two reigns.[12] The death is formal only when it is announced and the death of the king is announced at the same time that the new king's name is proclaimed. This double public announcement holds the two generations together and provides the necessary continuity of kingship within the same dynasty in the same way as the French used to shout: 'Le roi est mort, vive le roi!' A very short coronation ceremony takes place before the previous king is cremated. The new king is forbidden to take any part in the funerary rituals of his predecessor.

The funerary rituals of the Shah kings comprise two central features that distinguish them from those of ordinary men. First of all, as we have just seen, the eldest son, conventionally the main mourner, does not lead them. Second, they include a ceremony of expulsion of the dead king. These two characteristics can be read as transgressions that permit the establishment of the new kingship.

The king manifestly breaks the family rules of the patriline at the time of his initial installation by not leading the funerary duties for his father (or elder brother). This initial transgression is particularly striking since not only does the king not fulfill his filial duty, which, for a Hindu, is the main purpose of pro-ducing a son, but he also displays no sign of mourning. He does not shave his head and he is not prohibited from taking salt. What is more, he is the main figure in an auspicious ceremony that takes place while impurity prevails in the whole kingdom. To minimize the danger arising from this situation, the first coronation ceremony is short and is performed before the cremation of the royal body since the cremation causes a greater impurity to prevail throughout the kingdom than the death itself. Following the royal cremation, the kingdom remains closed for three days and then goes into a state of mourning that progressively diminishes in intensity over the succeeding ten days. The most usual explanation of the anomaly that the king does not mourn his father is the idea that the king should never be impure. However this argument contradicts the widespread belief that the king, like fire, can never be soiled. The king is not polluted by contact with low castes for instance, since he is partly created by one of them and since he himself places *tika* marks on the forehead of all his subjects during the ritual of Dasai, irrespec-tive of their caste or creed. He is, we should note, the only one who can do this without being polluted himself or polluting others – another sign of his exter-nality.[13]

In fact, in a more general way, it is said that whoever carries the crown should not see death. His participation in any funerary ritual is prohibited, be it for a member of his own family or not. It is not simply that the king should not see the dead king, but rather that he should not be exposed to death in any form.[14] Whatever the reasons for this prohibition, the Shah kingship displays this paradox. It is presented as an uninterrupted line of descent, yet the king stands apart from his forebears at a crucial moment by not taking part in the mourning for his pred-ecessor. Among 'ordinary' people the continuity of the patriline is ensured by a joining together of the dead father and the surviving eldest son. The mourning son is literally superimposed on his dead father. He is said to take upon himself his pain and to suffer his sufferings by avoiding certain food, salt and clothes; and if he is involved in misconduct it has a direct effect on the fate of his dead father. Through the royal mechanism of delegated mourning, the king is somehow detached from his patriline and the succession of kings through sons appears almost as a parallel line. The king is also detached from his subjects in another way during the royal mourning, since they are all polluted by it while he is not. On the other hand, he is re-attached to all of them after his death since three generations of dead kings, together with the three generations of one's own ancestors, are worshipped during the *shraddha* rituals.

Royal funerals have a second notable characteristic: to pollute brahmans and to degrade one of them. Indeed the royal corpse is not carried by close kinsmen, as is the case for ordinary people, but by brahmans who are employed in the army. The role played by the army in the funerals of the Shah kings is crucial.[15] When there is a particularly problematic royal funeral, as occurred in 2001 when Crown Prince Dipendra committed regicide, patricide and matricide before taking his own life, even the kinsman who normally lights the pyre can be replaced by a brahman.

The second extraordinary characteristic of the Shah royal funerals is seen on the eleventh day following the cremation. During the ten previous days, as for any ordinary man, the kinsman who acts as the mourner of the sovereign constructs a 'subtle body' of the dead king from an offering consisting of ten rice balls. This is a dangerous body that should be sent towards the resting place of the ancestors. For the Hindus of the hills of central Nepal, where the Shahs come from, this stage is usually symbolized by the destruction of a small mound of earth that represents the body of the dead, while gifts are offered to the family priest in the name of the deceased. These gifts are not accompanied by food offerings and are not presented as particularly polluting.

However the modern royal ceremony is very different. On the eleventh day following the cremation, a Brahman is invited to consume a dish called *katto* whose consumption transgresses conventional boundaries in an extreme way. Different sources provide widely varying accounts of the exact composition of this dish. According to some, it contains some brain tissue of the dead king, or the bone of his forehead made into a powder, or it is sprinkled with ashes from his pyre, or it contains two products which should not be consumed at the same time: milk and meat. Whatever the ingredients of this dish, most accounts indicate that the *katto* contains a part of the body of the dead sovereign. In fact it also goes against convention simply by virtue of the prohibition against eating anything at the place of the funerary rituals on the eleventh day following the cremation.

Immediately following this, the Brahman (in this context referred to as *katte bahun*) is dressed as a sovereign. He is made to wear brocaded clothes, a replica of the royal crown, and some personal objects of the deceased sovereign, in particular his shoes and glasses. These last two are important symbols of sovereignty, since the king must never walk barefoot on the ground and his glasses have the function of reinforcing his 'holy vision', which confers merit on those on whom it falls. The *katte bahun* is then perched on an elephant, sheltered under a royal umbrella. Astride the elephant, he crosses a river that marks the symbolic border of the kingdom. Theoretically he is thereafter expelled from the kingdom forever,[16] but, again theoretically, he receives whatever he asks for in exchange.[17]

Conclusion

High status Brahmans are regarded as terrestrial gods (*bhu devata*). In the funeral rituals of the Shah kings one is brought to commit the most odious crime of consuming the body of the king. This Brahman dies in order to allow the new sovereign to reign over his kingdom. The procedure may be linked to the installation ritual during which *brahmans* create *ex nihilo* a terrestrial divinity, an avatar of Vishnu, who is the king (see Witzel 1987). This creature may be destroyed only by the degradation and subsequent exile of a brahmanic terrestrial god, at whom the people throw stones and shout abuse.[18]

As soon as he has consumed the sacrilegious meal of the king's body, the brahman becomes a monstrous untouchable brahmanic king. It is as if the destruction of kingship was a symbolic destruction of the two main pillars of the caste hierarchy and subsequently of its whole order. The representatives of the two great powers, spiritual and temporal, are merged into one figure who is in turn relegated to the margin of the hierarchy. This very particular ceremony only concerns the sovereign, since the gifts made in the name of the queen and of a prince who is not heir to the crown go to the priests of the palace, as usual. As in many African cases, the king is thus ritually expelled from the kingdom. Perhaps he is even symbolically put to death. This interpretation gains strength if one considers the stoning and the fact that the degradation of a Brahman is a punishment equivalent to his death. The capital punishment of a Brahman is normally prohibited.

The king thus revived after his death in the person of a Brahman nullifies the concept of interregnum. Instead we see a kind of double royalty that lasts until the end of the funerary rites. The coexistence of two kings is equally evident if we consider the altars of the dead king established everywhere in the kingdom during the mourning, and in particular in front of his palace. During this time the new king remains hidden, except on two occasions that frame the crucial moment of the cremation of the body of his predecessor. He appears publicly during his ascent to the throne and the following short parade in the city that precedes the cremation, and he gives an official speech at the end of the cremation.

Like the coronation, the expulsion from the kingdom underlines the close relation of the sovereign to the earth whose husband, *bhu-pati*, he is presented as being. While his vital principle is thus expelled, another part of his person, the material remains, is scattered in various holy places, so as to return to the elements from which he emanated and to regenerate them.

The three transgressions linked to the Shah kingship may be understood as manifestations of the ambiguous nature of kingship in general and may be linked to the model of sacred kingship defined by Frazer and then refined by Luc de Heusch within the African context. This exercise of decontextualization and comparison allows for an original reading of Hindu kingship in Nepal by leaving to one side considerations of its internal logic. De Heusch (2000: 31) showed that during their installation the kings of Kongo are radically separated from the conventions of normal kinship through an act of incest or the consumption of a newborn child from their own lineage (see also de Heusch's chapter in this book). The Thakuri caste, from within which all the kings of Nepal are recruited, is noted for having a marriage preference for the matrilateral cross cousin. This alliance is considered incestuous by all the other high status groups since they see the matrilateral cross cousin as a classificatory sister.

The Thakuris themselves have endorsed this view with regard to other groups since, as kings, they have administered fines and punishments to groups other than theirs who have practised this form of marriage. That said, the Shah dynasty have imposed this incestuous rule on a group which does not practise it otherwise. These are the Ranas, who have been their main matrimonial allies since 1850, and who normally regard the father's sister's son as a brother.

With respect to marriage, nothing distinguishes the king from other members of the Thakuri caste. But it is noteworthy that the king comes from a group that practises a form of marriage that others regard as incestuous, and does so without penalty.[19] This anomaly is viewed by the common man as a sign of the foreign origin of the Thakuris, another point that may be compared with the African models where 'the king comes from elsewhere' (de Heusch 2000: 49).

We have seen how the Shah king undergoes a cultural demise. This does not require, as in many African cases, ending his term of office when he shows signs of ill health due to age. But it has the similar function of leaving the field free for the new sovereign. However, as is common in African kingship, the Shah king is thus dependent on the presence of monstrous figures: the degraded royal sacrifier, the younger brother mourner and the king-eating Brahman. In contrast to the African cases, the monstrosity of these figures is not physical but wholly cultural: kingship compels them to transgress kinship and caste rules, and does not spare them from the consequences of this transgression.

The first transgression takes the form of a degradation of a royal heir. It is presented as a disinterested act, a self-sacrifice of the royal figure in order to tame the wild local forces by means of an impure sacrifice. This is the preliminary to the establishment of the kingship in a new territory. It is an initial condition that is not repeated, but is perpetuated by a member of the new group that has been formed or the existing group that has been infiltrated. This person, who is degraded by his function, remains at a low but pure status, in the class of pure *shudras*.

The second transgression is against the normal rules of kinship at the time of the coronation. Although it temporarily pollutes the younger brother of the king, it does not degrade him. It allows the king to be detached from his group for the impure period of the mourning and for his coronation, which takes place at the same time. The third transgression aims at sending the dead king away from his kingdom. It may be understood as the last step of the detachment process that characterizes kingship. This last transgression has consequences for others besides the king and it is thus different from the first two we have examined. Contrary to these, the double is taken not from the royal family but from the Brahman caste. And while the other two transgressions appear to have somehow noble (or royal) characteristics, the motivation of the king-eating *katte bahun* is as monstrous as it is possible to be since it involves the voluntary self-desacralization of a Brahman for money. Through these complex mechanisms of transgression, the king masters both pure and impure while remaining, by definition, pure.

Of the three great models of the origin of kingship – the magical origin, conquest and the contract – none truly corresponds to the Himalayan case. It combines elements of all three models, but the main emphasis rests on the initial transgression that precedes the establishment of kingship. This transgression can certainly not be ranked in the blurred category of 'magical origin' since in both the Shah and the Malla cases a very precise process leads to the symbolic death of a potential king in the person of the closest heir to the throne, and the subsequent birth of an impure ritual specialist linked to royalty. This transgression transforms a potential king into a low caste individual of a particular type, a sacrificer.[20] Now the king is the supreme sacrificer in the kingdom, and the transgression has the result of splitting the royal function. This sequence, whereby a royal sacrifice precedes the establishment of the kingship, may be interpreted as one answer to the paradoxical position of the king in Nepalese Hindu society. He is simultaneously a member of a specific group (a lineage of a sub-species of *ksatriyas* known as Thakuris) whose members are all somehow apart from the rest of society and yet someone who is detached from this group during his installation. In fact the detachment brought about by the coronation rituals is usually described as a sacrifice and a rebirth. The king is said to die to himself and to the interest of his group in order to adopt a universal role. The royal function brings about a bifurcation of the king's initial *ksatriya* status – on the one hand elevated to his divine aspect, on the other degraded to his impure doubles. Both are necessary for the prosperity and functioning of the kingdom.

The transgressive character of Shah kingship is particularly apparent in the use of a high status Brahman in place of the *mahabrahman* traditionally charged to take upon himself the impurity of death. The splitting of the ritual function between specialists in impurity and specialists in purity that Hocart sees as constitutive of the caste system cannot be said to be fully transgressive. This splitting was institutionalized among the Mallas and in several regions of India. In the Malla kingship, the two main impure doubles of the king were recruited from a specific caste, the butchers (*Kasai*, Khadgi), who were, as we saw, created by the requirements of kingship, in the same manner that the *mahabrahman* was recruited from a specific low caste.

Shah kingship, on the other hand, is, as we saw, more transgressive. Its ritual process is individual and real, and affects all members of the Brahman caste, who are viewed as potential eaters of dead kings. The Brahman thus acquires an eminently paradoxical status with respect to the system he heads and towards the king who rules over it. He holds the two ends of the caste system: he makes and eats the king. It might also be said to affect all of Nepal's tribal groups since the degraded royal sacrificer of pig became a member of one of these groups, the Magars (see Lecomte-Tilouine 2002). Thus the tribal groups also have a considerably ambiguous role, sacrificing for the sake of their conquerors to their own chthonic gods in the person of the degraded royal/tribal sacrificer. If the organization of caste allows the different groups and individuals to deal with impurity according to their respective rank, the paradoxical position of the king, embodying all the castes and remaining always pure, leads to a ritual decomposition of the royal function, creating a parallel caste system within kingship itself.

Notes

1. All diacritical marks have been deleted from the transcription of words from Indian languages, including from passages in quotation, for the benefit of the reader unfamiliar with these languages. Note that the word 'Brahman' denotes a member of a caste, while the word '*brahman*' (lower case italics) denotes a *Varna*, i.e. a class of functionaries, normally priests and preceptors. The difference is the same as that between the English family name 'Smith' and the occupation 'smith'.

2. To qualify this remark somewhat, it should be said that the chronicles of the Kathmandu Valley often follow the dynastic history of a line, recounting how such and such a king came to settle in 'Nepal' (i.e. the Kathmandu Valley). Following the division of the Valley into three kingdoms the text deals with each line and kingdom independently until their conquest by the Shahs of Gorkha.

3. For an Indian parallel, see Gell (1997: 437).

4. The difference concerning who may legitimately compete for the throne is illustrated in other ways. For instance, King Pratap Malla is represented in the centre of four of his sons, whereas the Shah king is ideally surrounded by his four brothers, representing his 'limbs'. In both cases, the model shows the king forming the centre of a group, surrounded in the four directions of the universe by a prince, be it a son or a brother. The brothers of the Shah kings are his *cautara*, his four protectors who hold the role of ministers or advisers and lead the army at his side. The Rana ministers, who originate from the same area of central Nepal as the Shahs, developed this principle, which places the royal brothers on a relatively equal footing regarding access to the

throne. The Rana prime ministers usurped the throne between 1849 and 1951. They were made kings of the Nepalese provinces of Kaski and Lamjung by the king of Nepal in 1856 and instituted a particularly interesting type of kingship since succession was not from father to son, but from one brother to the next eldest. This model is recognized in the Shahs' mythical and symbolic representations of kingship.

5. This is documented at the two stages of the spreading of the Shahs of Gorkha. It is well known that Prithvi Narayan Shah changed his *gotra* from Bharadwaj to Kasyapa. Dharmaraj Thapa (1984: 71) writes that King Narahari Shah of Lamjung, who was Kasyapa, changed his *gotra* in order to attack his younger brother, the king of Gorkha.

6. Father Cassino, a rare witness of the Malla institutions, described one of them in these terms: 'Therefore, he [Ranjit Malla] called a general council of his people on the 26th of April, 1742. In the meeting they were to freely express their feeling and give their opinion … All of them had their faces covered to hide their identity and spoke in affected tone not to be recognized. Some scolded the king, even called him bad names; others threatened him with dire consequences' (D.R. Regmi 1966: 247).

7. This rule is sometimes applied to divinities other than Taleju: to the chariot of Matsyendranath in Patan, for example.

8. This essential detail relating to the dimensions of the principal court of the palace has never been published to my knowledge, nor is it mentioned by the Nepalese nowadays. Admittedly, many elements relating to the Malla kingdoms were forgotten and not recorded, but this fact does not explain this amnesia totally. Indeed, in 1792, when Bahadur Shah, the youngest son of Prithvi Narayan who continued the fabulous conquest undertaken by his father, while he was regent, under the reign of his young nephew Ran Bahadur Shah, ordered that a land register of the new kingdom be drawn up, the chronicle tells that he died, 'on account of this sin of ascertaining the limits of the earth' (Wright 1970: 261). Beyond the prosaic interpretation advanced by Sylvain Lévi (1905 vol. 1: 299), who sees there the suspicious attitude of the people towards the action of the sovereign, we may wonder if the regent did not usurp a royal prerogative or if he did not import a Malla tool of governance too quickly.

9. Interestingly, although the Shahs established their kingship within the Malla palace, they always distanced themselves from this symbolic centre. The first Shah conqueror of the Kathmandu Valley, Prithvi Narayan Shah, rarely resided there. During the nineteenth century, the Shahs constructed another palace for their residence even though the royal rituals still took place at the old Malla palace. The new palace at Narayanhiti, just outside the old city of Kathmandu, has frequently been modified and presents a modern image of the

kingdom since each of its rooms is named after a district of the country. The throne is located on a dais in the room named Gorkha, an ambiguous appellation since it refers not only to one of the seventy-five districts of Nepal but also to the original kingdom of the Shah dynasty. In a way, the Shahs are still reigning from Gorkha but have transported it to the Kathmandu Valley. Nevertheless, to this day, '[t]radition requires the King to spend at least the auspicious coronation night in the old palace' (Shrestha 1975: 35).

10. The universal problem of the transmission of monarchy was further complicated in this context by the specific difficulties connected with polygamy. Monogamy did not, however, mean that the problem was absent. For instance, Bloch (1983: 85) showed that in medieval Europe the strength of monarchic ideas led some to consider as king not the eldest son but the first son born after the coronation of his father. In this way, in order to ensure a perfect transmission, the king would be the son of a king and not of a prince.

11. As can be understood from this statement, it is the universe that benefits from the contact of the king, rather than the reverse.

12. Mayer (1985) showed that this negation is characteristic of numerous Hindu kingships.

13. In fact the king shares these characteristics with other humans who are incarnations of divinity – the *dhami* oracles of Western Nepal. The *dhami* may not perform death rituals even for their own parents, and may apply the *tika* mark on the foreheads of members of impure castes without being polluted (see Shrestha-Schipper 2003).

14. Perhaps we see here a conflict between kings since it is well known that the god of death, Yama, is himself royal. He is the king of *dharma* who calls the living from his own kingdom when his time has come.

15. All the actors in the royal funerals of the Shahs are recruited from within the army, underlining the warlike character of these kings.

16. It is perhaps revealing that the double of the king is expelled from the Kathmandu Valley, as if the Shah kings had retained something of the specific nature of the Malla kingdoms when they established their capital there.

17. To my knowledge, there is no mention of this ritual among the Shahs before their conquest of the Kathmandu Valley. Shortly after the conquest, however, full status Brahmans have been used, for instance for the Shah king of the Gulmi kingdom. On the other hand, the Malla sovereigns, as well as their subjects, practised this ritual, for which they employed a local Brahman of low status or certain Brahmans from Vaijanathdham, i.e. Jaganath in Orissa. These *brahmans* called *patra brahman*, *mahapatra brahman* or *mahabrahman*, may not enter in any house and nobody drinks the water they have touched. Additional research is necessary to document the former practices of the Shahs in this field, but for Ran Bahadur, the first Shah king crowned on the

throne of Kathmandu, a *mahabrahman* of central India, living across the Narmada river, was called. It is apparently only very recently, since the return of the Shah monarchy following the demise of the Ranas in 1951, that Brahmans of high status began to be used again. Bhatta Brahmans of Indian origin acted as *katte bahun* for Tribhuvan and Mahendra while Nepalese Upadhyaya Brahmans were selected for the last two monarchs, Birendra and Dipendra, in June 2001 (see Bhattarai 2001). With time, and perhaps because it corresponds particularly to their transgressive nature, the Shah kings thus operated an increasing sacrilege or returned to their former traditional sacrilege. The convention of returning to the other world a *mahabrahman*, a ritual specialist who is already very marginalised, was adopted by the Shahs after they established their dynasty in Kathmandu in the late eighteenth century. However, the more recent practice of using a high status Brahman in royal rituals is shocking for many Nepalese, particularly Brahmans (see Timsina: 2001).

18. This practice was not observed for the last two kings, probably because of the great shock that surrounded their violent death. It was documented for King Mahendra, as the report of the French ambassador to Nepal, dated 23 February 1972 shows: 'il fut obligé de quitter la vallée sous les huées et les lapidations de la foule' (Toussaint 1972).

19. This type of alliance is usually said to have been borrowed from the Muslims or from the Nepalese tribal groups.

20. It is common in the Indianist literature to distinguish between a 'sacrifier' – the person who commands, or patronizes, a sacrifice – and the 'sacrificer' – the person who performs the sacrifice.

References

Anonymous 1969–70. 'Nepalko itihas rajbhogmala', *Ancient Nepal* 7: 1–24; 8: 1–24; 9: 1–24; 11: 1–17.

Bhattarai, H. 2058 VS [2001]. 'Kattekhane-khvaune itihas', *Madhuparka* 34: from www.nepal.news.com.

Bista, K. 1975. 'The Crown and Nepal', *The Rising Nepal, Coronation Special*, February 24: 57–58. Kathmandu.

Bloch, M. 1983. *Les Rois thaumaturges* (with an introduction by J. Le Goff). Paris: Gallimard.

Dumont, L. 1966. 'La Conception de la royauté dans l'Inde ancienne', *Homo Hierarchicus*, Appendix, pp. 351–75. Paris: Gallimard.

Gell, A. 1997. 'Exalting the King and Obstructing the State. A Political Interpretation of Royal Ritual in Bastar District, Central India', *Journal of the Royal Anthropological Institute* 3(3): 433–55.

Hasrat, B. J. 1970. *History of Nepal*. Hoshiarpur: Research Institute Press.

Heusch, L. de. 1997. 'The Symbolic Mechanisms of Sacred Kingship: Rediscovering Frazer', *Journal of the Royal Anthropological Institute* 3(2): 213–32.

—— 2000. *Les Rois de Kongo et les monstres sacrés*. Paris: Gallimard.

Hocart, A. M. 1978. *Rois et courtisans*. Paris: Editions du Seuil.

Hodgson, B. H. n.d. Hodgson Papers, vol. 14, London: British Library, India Office Collection.

Inden, R. B. 1978. 'Hierarchies of Kings in Early Medieval India', *Contributions to Indian Sociology* New Series 15: 99–125.

Lecomte-Tilouine, M. 2002. 'The Enigmatic Pig. On Magar Participation in the State Rituals of Nepal', *Studies in Nepali History and Society* 5(1): 3–41.

Lévi, S. 1905. *Le Népal. Étude historique d'un royaume hindou*, 2 vols. Paris: Leroux.

Mayer, A. 1985. 'The King's Two Thrones', *Man* (N.S.) 20: 205–21.

Munamkarmi, L. 2047 VS [1990]. 'Bhaktapur darbar ra 99 cok', *Nepali samskriti* 6(3): 38–50.

Naraharinath, Y. (ed.) 2021 VS [1964]. *Gorkha Vamshavali*. Kasi: Aryabirsangh.

Pant, D. 1992 VS [1935]. *Shahavamsha-caritam*. Kashi (India): R. M. Pallasule.

Paudel, N. 2020 VS [1963]. *Bhasa vamshavali*, 2 vols. Kathmandu: Puratva Bibhag.

Poudyal, R. R. 1975. 'The Coronation – Some Interesting Rituals', *The Rising Nepal, Coronation Special*, February 24, p. 84. Kathmandu.

Quigley, D. 2000. 'Scapegoats: The Killing of Kings and Ordinary People', *Journal of the Royal Anthropological Institute* 6(2): 237–54.

Ramjham, 1975. 'The Hanuman Dhoka Royal Palace: A Brief Introduction', *The Rising Nepal*, Coronation Special, 24 February, pp. 9–15. Kathmandu.

Regmi, D. R. 1966. *Medieval Nepal, Part II. A History of the Three Kingdoms 1520 AD to 1768 AD*. Calcutta: Firma Mukhopadhyay.

Regmi, M. C. 1978. 'Preliminary Notes on the Nature of the Gorkhali State and Administration', *Regmi Research Series* 10(11): 171–4.

Sharma, J. P. 1975. 'Coronation: The Indigenous Way to Ideal Government', *The Rising Nepal, Coronation Special*, 24 February, pp. 97–100. Kathmandu.

Shrestha, C. B. 1975. 'Religious Aspects of the Auspicious Coronation', *The Rising Nepal*, Coronation Special, 24 February, pp. 33–5. Kathmandu.

Shrestha-Schipper, S. 2003. 'Religion et pouvoir chez les indo-népalais de l'ouest du Népal (Jumla)', Thèse de doctorat, Université Paris x, Nanterre.

Thapa, D. 2041 VS (1984). *Lok Samskritiko gherama Lamjung*. Kathmandu: Sajha Prakashan.

Timsina, N. N. 2001. 'Ridiculing Brahmanism', *The Kathmandu Post*, 21 June.

Touissant, F. 1972. 'Mort et crémation du roi; Rites funébres pour le roi'.

Unpublished reports from the French ambassador in Nepal to the French foreign minister.

Vajracarya, G. 2033 VS [1976]. *Hanumandhoka rajadarbar. Nepal ra esivali adhyayan samsthan,* Kirtipur: Tribhuban University.

Witzel, M. 1987. 'The Coronation Rituals of Nepal, with Special Reference to the Coronation of King Birendra (1975)', in N. Gutschow & A. Michaels (eds) *Heritage of the Kathmandu Valley.* Sankt Augustin: VGH Wissenschaftsverlag, pp. 415–67.

Wright, D. (ed.) 1970 [1877]. *History of Nepal.* Delhi: Cosmo Publications.

–7–

Kingship and Untouchability

Declan Quigley

Kingship and Caste Organization

Caste is typically defined, in opposition to organization by class, estate, slavery or tribal groupings, as a system where statuses are ritually defined by using concepts of purity, pollution and inauspiciousness. To Western, (relatively) liberal, egalitarian eyes the apparently constant preoccupation with maintaining differences between groups through these concepts is difficult to fathom and is often branded as unreasonable or barbaric or even inhuman. Interestingly, those who practise caste sometimes say just the opposite: that it is precisely these differences that are the hallmark of culture and of humanity. From this viewpoint, *not* to have permanent distinctions among social groups is to be animal-like.

This chapter will be concerned with caste and kingship in the Hindu world though I should state unequivocally that, unlike many commentators on caste in India, I do not believe that caste is irrevocably linked to Hinduism.[1] Caste groups are based on lineal kinship and tightly regulated marriage alliances between households of different lineages, mechanisms that prevent one's 'own kind' from being contaminated. In India and Nepal, the regulation of marriage on the part of wealthy households is often also used to inhibit the dispersal of land ownership. However, non-landowning lineages, whether wealthy merchants or impoverished groups, regulate their marriages just as strictly as members of landowning lineages. It is as if they believe that they belong to different species whose miscegenation would be unnatural. The most common word for 'caste' in Indian languages is *jati*, which means precisely 'species': the concept is a cultural denial of the natural fact that there is only one human species.[2]

The prohibition on inter-mixing is shown more clearly still by the fact that it is not restricted to sex, marriage and procreation. All of those 'ritual' domains that are regarded as the basis of constituting people as fully social beings are regarded as taboo areas for the mixing of people from different castes. Of these, perhaps the most subject to regulation is everyday eating and drinking since food and drink are normally shared with one's 'own kind'.

Hindu communities typically comprise a large number of castes whose members all fastidiously avoid any kind of fundamental contact. But normally one caste predominates in every sense – politically, economically, numerically and as the provider of the main patrons of rituals. Conventionally referred to as the 'dominant' caste (following Srinivas 1959), they are more accurately entitled the 'noble' or 'kingly' caste, it being understood that nobility is an attenuated form of kingship. The other castes tend to have less or no land, and, with the common exception of merchants, have an obligation to provide people who will perform specialized ritual duties for the noble caste or to the community as a whole. To default on these obligations always incurs some kind of sanction, which is frequently underpinned by the threat, if not the actual use, of violence. Since landownership, as the principal form of wealth, confers power, the only people who can easily escape from ritual obligations to the noble caste and the community are those merchants who are not dependent on landowners, or renouncers, who choose to leave the sedentary communities organized along caste lines and wander from place to place seeking alms wherever they go.

Hindus often claim that Brahmans are the 'highest' caste and untouchables the 'lowest'. This common popular formulation of the order of castes does not, however, sit easily with the ethnographic facts or ancient textual exegeses. There are thousands of Brahman castes whose members daily dispute each other's status.[3] Evidently, if one Brahman caste claims superiority over another Brahman caste, not all of them can be the 'highest'. And if some Brahmans are 'higher' than others, then the criterion of being 'higher' must be something other than simply being a Brahman.

The reason that Brahmans are divided into different castes revolves around the nature of priesthood. A priest is, by definition, someone who provides ritual services for others, not for himself, and the status of the priest depends crucially on to whom he is linked and in what capacity. The first issue, then, is whether a lineage provides priests at all, and many Brahman lineages do not. If the lineage does provide priests, the second question concerns the kind of priestly activity undertaken and for whom. Family priests enjoy more esteem than temple priests, and the family priest of a noble household enjoys greater prestige than the family priest of an artisan household. Funeral priests have a particularly ambiguous status because of their constant association with death, but the words 'particularly ambiguous' must be stressed since all priestly activity is regarded as dangerous and thus perceived with a mixture of awe and contempt.[4]

For those castes who deal overtly with death or the disposal of liminal substances such as cut hair and nails, faeces, menstrual blood and afterbirth, this may seem easily understandable – though it still requires explanation since dirt and impurity are quite different things, as Mary Douglas pointed out long ago in her seminal book *Purity and Danger* (1970). What is perhaps more difficult for the modern Western imagination to grasp is that it is not just castes such as barbers and tanners, washermen and sweepers, i.e. those dealing in the by-products of human waste and decay, whose status is endangered by their activities. So too is the status of Brahman priests who are normally conceived of as belonging to the 'highest' caste(s) because of their alleged distance from the polluting functions of untouchable and other 'lowly' specialist castes.

The distinction between occupation and ritual function is crucial here. It is not the removal of physical dirt that is defiling; it is the association with evil and death and all that is symbolically linked with these. Priestly activity of every kind is feared because it involves the acceptance of prestations which act as vessels for the threatening, inauspicious qualities which the patron of the ritual is attempting to shed in order to guarantee his own good life. Members of Brahman castes who function as priests are compromised by their ritual activities in the same way as any other ritual functionary. They attempt to mitigate this by delegating particularly harmful aspects of the disposal of inauspiciousness to others, but such attempts can never be wholesale or the *raison d'être* of their priesthood would be lost. Many Brahmans are acutely aware of this problem and refuse to take on priestly duties. These non-priestly Brahmans, we are told in one particularly revealing ethnography, 'widely despise Brahman priests' (Fuller 1984: 50; see also Guneratne 2001: 539).

The relative evaluation of caste statuses is always a matter of dispute for two reasons. First, the orientation of castes is to the royal centre rather than to each other. This means that most castes often have no good reason to rank themselves above or below others except in so far as they are more or less attached to the court or noble families. Second, the paradigmatic ritual that connects members of noble castes to others is sacrifice, and this is, by its nature, simultaneously concerned with death and rebirth.[5] The Brahman normally represents himself as being removed from the violent aspect of sacrifice (see Heesterman 1985) but this is always relative and, in the final analysis, something of an illusion (or delusion) if he or members of his lineage are engaged in ritual duties which connect them to the inauspiciousness of others. Those Brahman lineages that do not supply priests are really Brahman in name only since their caste function, like that of noble castes and those who aspire to nobility, is to patronize ritual.

Since the performance of all ritual functions is degrading or compromising, only the renouncer, who is by definition outside caste-organized society, can claim to be 'pure'. The concept of 'most pure' cannot then be equated with 'highest' since 'highest' indicates 'inside'. For this reason, the common idea that 'Brahmans are the highest caste' makes no sense, or is a kind of illusion, irrespective of the fact that it is very widely held by Hindus themselves and by commentators on Hinduism.

An alternative representation of caste organization and values, which avoids concepts of highest and lowest, draws on the fact that caste is an expression of kingship.[6] In contrast to the idea that caste is orientated to a pure–impure axis with brahmans and untouchables at polar ends, Hocart (1950) argues that what is at stake is the integrity of kingship, the single institution to which everyone in the society is connected. The kingship is protected by the repeated performance of rituals that expel any inauspicious qualities generated either by natural forces (disease, decay, death) or the perpetually changing nature of social relations. All social changes are potentially disruptive and dangerous, and the most important (brought about by birth, marriage and death) are generally marked by ritual in every society in order to dissipate any negative consequences they may bring in their train. Kingship provides a model for others to emulate by replicating the king's rituals on a lesser scale.

What is at stake here is legitimation, and the capacity of a particular figure to secure this by transcending the ordinary rules of kinship (without a 'g') so that he represents all lineages before the gods through the repeated sacrificial re-creation of a perfect, timeless centre. Those who prefer materialist certainties like to portray caste as a peculiarly rigid form of stratification where the central problem, as in all systems of inequality, revolves around the wielding of temporal power. Hocart's argument is that it is much more revealing to view caste as a complex manifestation of kingship where, as in all forms of kingship, ritual and temporal functions are collapsed.

Hocart's approach endorses the assertion of Louis Dumont that the opposition of king and priest is central to the understanding of caste. But it shows that Dumont was quite wrong in echoing popular Hindu opinion by constructing a ladder-like structure that implied that the dynamic of caste relations placed priests 'higher' than kings, with untouchables at the 'bottom' as the polar opposites of priests. *All* ritual functionaries must be kept apart from kings: this is the crucial principle. How ritual functionaries are then differentiated from each other is a secondary matter: very important no doubt, but secondary.

Dumont's mistake was to insist that kingship in India became secularized from a very early date. As elsewhere, the primary concern of kingship in the subcontinent is with the generalized well-being of society, and this requires the ability to command rituals that bring the community together and expurgate whatever threatens communal well-being. Kings cannot perform the rituals themselves because to do so would be to interiorize the accumulated evil/sin/death that the rituals are designed to expel. Priests are the instruments who perform this purging function and who, in doing so, make possible kingship and nobility. Untouchable castes provide certain kinds of 'priests' whose tasks are regarded as particularly dangerous, but, as Parry has written, the priests provided by Brahman castes also have a profoundly ambiguous status:

> The priest's status is highly equivocal; and he is seen not so much as the acme of purity as an absorber of sin. Just as the low caste specialists remove the biological

impurities of their patrons, so the brahman priest removes their spiritual impurity by taking their sins upon himself through the act of accepting their gifts ... I stress that my observations here relate to the whole range of priestly specialists (Parry 1980: 89; 102)

Caste organization could thus be said to be based on a structural principle that separates noble and kingly families from priestly families. However, this is complicated by the fact that any priest or member of a priestly lineage may also act as the patron of other ritual specialists. This is yet another reminder not to essentialize caste in the manner of the vast majority of sociologists and anthropologists (as well as most Hindus). One must distinguish priesthood from Brahmans, kingship from dominant castes, untouchability from untouchables.

The disappearance of kings from the political scene in modern, ostensibly democratic, India has not led to the disappearance of king*ship* as an organizing principle of ritual and social relations in caste-organized communities. Members of noble castes continue to be mini-kings, not just materially, but in terms of their political/ritual function. They are 'at the center of a complex ritual organization that permeates nearly every aspect of the everyday life of the village' (Raheja 1988b: 517). The king's exemplary centre is seen as offering the key to the structure of caste relations in both ancient Sanskrit texts and recent ethnography on caste-organized communities:

[F]ar from being simply a matter of secular power and force, the role of the king is ritually central to the life of the kingdom ... Kings are enjoined, in the textual traditions, to give gifts if they wish to wish to enjoy sovereignty [here the work of Gonda 1965, 1966 is cited]; and to give is seen as an inherent part of the royal code-for-conduct, rajadharma. (Raheja 1988b: 514–15)

that brings us to the real nature of *rajadharma*, the teachers of which (all of them brahmans) regarded kingship as a practical and religious necessity, for they feared nothing more then chaos ... *Rajadharma* is 'the way a king should comport himself in order to be righteous'. (Derrett 1976: 606)

This connection between kingship and the prevention of chaos made by ancient Indian authorities finds strong echoes in the literature on African royal ritual, as we see below.

Precisely the same ambiguity – of setting apart and belonging – characterizes the institutions of caste and kingship. What distinguishes caste as a form of social organization is that the concept of setting apart applies so rigorously to all castes by virtue of the ritual function their members perform. The setting apart of untouchables may appear extreme to modern Western eyes, but it is no different in principle from the setting apart of other castes.

Dumont was mistaken to say that the king's function was secularized at an early period in Indian history with Brahman priests taking over the king's erstwhile ritual role. What did happen was that there was a parcelling out of ritual functions so that inauspiciousness would be continually removed from the kingly centre by a variety of specialists. The king's role cannot be said to have become de-ritualized because his primary function has always remained the commanding of these specialists to ensure that the kingship remained free from blemish. In other words, the king plays a primary role in the constant rituals of purification; he is not outside them. As others aspired to emulate the kingly role, they replicated it in miniature using whatever resources were at their disposal. Those whose ritual role was regarded as particularly dangerous and came to be classified as untouchables used this strategy no less than members of other castes to set each other apart, as Deliège has shown.

Perhaps the main reason for failing to understand that the setting apart of untouchables and kings derives from the same sociological and ideological complex is the concept of ritual employed by the great majority of observers of caste. This comes from a general way of seeing certain phenomena as 'religious', as opposed to political or economic, whereby the concept of ritual becomes subsumed by the concept of religion. There are two related problems with this perspective.

The first is that while the separation of the religious from the political and economic may be far-reaching, as in the typical modern democratic separation of Church and State, this separation can never be absolute. The powerful residual connection between the religious and the political is brought out in many ways, whether through memorial celebrations of the war dead or the attempts by states to regulate core areas of morality such as euthanasia, abortion and the rights of children. The second mistake is to see ritual in an essentialist rather than a processualist fashion. Ritual is the cultural means of binding people together in meaningful ways. As such, it pervades all aspects of human behaviour, not merely the religious as understood from a modern Western perspective. Other people's rituals always appear 'religious' in so far as they indicate values and practices that are alien to those of one's own group but this works both ways. When I was living in Nepal, I was continually upbraided by my hosts for the lack of values in Western society demonstrated particularly flagrantly by women traveling alone and being improperly dressed, and the fact that elderly people were left to die alone in nursing homes, uncared for by their families. This, I was often told, was because Westerners had no religion or no culture, the two ideas being used synonymously. It is very revealing that both examples – single women and abandoned parents – stress the aloneness of individuals and the failure of the community to absorb them.

In order to see more clearly the ideological juxtaposition of untouchability and kingship, it is useful to look at the idea of the exemplary centre, which comes from such thinkers as Hocart and Geertz, alongside the theory of the scapegoat king proposed by Frazer. In fact, as both de Heusch and Scubla point out in their respective chapters in this volume, Frazer offered two theories of the scapegoat. Only one of these, the lesser known, is relevant here.[7] In the thesis that is widely held to be the central idea of Frazer's *magnum opus*, *The Golden Bough*, the king is held responsible for the well-being of the kingdom and this is thought to be made manifest in his own bodily health. Should the king become ill, this would threaten the health of the kingdom and it would therefore be expedient to hasten his death.

In Frazer's second version of the scapegoat king, the king's well-being is again a barometer of the well-being of the community he presides over. But this time his well-being is not measured principally by his physical health. According to this view, which receives very many ethnographic illustrations, the king is *always* believed to attract the sins/evil/death/inauspiciousness of his people and some means must continually be found to rid himself of the contagion he absorbs lest his putrefaction endanger the kingship and the kingdom. This means is the setting apart of the king from 'ordinary' people through constant ritual.

As we have seen in earlier chapters in this volume, de Heusch and Scubla differ as to the importance of the scapegoat dimension. As I have pointed out in the Introduction, I am inclined to agree with Scubla that scapegoatism is the fundamental element of the institution, though I am less sanguine about his invocations of Girard and Freud to explain this phenomenon. It seems to me that one can take another path to explain the prevalence of the scapegoat phenomenon – and the institutions of caste and untouchability provide particularly good illustrations of this path.

As I have outlined in the Introduction, kingship is built on a central paradox. The king must be of the people but unlike them: he is a human being, but he is set apart from other human beings in order to be kept in a state of purity. However, the purity attained through separation from others can only be held for a fleeting instant. It is made possible through the performance of rituals that transmit to others the inauspicious qualities he has accumulated. These others are conventionally identified in the ethnographic literature as ritual specialists, but one might just as easily describe them as fulfilling a particular *sociological* function. Very simply, they must be unlike kings, and to demonstrate this they do something that kings cannot do: they absorb impurity. Since rituals inevitably come to an end, the king can only be set apart for the duration of the ritual, and then, strictly speaking, only at the moment of sacrifice, which is the paradigm of all ritual. Once this moment of release has passed, the king again becomes attached to others and begins anew to absorb the inauspiciousness that their relations generate. And so the ritual procedures, culminating in the sacrificial moment, must continually recommence. The rituals surrounding kingship are never-ending because if they were not, the king would quickly revert to the status of a 'normal' human being.

Frazer gave some nice illustrations of this process. Of these one of the clearest is the following:

In Travancore [in South India], when a rajah [king] is near his end, they seek out a holy brahman, who consents to take upon himself the sins of the dying man in consideration of the sum of ten thousand rupees. Thus prepared to immolate himself on the altar of duty as a vicarious sacrifice for sin, the saint is introduced into the chamber of death, and closely embraces the dying rajah, saying to him, 'O King, I undertake to bear all your sins and diseases. May your Highness live long and reign happily.' Having thus, with a noble devotion, taken to himself the sins of the sufferer, and likewise the rupees, he is sent away from the country and never more allowed to return. (Frazer 1994: 566)

Still today, without the constant purificatory rituals performed by specialists from other castes, the Hindu king accumulates the evil and death of his people to become the greatest of threats to his people. Following tradition, exactly the same ritual as described by Frazer above was performed twice in Nepal in the summer of 2001 following the massacre of the royal family by the crown prince who then killed himself (see Kropf 2002). For each a Brahman priest took upon himself the inauspiciousness of his monarch and was ritually expelled from the Kathmandu Valley.[8] The reasons for this are not as exotic or impenetrable as they might at first appear. Since the king is that individual who is uniquely connected to everyone, he is, as such, the target equally of everyone's sinful qualities as their beneficence.

Untouchability

In Hindu communities in India and Nepal the most obvious functionaries who channel pollution are certain members of so-called untouchable castes who perform tasks that are clearly ritually defiling. For the reader who is not familiar with the ethnographic writing on this region, it is very important to stress that we are dealing here with symbolic dirt, not actual dirt. For example, certain musicians are deemed untouchable because their services are required at funerals: it is their permanent association with death that defiles them (see, for example, Gellner 1995: 268–9).

As we have seen, the underlying purpose of royal ritual is always to keep the kingship free from pollution. Untouchability and kingship are thus mirror images of each other. At base, they derive from a structure of social relations which is common in complex agrarian societies throughout history but which is found in a particularly pronounced form in the caste-organized societies of the Indian sub-continent. In this section I will look at the institution of untouchability by using a foil: Robert Deliège's impressive (1999 [1995]) survey *The Untouchables of India*, the most comprehensive book to appear on this subject. My linking of untouchability to kingship is somewhat at odds with Deliège's analysis in three respects. Where Deliège's focus is untouchables, mine is untouchability; where he stresses inequality, I emphasize separation; and where he is most interested in the situation of untouchables in post-colonial times, my concern is less tied to any historical period though it depends on an understanding of caste in the pre-colonial era.

Deliège's position is straightforward: whereas others have explained the situation of untouchables with reference to an ideology of purity and pollution, he believes that their position is explained by a combination of ideological and economic factors and cannot be reduced to ritual notions alone. As Deliège sees it, untouchables perform 'menial' tasks because they are victims of economic exploitation and therefore their status 'cannot be reduced ... to a question of ritual' (Deliège 1999: 7) in the manner of the two most celebrated theories of caste. Here Deliège brackets together, and rejects, the different approaches of Dumont (1980 [1966]) and Hocart (1950 [1938]) both of whom lay stress on the ritual aspects of caste, though in radically different ways. Dumont, easily the most influential theorist of caste, emphasizes the purity of the Brahman priest *vis-à-vis* the impurity of the untouchable. Untouchables *per se* do not play a prominent role in Hocart's explanation of caste, which stresses the ritual centrality of the king. In his theory, the function of all groups in the society is to keep the king free from pollution.[9]

From the very beginning of his book, Deliège refers to untouchables as 'these most depressed categories of Indian society' (Deliège 1999 [1995]: vii) who are '*par excellence* those groups that carry out the various menial tasks that keep the village running' (1999: 6) and who are 'unfree labourers *par excellence*' (1999: 59). Yet he is also careful to state that it is not always the case that untouchables are poorer than their neighbours. Even when they are not, however, their neighbours invariably insist that untouchables should not transgress their ritually polluted status by engaging in any kind of relation which could be said to be constitutive of social status: pre-eminently, sexual relations, marital relations, commensality and the performance of certain rituals.

Deliège points out that untouchables are not the only people to carry out polluting tasks: so too do others such as members of the barber castes and certain 'Brahmans' who work as funeral priests. But these, he writes, are not regarded as untouchable, so there must be some other factor that gives an untouchable his uniquely 'depressed' status. It is, he says, a question of a combination of circumstances. Untouchables are 'those sections of Indian society that are [1] economically dependent and exploited, [2] victims of many kinds of discrimination, and [3] ritually polluted in a permanent way' (Deliège 1999: 2).

Deliège is particularly explicit about violence, including murder, perpetrated against untouchables. While this can be compared to other forms of 'social oppression and economic exploitation' in other parts of the world, there is, nevertheless, he believes, 'something unique about Indian untouchability' (1999: 3). One such feature is that untouchables have an ambiguous ritual status, simultaneously set apart from the rest of the community yet integrated into it. Another is that untouchables are divided into many castes and these are just as determined to avoid contact with each other as other castes are to avoid contact with them *en masse*.

The situation is greatly complicated by the modern reality of 'Scheduled Castes', the latest in a line of classifications of untouchables by the Government of India since Independence in 1947. As Deliège notes, the collective labelling of untouchables by the central government has given them a unity which they did not have before – for example in the reserved allocation of parliamentary seats and public posts, and their political associations which transcend localized 'traditional' caste-organized communities which are always framed in terms of agricultural landownership. But while he is careful to point out that the untouchables of pre-colonial India were fragmented in every sense, and remain divided today in most contexts even though some among them unite for modern political purposes, he tends to write about them as a corporate group from the point of view of economic exploitation. This leaves unsolved the question of why different untouchable castes are fastidious about separating themselves from each other for the purposes of commensality, marriage and ritual. This relative quality of untouchability, which makes some untouchable castes perceive themselves to be in danger of pollution from contact with other untouchables, seems to me to be at the heart of institution of caste.

In contrast to Dumont and Hocart, who focus on priesthood and kingship respectively, Deliège prefers the Marxist-leaning Béteille (see especially 1966, 1992) who, he says, judges the question of untouchability to be 'above all a problem of economic and social deprivation' that can be explained by 'nothing except certain political and economic considerations' (Deliège 1999: 49). Deliège seems to find unproblematic the fact that non-untouchable castes are also set apart from each other in terms of pollution concepts since they are not reduced to 'sub-human status' in the manner of untouchables. He does not offer any general theory of caste. But if the 'extreme' case (to modern Western eyes) of untouchables is explained by political and economic factors, how are we to explain other caste divisions? Deliège does not appear to endorse a materialist explanation of how caste works in general, and thus appears to argue for an explanation of untouchability that would not be subsumed under a more embracing theory of caste. It is not obvious how this could be so.

Contrasting the position of untouchable castes with those, like barbers, who also deal in pollution but who are not assigned untouchable status, Deliège states that the difference is that untouchables 'are also forced to perform all the socially debasing tasks, and a variety of means are employed to keep them in this state of inferiority and abjection' (Deliège 1999: 50). Primary among these means are violence and the denial of any right to landownership. Deliège, implicitly championing the cause of liberal egalitarianism at the expense of the anthropologist's more agnostic comparative perspective and political neutrality, refers to this as the 'insidiousness of caste ideology' (1999: 88). Of course reduction to subhuman status is the logical conclusion of being set apart to deal with the most polluting, or inauspicious, aspects of life and death. And such setting apart requires some means to achieve it, the options are not many, and these options must include violence as a last resort. This may be deeply unpalatable from a Western point of view but, as Dumont quite correctly pointed out, the values of caste, as of traditional society generally, are quite alien to the values of modern individualism.

If Deliège parts company with Dumont in devaluing caste ideology in comparison with modern Western individualism, he follows him in slipping between two quite different concepts of 'hierarchy'. On the one hand, Deliège defines this in the pre-eminent Dumontian sense as 'a way of ranking in relation to the whole' (1999: 59). On the other hand, he repeatedly refers to hierarchy in its ordinary (French or English) sense as a 'scale running from high to low', though this is qualified in the caste context as being 'based on association with death, on certain dietary rules and on degrading social practices' (Deliège 1999: 58). It is important to distinguish carefully between these two different senses of hierarchy because they have contrasting implications. When Deliège writes that 'separation does not necessarily mean hierarchy' (1999: 59), this is perfectly true if by hierarchy he means a ladder-like system of ranking. But it is the exact contrary of the sense of hierarchy as a system of elements that perform different functions in contributing to a coherent whole. Difference requires separation.

Deliège also states that '[g]enerally speaking ... the divisions between the various castes are particularly strong (even militant Untouchables admit that doing away with endogamy is unthinkable), but ... there is often an absence of interdependence between the untouchable communities and no real hierarchy' (1991: 59). Here he appears to consider the possibility that untouchable castes might form a separate system apart from other castes. But this is not a possibility. The presence of untouchable castes only makes sense if they are systematically linked to others who are not untouchable and for whom they perform a service.

Often, however, as with many other castes, it is not possible to rank untouchable castes one above another even though they are fastidious about keeping apart from each other. This is not something that generally bothers us if we look at other areas of human relations where differentiation is pronounced: gender or sibling difference, or the fact that neighbours must, by definition, be apart. Separation – being different or apart – does not automatically imply ranking. It *may* do, given other factors, but it need not. Similarly, the separation of castes does not automatically imply their inequality. According to Deliège, '[r]itual impurity cannot be separated from servitude or powerlessness' (Deliège 1999: 67), but this is clearly false in the sense that Deliège implies, where servitude is equated with economic and political powerlessness. Very frequently castes are ritually separated even though they are not in a position of economic servitude to each other, or perhaps to anyone.

If, however, one reads Deliège's proposition in a different sense, *viz.* that 'servitude' means 'serving society', it becomes true. In this latter sense, however, *all* castes are subject to ritual impurity, not merely untouchable castes. Untouchable castes are *more* polluted than others, but it is only a matter of degree, not of an absolute break. This may appear to be contradicted by the fact that untouchables are excluded in ways that others are not: where they live, where they may draw water, the kinds of clothes and ornaments they may wear and so on. But two facts militate against such a conclusion. First, the placing of the line that separates untouchables from others is always arbitrary. It is precisely because it *is* arbitrary that violence is required to uphold it. Second, it is not only untouchables who are categorically separated from the rest of society. So too is the king, as we have seen above, and as many of the other contributions to this volume make plain.

There is an underlying problem with Deliège's perspective that derives from his tendency to focus on the plight of untouchables today. Thus, he writes: 'while untouchability persists, it is no longer expressed in terms of ritual purity' (idem: 87). But as he himself notes, some untouchables have managed to improve their political and economic standing, yet have remained, for all that, untouchables. There is clearly some characteristic of untouchability that defies material improvement. Deliège admits this when he says that still today, '[a]s a direct result of their ritual impurity, untouchables incur a series of religious disabilities, the most common being that they are forbidden to enter temples and religious edifices' (1999: 91). So clearly, in important ways, untouchability *is* expressed in terms of ritual purity.

In any case, if it were true that the status of untouchables today was no longer expressed *primarily* in terms of ritual purity, this would clearly indicate (a) that in the past untouchability *was* expressed in this way, and (b) that comparing the situation of untouchables today with their counterparts in the past is to compare different entities. Deliège is perfectly correct that we cannot explain all aspects of the contemporary situation of untouchables with reference to the system of ritual offices that we conventionally describe as (traditional) caste organization. The advent of colonialism allowed untouchables from different regions to unite in ways that were not previously possible and to seek new means of earning their livelihood, in particular outside the locality of their birth. The whole nature of what it means to be an untouchable in the post-colonial world has changed fundamentally in political and economic terms in such a way that to compare today's untouchables with yesterday's is not to compare like with like.

It could be said that my aim here – the explanation of untouchability, an abstract idea that is at the heart of certain kinds of social relations – differs from Deliège's project – the explanation of the situation of untouchables in the modern world. But today's untouchables have a great deal in common with their pre-colonial forebears, and Deliège's analysis tends to obscure this. Untouchables in the twenty-first century could not exist were it not for persisting beliefs in untouchability and other ideological devices that are central to caste organization. They have acquired a variety of new economic and political mechanisms that allow them to forge alliances and prosecute political agendas that were simply impossible, even inconceivable, in the pre-colonial era. But in general they have not been able to shed their pre-colonial status.

While Deliège strives to move the understanding of the position of untouchables away from pre-modern symbols of pollution in order to focus attention on the political and economic plight of twenty-first century untouchables, it seems to me that one cannot brush over the fact that untouchability is an archaic cultural device. Indeed, it could be said that the situation of untouchables in the modern era is the reverse of what Deliège suggests. In pre-colonial India, it was possible to exclude untouchables because they were generally landless and powerless. However, as the fruits of modernization and greater democracy have become increasingly available to all, and new economic and political possibilities have opened up for untouchables, their setting apart has only continued to be possible by continually falling back on archaic ritual concepts.

Under modern political and economic conditions, the traditional bonds that connected members of untouchable castes to members of other castes have been attenuated by increasing political and economic centralization. However, the concept of untouchability has been strengthened by modern conditions for the paradoxical reason that the pervading liberal notion of equality for all has produced systems of protection and positive discrimination. (Notional) equality has not brought about an end to separation: on the contrary it has reinforced it. There is often, as many others have noted, an ironic advantage in claiming to be an untouchable today since this allows access to certain reserved places in public life. One cannot have quotas for untouchables (for example, in universities or civil administration or parliament) unless there *are* untouchables.

Conclusion

The conventional picture of caste organization, which presents untouchables at the bottom of a hierarchical ladder, obscures the fact that other groups also play a scapegoating function. Indeed it could be said that everyone shares in this function. Most commentators on caste believe that it is a phenomenon that is uniquely Indian or Hindu (the two not, of course, being the same thing). But if we see caste as an expression of kingship – that is to say, of a social structural form, rather than as a geographically confined ideology designed by priests to bolster their superiority – then the possibilities of comparison immediately open out. The Indian king, like his African counterpart, is simultaneously inside and outside. He is a paragon of purity who is forever contaminated by the relations that bind him to his people (not 'subjects' since he is as much of a subject to the kingship as they are). Where there is caste, everyone is, to a greater or lesser extent, attempting to replicate the rituals of the king and to reproduce the structure of social relations that this entails: i.e. to have their own priests. Thus untouchables, like everyone else, have their priests whom they must in turn keep separate from themselves.

Understood this way, pollution is not something that attaches merely to those who perform the most 'menial' of tasks in the society, as Deliège puts it. Rather, beliefs about pollution and the ritual practices that go with them provide means of separating out lineages from one another. In particular, pollution beliefs ensure that a sacred space is kept around the patron of a ritual, with members of noble and kingly lineages providing the model for this. Lineage organization in general provides a very convenient method of transferring ritual functions from one generation to the next. It is not the *only* means, but it has advantages and is a very widely chosen mechanism throughout history.

The institution of kingship provides, then, a kind of ideological complement to the institution of untouchability. Both deal with the same problem: the creation of order in a society where lineages provide a basis for social organization though – because of political and ecological factors – an insufficient basis. Caste emerges in agricultural societies, and where it is found the process of centralization is too well established for the possibility of a society based on lineage organization alone to re-assert itself. Caste organization, with its orientation to the royal centre, is of quite a different, more complex order. On the other hand, it is a rather weak form of centralization, as monarchical systems typically are, unable to displace lineage organization altogether, in the way that it is typically displaced by industrialism (see Quigley 1993: ch. 7).

The inadequate consideration of the role of lineage organization in caste organization is one of the main factors that pushes certain commentators to provide a materialist thesis for untouchability. As we have seen, it is more profitably explained with reference to the manner in which lineages sustain kingship both in practice and as an ideal.

Notes

1. See Quigley (1993) for a full explanation of the institution of caste. The chapters by Tamari and Ohnuki-Tierney in this volume are particularly good demonstrations of the utility of the concept of caste for comparative purposes.
2. All diacritical marks have been deleted from the transcription of words from Indian languages, including from passages in quotation, for the benefit of the reader unfamiliar with these languages.
3. Levy (1990) is a brilliantly encyclopaedic survey of ritual practitioners in one of

the most complex examples of caste organization on the Indian sub-continent.

4. This issue is explored in some detail in Chapter 4 of Quigley (1993).
5. Among the many texts on sacrifice, see Bloch and Parry (eds) (1982) and Scubla (1995).
6. Apart from Quigley (1993), see especially Hocart (1950 [1938]), Yalman (1989), Galey (1989), and Raheja (1988a,b).
7. For further elaboration on this, see the Introduction in this volume and the following chapters by de Heusch and Scubla.
8. Breaking with tradition, these priests were later allowed to return to their homes, apparently because they were not happy with the payment they had received for such inauspicious work. This goes against the entire rationale of their acceptance of the king's sins. Kropf (2003) explains this modern development as a weakening of the hold of ritual practices in the face of the onslaught of modernity.
9. I have reviewed the theories of caste of both Dumont and Hocart at some length in Quigley (1993).

References

Béteille, A. 1966. *Caste, Class and Power: Changing Patterns of Stratification in a Tanjore Village*. Bombay: Oxford University Press.

—— 1992. *The Backward Classes in Contemporary India*. Delhi: Oxford University Press.

Bloch, M. and Parry, J. 1982. *Death and the Regeneration of Life*. Cambridge: Cambridge University Press.

Deliège, R. 1999 [1995]. *The Untouchables of India*. Oxford: Berg.

Derrett, J. D. M. 1976. Rajadharma. *Journal of Asian Studies* xxxv(4): 597–609.

Douglas, M. 1970. *Purity and Danger: An Analysis of Concepts of Pollution and Taboo*. Harmondsworth: Penguin.

Dumont, L. 1980 [1966]. *Homo Hierarchicus: The Caste System and its Implications*. Chicago: University of Chicago Press.

Evans-Pritchard, E. E. 1962. 'The Divine Kingship of the Shilluk of the Nilotic Sudan', Frazer Lecture, reprinted in *Essays in Social Anthropology*, 66–86. London: Faber & Faber.

Fortes, M. 1968. 'Of Installation Ceremonies', *Proceedings of the Royal Anthropological Institute 1967*: 5–19.

Frazer, J. G. 1994 [1980]. *The Golden Bough*. London: Oxford University Press.

Fuller, C. J. 1984. *Servants of the Goddess: The Priests of a South Indian Temple*. Cambridge: Cambridge University Press.

Galey, J.-Cl. 1989. 'Reconsidering Kingship in India: An Ethnological Perspective', *History and Anthropology* 4: 123–87, reprinted in J.-Galey (ed.)

1990. *Kingship and the Kings*, Chur, Switzerland: Harwood Academic Publishers.

Geertz, C. 1980. *Negara: The Theater State in Nineteenth-Century Bali*. Princeton, NJ: Princeton University Press.

Gellner, D. N. 1996. 'Low Castes in Lalitpur', in D. N. Gellner & D. Quigley (eds) *Contested Hierarchies. A Collaborative Ethnography of Caste Among the Newars of the Kathmandu Valley*. Oxford: Clarendon Press, pp. 264–97.

Gonda, J. 1965. *Change and Continuity in Indian Religion*. The Hague: Mouton.

—— 1966. *Ancient Indian Kingship from the Religious Point of View*. Leiden: E. J. Brill.

Guneratne, A. 2001. 'Shaping the Tourist's Gaze: Representing Ethnic Differences in a Nepali Village', *Journal of the Anthropological Institute* 7(3): 527–43.

Heesterman, J. C. 1985 [1964]. 'Brahmin, Ritual and Renouncer', in J. C. Heesterman *The Inner Conflict of Tradition: Essays in Indian Ritual, Kingship, and Society*. Chicago: University of Chicago Press.

Heusch, L. de 1997. 'The Symbolic Mechanisms of Sacred Kingship: Rediscovering Frazer', *Journal of the Royal Anthropological Institute* 3: 213–32.

Hocart, A. M. 1950 [1938]. *Caste: A Comparative Study*. London: Methuen.

—— 1970 [1936]. *Kings and Councillors. An Essay in the Comparative Anatomy of Human Society*. Chicago: Chicago University Press.

Izard, M. 1987. 'De quelques paramètres de la souveraineté', in L de Heusch (ed.) *Systèmes de pensée en Afrique noire*, vol. 10: *Chefs et rois sacrés*. Paris: CNRS, pp. 69–91.

Kropf, M. 2002. 'Katto Khuvaune: Two Brahmins for Nepal's Departed Kings', *European Bulletin of Himalayan Research* 23: 56–84.

Levy, R. with the collaboration of K. R. Rajopadhyaya 1990. *Mesocosm: Hinduism and the Organization of a Traditional Newar City in Nepal*. Berkeley: University of California Press.

Parry, J. P. 1980. 'Ghosts, Greed and Sin: The Occupational Identity of the Benares Funeral Priests', *Man* (NS) 15: 88–111.

—— 1986. '*The Gift*, the Indian Gift and the "Indian Gift"', *Man* (NS) 21: 453–73.

Quigley, D. 1993. *The Interpretation of Caste*. Oxford: Clarendon Press.

—— 2000. 'Scapegoats: The Killing of Kings and Ordinary People', *Journal of the Royal Anthropological Institute* 6: 237–54.

Raheja, G. G. 1988a. *The Poison in the Gift*. Chicago: Chicago University Press.

—— 1988b. 'India: Caste, Kingship and Dominance Reconsidered', *Annual Review of Anthropology* 17: 497–522.

Scubla, L. 1995. 'Repenser le sacrifice: esquisse d'un projet d'anthropologie comparative', *L'Ethnographie* 91(1): 133–46.

Srinivas, M. N. 1959. 'The Dominant Caste in Rampura', *American Anthropologist* LXI: 1–16.

Yalman, N. 1989. 'On Royalty, Caste and Temples in Sri Lanka and South India', *Social Analysis* 25: 142–9.

—8—

Kingship and Caste in Africa: History, Diffusion and Evolution

Tal Tamari

Introduction

A large number of sub-Saharan African societies, located in geographically discrete portions of the continent, include institutions that have been labelled 'castes'. A major subset of these institutions consists in specialists – in crafts, music, hunting and/or overtly ritual activities – that form endogamous minorities within a larger society. Some societies (in the West African savannah and Sahara, Ethiopia, Somalia and the Nilotic Sudan) distinguish several minorities, while others (in the central savannah and Sahara, the Mandara and Alantika mountains of northern Nigeria and northern Cameroon, and northern Kenya) distinguish only one minority, which may, however, have several specializations.

The emergence of most of the endogamous specialist groups appears to depend on economic factors and symbolic representations that are common to all, or most, agricultural or pastoral pre-industrial societies, and certain contingent triggering factors. In Africa, the triggers seem to be of just two types. One involves kingship; the other sees the subordination and encapsulation of one population by another. Though at first blush these might seem to involve very different processes, in practice it is possible to identify links between the two.

One must postulate factors common to all or most pre-industrial societies in order to account for the extremely varied settings in which the institutions are found: agricultural, pastoral, with or without urban centres and significant long-distance trade, with or without writing, the existence of several 'world religions' and an apparently infinite diversity of 'traditional' belief systems. Particularly significant among these factors are symbolic representations with respect to crafts and music (which are themselves symbolically linked), whose range is remarkably similar within the whole gamut of pre-industrial societies based on agriculture or pastoralism. These representations explain why one repeatedly finds endogamous groups associated with the same activities, why their practitioners may be subject to avoidance behaviour or form hereditary groups even when they do not form endogamous ones. They suggest that the attribution of special status to regular practitioners of these activities is an inherent potentiality of most traditional societies – and one that may be realized through several different processes.[1] Specific events or processes seem to generate the structure because it is already latent.[2]

One must also postulate contingent factors in order to explain why not all societies have endogamous specialist groups, in spite of the fact that these symbolic representations are very widespread. The emergence of at least some of the West African and Chadian specialist groups involved modification of the status of 'blacksmith kings' (or groups with blacksmith kings), while the great frequency and importance of the institution of kingship in Ethiopia argues for its pertinence there. Other groups in Ethiopia, the central Sahara and savannah, however, seem to have been formed through the subordination of once autonomous, typically hunting populations. Thus, there appear to be at least two models for the formation of endogamous specialist groups. However, the emergence of some groups partakes, in a sense, of both models. For example, a blacksmith king may be thought of as originating in a population whose identity differs from that of the newly dominant one (which proceeds to transform persons associated with the erstwhile ruler into a segregated and ultimately endogamous group). On the other hand, a population that has initially been primarily agricultural and once had its own kings (such as the Falasha) may become an endogamous group primarily associated with crafts, even though its erstwhile kings were in no way associated with such occupations. Moreover, in this second case, the vocationally specialized endogamous group comes to acquire its latter-day characteristics largely through manipulation by rulers who are culturally identified with other populations. Thus, although superficially the two triggering factors appear to be very different and even opposed, the former, involving kingship, may be viewed as a special case of the latter, while transformation of hunting groups into hunter–craft or craft groups may be viewed as another special case.

The data assembled here lend new meaning to the currently unfashionable concepts of evolution and diffusion. On the one hand, they suggest that complex institutions with similar characteristics may develop independently of each other (evolution). The specialist groups of at least three regions – West Africa, the central Sahara and savannah, and Ethiopia – seem to have arisen without reference to each other. Yet this is not a monochrome kind of evolution, since these widely separated institutions achieved similar characteristics through partially differing processes. Nevertheless, common symbolic representations intervened to bring about similar results in the long run.

On the other hand, these data indicate that the movement of specialists within each of the above culture areas is a major factor accounting for their current or recent distribution (diffusion). Despite the fact that interaction among the clusters appears to have been limited historically, by the early twentieth century a pan-African – or at least pan-savannah, Sahelian and Saharan – social system involving endogamous specialists was emerging. Societies with this characteristic cut a significant swathe across the continent, stretching in an almost unbroken chain from the Atlantic to the Red Sea and the Indian Ocean, from the northernmost fringes of the forest through the southern Sahara.

Resemblances between institutions located in different parts of the continent have not gone totally unnoticed. Thus, the scholar–administrator Maurice Delafosse stated in 1894 that those in savannah West Africa appeared to be similar to those of the Somali. Randi Haaland (1985) similarly pointed out resemblances in the social status of ironworkers and other craftspersons she had studied in the course of her fieldwork in the western Republic of Sudan, and those of both Ethiopia and West Africa. Olivier Gosselain, in a conference paper presented in 1999, recognized the same clusters of craft castes mentioned here, and also posed the question of their historical interrelationships, arguing for diffusion within the clusters on the basis of uniformity of pottery fashioning techniques.[3]

A. M. Hocart (1950 [1938]), of course, thought that caste was fundamentally about kingship.[4] He made a very broad use of this term to mean any largely hereditary (not necessarily endogamous, nor even strictly hereditary) group, whose activity involved a ritual aspect (though it might, and usually did, have an economic one as well). He had in mind primarily the *varna* classifications of India and Sri Lanka, and all-encompassing hierarchies of Fiji and other Pacific societies, but also minorities endowed with a distinctive status, such as the barber–doctors of Egypt and the carpenters to the kings of Fiji (who constructed the royal shrines and palaces, ate apart from all other Fijians and only married amongst themselves).

The African data presented here, on the basis of a narrower interpretation of 'caste', bear Hocart out insofar as they show that when kingship and specialized endogamous groups coexist in the same society, they are strongly implicated with each other. However, these data also show that these institutions may be found in societies that are, at least temporarily, not characterized by kingship, and that kingship is a factor in the formation of some (but not necessarily all) such groups. On broader methodological issues, however, this essay is very much in the line of Hocart. He too identified far-reaching structural similarities among culturally diverse and geographically remote societies, yet recognized the significance of common heritage and the mutual influence of neighbouring societies.

The data surveyed here also suggest that there is a connection between kingship and 'untouchability' – as Quigley (this volume) has noted on the basis of his research on India and Nepal. The relationships between kings and specialists are most intense precisely in the societies where the latter are subject to the severest segregation. Thus, among the Maba of Chad, the designated head of the musician–blacksmith–executioners is responsible for providing bodily care to the king; among the Marghi of northern Nigeria, the king is buried in the manner of a blacksmith; and the founders of some of the dynasties of southwestern Ethiopia are said to have been brought up by specialists. Among the Bari of Sudan, the rainmakers are assisted by *dupi* 'serfs'.

I shall proceed in geographical order, from west to east.

Western Savannah and Sahara

Endogamous groups of artisans and musicians are found among most of the peoples of savannah West Africa, the adjoining portions of the Sahara and the forest fringe. These include the Manding-speaking peoples (Malinke, Bamana, Dyula, and several lesser-known groups), Soninke, Wolof, Fulani, Tukulor, Songhay, Dogon, Senufo, Moors and Tuareg. Each of the above peoples distinguishes at least two, but usually three to seven named endogamous groups, each with different, though sometimes partially overlapping, technical and musical specializations. Traditional (as well as, of course, modern) urban and commercial centres may include representatives of an even larger number of castes, with differing ethnic affiliations.[5]

Members of the endogamous groups constitute one of three basic social categories, the others being the well born ('nobles' or 'free') and the slaves. The well born usually constitute at least half, but sometimes nearly the whole, of the population. 'Caste persons' have been estimated to constitute about five per cent of the population among most peoples where the institution is well established, but up to twenty per cent among the Wolof. A few peoples of the region, such as the Moors, Tuareg and Tukulor, make internal distinctions among the well born, differentiating among tribes or lineages preferentially associated with either warfare or religion, and 'vassals' or 'commoners'; however, none of these groups is endogamous, and their relative status is subject to continuous negotiation and change.

Metalworking, pottery, woodworking, leatherworking, praise singing and the playing of musical instruments are the professions most usually assigned to the endogamous groups. Pottery is usually a specialty of women of blacksmith, more rarely of bard, status. Woodworking is most often a secondary specialization of metalworkers, but two groups specialize primarily in this activity. There is one weaver group, while another group specializes both in weaving and bardship. However, among most peoples of this region, weaving is open to the majority of males, while spinning is a typical female activity. In most of the above societies, 'caste people' are the only ones allowed to engage in metalwork, leatherwork, most kinds of woodwork and musical performance, but they may generally also engage in all other recognized economic activities. The Dogon constitute an exception as, at least in some areas, they did not allow blacksmiths or bards to cultivate.

In nearly all the societies said to have 'castes', specialists could not marry members of the majority population; intermarriage between members of certain specified castes (for example, bards and blacksmiths among the Manding and Soninke) was tolerated but not favoured, while some castes were strictly endogamous. Persons belonging to castes practising analogous occupations, but living amongst different peoples and sometimes speaking different languages, could often intermarry, since they were believed to share a common origin. There are few other forms of inter-group avoidance. As Delafosse noted in the early twentieth century, 'the noblest inhabitant of a land would never hesitate to make friends with a casted individual, to allow him into his home, to shake his hand, or to share a meal with him'.[6] Nevertheless, some Soninke, Fulani and Senufo refuse to sit on the same mat as certain caste persons. Among the Bamana, *funè* were traditionally not allowed into the fields of others during the sowing season.[7] Dogon do not partake of food or drink with members of some groups associated with speech and leatherworking.[8] Some regions of Senegambia were formerly characterized by severe avoidance behaviour, as shown in the sixteenth-century Portuguese-language sources. For example, bards could not take water from a spring or well as long as others were present, had to obtain permission from the lord of the village before they could enter it and were not allowed into other persons' homes. They were not buried, but rather had their corpses exposed in baobab trees – a practice which persisted in Senegal through at least the mid-1950s.[9,10] Wolof still avoid making friends with, or coming into any kind of close physical proximity to, members of the minorities.[11] Although this has recently been contested,[12] it seems certain that all or nearly all West African societies with minority groups adhered to a notion of hierarchy. This is the opinion not only of the early French writers, but, significantly, of all African ones.[13]

Relationships between kings and chiefs on the one hand, and specialists on the other, are strongly articulated. Oral epics (which are transmitted by the endogamous bards) always depict kings, princes and all other legitimate political and military leaders as accompanied by bards, and often craft specialists as well. The fourteenth-century Arabic descriptions of Malian courts and kings always show the sovereign attended by musician–spokesmen who may be identified as bards. One chronicler depicts the king seated on a dais, between his personal bard–spokesman and his sword-maker – precisely the image projected in the Sunjata epic.[14] Descriptions by European travellers, from the sixteenth century onwards, show rulers of this region constantly attended by bards, and sometimes by members of the other special status groups as well.

Correlations can also be established between the degree of development of endogamous groups and the presence of state structures (which, in this as in other regions of pre-colonial Africa, nearly always implied kings).[15] Thus, the state societies distinguish the largest number of different castes. The Senufo also distinguish a large number of castes, but they have very strong chiefs. The Dogon, most of whom have consecrated ritual leaders but only a few of whom have chiefs with executive authority, have a sketchy distribution of specialists, no group being present throughout Dogon country. The Minianka, who are chiefless, distinguish only two specialized minority groups – of which at least one (blacksmiths) does not seem to be fully endogamous. Among the chiefless Bobo, blacksmiths form a largely hereditary, but not an endogamous, group.

There are strong indications that the emergence of endogamous special status groups is itself related to ideological struggles among kings and the process of state formation. Linguistic evidence and oral traditions together imply that castes may have been developed independently by at most three peoples – the Manding, Soninke and Wolof – precisely the ones who founded the earliest states in the region.

Only five societies, speaking four languages (Manding, Soninke, Wolof and Fulfulde), have terms for collectively designating all the endogamous specialists living among them. These can be traced back to etymons in just two languages, Manding and Wolof.[16] Over forty terms used in twelve languages for endogamous bards, leatherworkers and woodworkers have been reported, but they can be traced back to at most fourteen etymons in just five languages (Manding, Soninke, Wolof, Fulfulde and Dogon). Only terms for ironworkers (as distinct from other metalworkers) are proper to each language, suggesting either that familiarity with this technique preceded its attribution to a special status group, or that each society developed such a group independently. (Other data, mentioned below, suggest that the first interpretation is the appropriate one.)[17]

Oral traditions, often backed up by detailed genealogies, link some of the specialist groups in each society to those of at least one, and usually several, other societies. They show that the overwhelming majority of specialists among the Songhay, Dogon, Senufo, Moors and Tuareg originated among other populations. This is also true of the Minianka and Dan, among whom the institution is little developed. Only among the Wolof, Soninke and Manding can the members of at least one metalworker, one leatherworker and one bard group not be shown to originate in another society. Thus, linguistic, genealogical and oral traditional evidence, taken together, show that West African castes originated in one or a very small number of societies, all of which have long been organized as states.

The Sunjata epic provides insights into some of the processes through which endogamous specialist groups might have come into being. This epic, told primarily by Malinke bards, but to an audience composed mainly of the well born, recounts the founding of the Mali empire – a development that may be dated, on the basis of Arabic external sources, to the mid thirteenth century. These sources also provide confirmation of the reality of some of the persons and events mentioned in the epic. Textual analysis – a considerable number of versions have been collected – indicates that some elements of the epic, particularly the praise songs, are extremely old. It thus has unusually strong claims to historical veracity, or rather to a definite, though not necessarily straightforward, relationship to past events.[18]

The plot centres on a conflict between a blacksmith king (Sumanguru Kante, ruler of the Sosso kingdom) and Sunjata – a hunter, son of a Malinke chief, and future founder of the Mali empire. Although Sumanguru is said to be a caste black-smith (there is no term for ironworker in Manding that does not imply this status), he marries well-born women, is a remarkable warrior and a strong (according to some versions, tyrannical) ruler. He thus utterly confounds what might be expected of a caste person, since in recent times the specialists have not been allowed to bear arms or hold political office. Although Bala Faseke is presented as Sunjata's bard, son of his father's bard, he is not familiar with the xylophone, the principal musical instrument at the medieval Malian court, and only discovers it in Sumanguru's secret chamber.

I submit that the epic obliquely refers to a change in the status of groups associated with ironworking and certain kinds of music. Objects that were once symbols of royal status, and vehicles of occult power, gradually became, as a result of the Sosso's defeat by the Malinke, symbols of inferior status. The new Malinke rulers, and groups formerly associated with Sosso power, were furthermore linked to each other in a perpetual alliance through a ritual contract – perhaps on the model of a 'bitter' joking relationship, i.e. one involving ceremonial blood exchange – which entails a prohibition on marital exchange and mutual violence, as well as an obligation of mutual assistance. It is not possible to dismiss as mere hyperbole the epic's claim that Sumanguru Kante was a blacksmith king, since such a claim is highly inimical to the interests of Malinke power, and therefore could only be based on fact – a fact which the Malinke princes could not completely dissimulate.

Once endogamous or quasi-endogamous groups had emerged at the Malian imperial court, they could have been rapidly accepted in other milieux, both courtly and rural. A medieval Arabic source depicts Malian provincial governors and military leaders as being accompanied by their own spokesmen–musicians.[19] Members of the castes in formation would have accompanied the Malian administrators and also travelled for their own reasons – as they are documented to have done in later centuries. They would have been welcomed not only because they met certain practical needs, but because their partial social segregation corresponded to symbolic representations that exist in nearly all traditional cultures, whether or not they are characterized by groups of endogamous specialists.[20] The current distribution of castes extends just slightly beyond the furthest limits of the Mali empire (which survived, though in reduced form, through the end of the sixteenth century).

The time framework implied by the above interpretation is precisely that indicated by written sources for the emergence of special status minorities. Arabic descriptions of the earlier, Soninke-dominated empire of Ghana (eighth to eleventh century CE) do not mention any intermediary between king and people, nor any of the musical instruments characteristic of modern times.[21] In contrast, and as we have already noted, the fourteenth-century Arabic descriptions of the Malian court depict musician–spokesmen whose activities are very similar to those of the modern bards. Furthermore, they are designated by the same term (*jeli*) and play some of the same musical instruments. The Arabic chronicles of Timbuktu report on the designations and activities of Soninke, Manding, Fulani, Tukulor and Songhay bards, and more rarely other specialists, in the fifteenth through seventeenth centuries. As we have already seen, Portuguese sources mention segregated artisans and bards among the Wolof, Serer and Manding-speakers of Senegambia, beginning in the sixteenth century.

There is no evidence that any of the endogamous craft and musician groups of the West African savannah and Sahara formed from an initially autonomous population, particularly one with a distinctive life style, in contrast to those of the central savannah and Sahara, as well as in East Africa, where that process seems to have occurred repeatedly. In the region considered, such a process seems possible only with respect to the itinerant, Fulfulde-speaking *lawbe* woodworkers, whose origins are unknown. In all other instances, castes emerged from other castes – except for the very first ones, which can only be understood in relationship to kingship.

The Mandara and Alantika Highlands

Many, perhaps most, of the societies of the Mandara and Alantika highlands of northeastern Nigeria and northern Cameroon have been described as having a 'caste' of endogamous 'blacksmiths'.[22] Among Mandara societies such as the Mafa (also called Matakam), Kapsiki (also called Higi) and Marghi, male 'blacksmiths' are also woodcarvers, leatherworkers, morticians and gravediggers. They are considered expert in curing certain diseases, are the only persons entitled to play certain musical instruments, and are sometimes also regarded as the best diviners. Women are potters and, often, midwives. In Alantika societies such as the Dii, Dowayo and Vere, male 'blacksmiths' often have one or more ritual specializations, while the women are potters. In both areas, smelting is sometimes but not always done by men of the 'blacksmith' group. Where iron ore is collected on the surface in the form of magnetite, as is often the case in these highland regions, this work is most usually accomplished by members of the majority, farming population. In marked contrast to most of the West African savannah societies described above, until recently men and women of the 'blacksmith' group were not allowed to farm, and were thus full-time specialists.

'Blacksmiths' have been estimated to form about five per cent of the population among the Mafa, among whom rigorous statistical and demographic studies have been carried out.[23] Mafa blacksmiths have also been shown to have been (through the 1960s) strictly endogamous, while more informal counting procedures applied to some Marghi populations (in 1959–1960) revealed no exceptions to group endogamy.[24] Among some Alantika societies, an association between black-smithing and pottery-making may be only incipient and these craftspersons do not form an endogamous group, though blacksmith–potter marriage is represented as ideal.

In those Mandara societies where they are endogamous, the specialists are also subject to other kinds of avoidance behaviour. They reside apart, and must eat and drink apart, using their own vessels. The specialists may accept gifts of food and beer from members of the farming majority, but the converse is not true. Among the Marghi and the Kapsiki, members of the majority believe (falsely) that specialists eat some items (such as snake) that they themselves consider disgusting. However, at least among the Marghi, relationships between majority and minority can be convivial, and personal friendships are sometimes formed.

In this geographical area, kingship has had a role in reinforcing and defining, and perhaps also in bringing about the emergence of, endogamous specialists. In a Marghi kingdom that James Vaughan has studied in considerable depth, a close symbolic and ritual relationship exists between the king and the specialists. The king's court included a blacksmith whose title also meant 'king', and who was responsible for judging disputes among his fellow blacksmiths. Both 'kings' styled their hair in the same manner. The king married a 'smith' woman shortly after his installation; he was the only person in the realm allowed, and indeed required, to transgress the rule of endogamy. Furthermore, the king was buried sitting upright on an iron stool, surrounded by charcoal – in the same position as a blacksmith.[25]

Although the Marghi and other peoples of the region are considered stateless, many have kings or chiefs who have significant ritual roles, great prestige and considerable decision-making power. Furthermore, it seems possible that kingship was even more highly developed in the past, and that many small chiefdoms were once the centres of, or alternatively were included in, large-scale states. Read together, a sixteenth-century chronicle from Bornu and Heinrich Barth's account of his travels in the mid nineteenth century imply that the kingdoms in this area were progressively weakened and destroyed as a result of centuries-long raiding by Bornu and other Islamic powers. The Marghi in particular seem to have suffered this fate and to have had strong kings at the times highlighted by these two written sources.[26] Thus, the Mandara mountains and adjacent flatlands may not always have been occupied by the naked, 'primitive', mutually isolated groups depicted in European accounts that date from the first half of the twentieth century.

The Lake Chad Area and the Central Sahara

Many of the peoples established near Lake Chad and on its islands, and most, perhaps all, those of the central Sahel and Sahara (northeastern Niger, northern Chad and western Sudan) are characterized by the presence of minorities that have been labelled 'castes' or, more rarely, serfs.[27] The best described groups include those found among the primarily agricultural Kanembu, and the primarily pastoral Teda, Daza, Beri-speakers (the Zaghawa and the closely related Bideyat) and Shoa Arabs. All groups are associated with craftwork, hunting and music, but the modalities vary; craftwork always includes ironworking (smithing and often smelting), but may include leatherworking, woodworking and weaving as well. Ironworking is the primary occupation of most Teda male specialists. Hunting and leatherworking are the primary occupations of most of the male specialists associated with other populations, but some engage primarily or exclusively in craftwork, certain skills – especially ironworking – being transmitted within particular lineages. Each of the above groups includes musicians, for whom provision of musical entertainment is a secondary, or, very exceptionally, a primary occupation; the use of certain instruments is restricted to men of the specialist groups. These men may also have various minor ritual roles, in both Islamic and non-Islamic ceremonies, while some specialist women dress the hair of higher status females. Specialist women, particularly ones from craft families, are often potters. The specialists of the primarily agricultural Maba population are exclusively associated with craftwork and music, but claim that they were once hunters. Traditionally, the specialists were not allowed to own land or more than a few small stock. In each language, a single term applies to all minority persons; additional qualifiers are used in order to distinguish them according to their occupations. *Haddad*, the term used to designate the specialists in colloquial Arabic, means 'blacksmith' in classical Arabic.

Each of these groups was endogamous with respect to the dominant populations, but there was no bar to the intermarriage of persons with similar occupations resident among different populations. On the other hand, among the Kanembu, families specializing in craftwork did not usually intermarry with hunting families.[28] Thus, differences in status and occupation that were of only slight significance to the majority population may have been crucial to the minorities themselves. Specific links existed between hunting families and lineages and their patrons in the majority population. Daza and Kanembu hunters exchanged game meat and other 'bush' products for milk and/or grain from their patrons. Through the 1970s, there seems to have been no commensality between members of the minority groups and the majority population. Among pastoralists, minority families camped behind and just a short distance away from their patrons. Among agriculturalists, they often formed their own neighbourhoods and/or villages.

Nicolaisen (1968: 92) estimated that there were no more than 30,000 special status hunters and craftspersons in Kanem in the 1960s. By contrast, Conte estimated that persons of this status constituted twenty to twenty-five per cent of the population of this region, reaching fifty per cent in the south, but that most had become tenant cultivators over the past several decades.[29]

Although, or perhaps because, these minorities were subject to strict social segregation, they were sometimes closely linked to kings or chiefs. The sultan of Wadai was attended by musicians drawn from the *kabartu* specialist group. Members of this group also acted as his torturers and executioners. The chief of the specialists was the sultan's personal barber and medical assistant, and was, furthermore, responsible for the ceremonial treatment of his corpse.[30] Zaghawa leaders named 'chiefs' among the blacksmiths, to assist them in carrying out their policies with respect to their group, and some Zaghawa leaders received regular tributes of game meat and smelted ore.[31]

The minorities seem to have been constituted from several quite diverse groups, classifiable in at least two broad categories: autochthonous hunting and gathering populations that were incompletely assimilated by the empire-building Kanembu, and remnants of populations prominently associated with ironworking, who had previously dwelled in walled city-states. Nicolaisen (1968: 92, 95) states that according to his informants, all the *duu* were originally hunters and gatherers. However, several detailed studies of the oral traditions and genealogies of some ironworking groups show that their members claim to originate in towns that were destroyed by other populations, sometimes ones with a different, pastoral lifestyle. Most of the survivors were assimilated by the newly dominant populations, but a few clung on to their identity, becoming dispersed lineages of smelters and blacksmiths. They thus were often assimilated to existing low status groups sharing the same profession. This was, in particular, the case of the Mbara, who still retained their own language in the 1970s, but also of the Kargu, Budugur, Kawalke, and Jorok.[32]

There is an uncanny resemblance here to one of the processes of caste formation posited for the Western Savannah area: modification of the status of a group simultaneously associated with kingship and ironworking following upon its military and political defeat. In these central Sahelian city-states, as among the Sosso, kingship was symbolically associated with ironworking, but a high proportion of the inhabitants may have known how to work iron. In both cases, the social status associated with ironworking abruptly shifted from royal to low. Contemporary Mbara, Kargu, Budugur and Jorok do not claim to descend from kings – as Manding blacksmiths do when they affirm a link to Sumanguru Kante – but they do claim to derive from a group that once had its own kings. Resemblances between Manding and central Sahelian ironworkers do not stop there. In both cases, despite their lowered status, the ironworkers were the major propagators of an initiation society. However, the Central Sahelian blacksmiths do not seem to have formed a ritual and social contract with the new rulers – perhaps because, in many cases, there simply were no rulers, in the newly dominant, often segmentary societies. Convergences between the oral traditions of majority and minority, as well as linguistic and archaeological evidence, suggest that the erstwhile prestige of some blacksmith groups is not merely a cherished belief, but corresponds to aspects of past reality.

The association of hunting and craftwork is intriguing but, as we shall see, far from unique. We shall encounter it again in Ethiopia and Kenya, and it is also found among the Twa of Rwanda and Burundi. It does not seem necessary to posit any intrinsic symbolic relationship between these two spheres.[33] Rather, insofar as a group already has low status, additional activities that are – for whatever reason – held in low esteem, may be attributed to it.

On a map, the 'caste systems' of the western and central savannah and Sahara seem to touch. There may indeed have been some relations of mutual influence or demographic interchange between the institutions of both areas. Tuareg and Fulani are nomadic in some portions of eastern Niger and Chad – and West African pilgrims pass through these lands on their way to Mecca. The Fulani of Chad designate 'blacksmiths' (here, really multi-purpose specialists) by the same term, *baylo*, used to the west, and also relate a similar story about the origin of the joking relationship that links them to these artisans.[34] One Mbara ironworking clan is said to descend from the 'Baylao'. Not only is this designation suspiciously like the Fulani one, but the Baylao are said to have been both ironworkers and herders, while their women were potters.[35] On balance, however, oral traditions, as well as their several specificities, suggest that the endogamous groups considered here developed primarily as a result of demographic and political processes specific to the area. These oral traditions mention considerable movement within the central Sahelian and Saharan area, but do not mention any movement to or from the west. On the other hand, there may be stronger connections to the endogamous specialists of the Mandara mountains, due south. Oral traditions do mention some movement of craftspersons, and trade in craft products, in the area extending from Kanem to the foothills of Mandara. Furthermore, some Chadian kings and blacksmiths are buried in the manner already described for the Marghi.[36]

The Bari of the Riverain Sudan

The Bari, who live along the White Nile in the southern Republic of Sudan, have been described as possessing a caste system, or – these terms may be used simultaneously by the same writers – as characterized by 'servile castes' or 'submerged classes'. The principal descriptions are based on field enquiries made in the 1920s and 1930s, but at least some aspects of this system persist into the present.[37]

The Bari traditionally distinguished six social categories: free persons (to use the earlier writers' terminology – one could as appropriately speak of 'the well born'); *dupiet*, pl. *dupi*, serfs, sometimes more fully designated as *dupi kaderak*, 'serfs who cook'; blacksmiths; hunters; aquatic hunters; and slaves or captives and their descendants. Certain clans or lineages provided 'rain chiefs' or 'rainmakers', who, according to Simonse (1992), wielded considerable executive and judicial powers in pre-colonial times, and fully deserve to be described as 'kings'. The Bari also recognized various 'masters of the land', 'masters of the mountain', and other specialized offices, transmitted within the well-born population, as well as 'masters of the forest', chosen among the hunters.

The *dupi* were, literally, hewers of wood and drawers of water for the freeborn, and also prepared and served their sacrificial food and beer. They also assisted them in cultivation, the care of their cattle and house construction, but could not, until well into the British colonial period, own cattle of their own. Each of the first five categories was almost, but not quite, endogamous. Although marital and sexual relations were ordinarily prohibited, a freeman who had lost his children by freeborn wives might wed a *dupiet* in the hope that henceforth all his children might live. On the other hand, the freeborn sometimes killed *dupi* children, on the pretence that the high fertility of the serfs was inimical to their own. Members of each of the first four categories had to eat and dwell apart.

The *dupi kaderak* have generally been thought to be a formerly autonomous, primarily hunting and gathering group, yet they have a definite relationship to the kings or rainmakers. Certain *dupi* acted as assistants to the rainmakers, and were sometimes entrusted with the transport of the rain stones and the performance of rain rites when the former could not be personally present. They were also entrusted with guarding the rainmakers' tombs (and, it seems, were at one time buried with the rainmaker they had assisted). Adult *dupi* could not be killed or harmed and, therefore, served as the rainmaker's messengers in times of war. The blacksmiths, aquatic and terrestrial hunters had to pay annual tribute to the rainmakers in appropriate products. Thus, though there is no reason to believe that the rainmakers created the specialized groups, they maintained multiple links with them.

Undoubtedly there would be more to say about the riverain Sudan if the ethnography were not so uneven. The Fulani of West Africa have been settling in Dar Fur and the riverain Sudan for the past three centuries, in several major migrations and also in a continual trickle; at least some of them come from regions long characterized by hereditary and/or endogamous craft and musical specialists. The persistence, or otherwise, of these Western institutions in the Sudan, and their possible encounter with Eastern ones, is a topic that merits investigation. Many of the Arabic-speaking populations claim to originate among the tribes of the Arabian peninsula, who are often serviced by hereditary, endogamous, low-status smith–musicians; did any such persons settle in the Sudan and maintain their status? Is there any historical relationship between the craftspeople of Sudan and those just to the east, in Ethiopia?

Ethiopia

Most Ethiopian peoples are characterized by endogamous specialist groups remarkably similar to those found in West Africa. These groups have been described among the Amhara and Oromo (who together constitute about seventy per cent of Ethiopia's population), the Gurage, Konso, Dime, Dizi and many other peoples. They have nearly always been labelled 'castes', 'low castes', 'despised groups', or 'pariahs' (sometimes simultaneously by the same authors), though a few late twentieth-century writers have preferred to designate them as 'marginalised minorities' or simply as 'minorities'.[38]

Until recently, most of these Ethiopian societies have had chiefs or kings, and some have founded powerful states. These societies typically distinguished between the royal clan or lineage, commoners, slaves and the endogamous specialists. Others, such as the Konso and the various Gamo populations, simply distinguished between well-born persons and the specialists, or, as in the case of the pastoral Oromo, between their members and the specialists, whom they regarded as discrete populations.

The activities most usually assigned the specialists are: hunting, leatherworking, ironworking (including both smelting and smithing), pottery and, more rarely, weaving and woodworking. Pottery is typically made by women of the iron-workers', hunters', or leatherworkers' groups. Several groups have music making and praise singing as a secondary activity, but it is the primary or exclusive specialty of very few groups. Members of the endogamous groups often have specific ritual roles, including the performance of circumcision, excision and midwifery. Among the Gurage, male ritual experts drawn from the specialist groups were entrusted with the initiation of well-born girls, while certain specialist women had a major role in the cults specific to Gurage men.

Thus, in comparison to West African ones, the Ethiopian groups add hunting to their professional activities, but omit the working of precious metals and limit music. Goldsmithing and silverwork have often been prestigious in Ethiopia, practised by high status Ethiopian families as well as by foreigners invited to settle in the realm.[39] Although Amhara society distinguishes many different kinds of music, including some performed by persons of distinctive status, music makers do not usually, if ever, form strictly hereditary or endogamous groups.[40] Most Ethiopian societies, like most West African ones, distinguish several different specialist groups. However, the Ethiopian specialist groups differ from West African ones in that, in many or most cases, their members were not allowed to engage in the main subsistence activities.

The Ethiopian groups, furthermore, differ from the West African ones in that they are subject to very strong avoidance behaviour. In this they resemble nearly all the other sub-Saharan groups that have been labelled 'castes'. Thus, the specialists may not eat or drink with, nor use the same utensils as, the majority population; they must locate their homes at a certain distance from the majority population and may not, under most circumstances, enter them. Gurage specialists were, furthermore, forbidden from entering markets, and therefore had to sell their wares to middlemen. Some specialists eat foods that are not consumed by the majority population, while being denied items that are highly valued by the latter. Several peoples, including the Amhara, believe that certain specialists, especially blacksmiths and tanners, can transform themselves into hyenas and, in this form, consume human corpses. Over the past few decades, however, restrictions placed on the specialists have gradually been softening.

No historical study of the Ethiopian specialists exists, but there is a consensus that no single model or sequence of events is likely to account for all the institutions observed. There is, furthermore, a consensus that migration is one of the factors that accounts for the present-day distribution of the specialists. Similarly named groups are found among different peoples; most specialist groups, especially in the southwest, have traditions of coming from other areas.

In view of the large number of special status groups with distinctive hunting traditions in Ethiopia and more generally in East Africa, several writers have argued that some, but not necessarily all, were once autonomous hunting populations, a social configuration that subsists in some regions of East Africa, but apparently not in Ethiopia. Given that some groups in Ethiopia (and in the central Sahel and Sahara and in Somalia) both hunt and engage in craftwork, I would suggest that some groups associated in the twenty-first century exclusively with craftwork may once have engaged in hunting as well.

That most Ethiopian societies have been – or neighboured upon, or were once included in – kingdoms or chiefdoms, suggests but hardly proves that there is a causal relationship between kingship and state formation and the emergence of caste. On the other hand, there is clear evidence that in Ethiopia kings and chiefs were greatly interested in, and manipulated, the specialist groups. According to the myths of the Seka and several other peoples of southwestern Ethiopia, their earliest kings were brought up by specialists.[41] Among these peoples also, some specialists participated in the king's installation and death ceremonies and acted as bards, singing his praises.[42] In Jimma Abba Jifar, the king named representatives and exacted tribute from among each of the artisan groups.[43] Commoners regarded the kings as the specialists' friends and protectors.[44] Among the Dime, one endogamous group, the Kaisaf, is said to have been created by newcomer chiefs from among the members of autochthonous clans, their sole specialty being the provision of ritual and police services to chiefs (Todd 1978). The model of caste formation involved here is not unlike that posited above for West African savannah societies, inasmuch as it involves deliberate modification of social status. Among the nearby Maale, the king chose his personal servants from among the members of an endogamous hunter–tanner group (Donham 1985: 46).

The history of the Falasha, which can be traced in some detail as far back as the thirteenth century, sheds considerable theoretical light on the development of professionally specialized endogamous groups, both in Ethiopia and elsewhere. Since the 1970s, the Falasha have been regularly compared to a caste or a quasi-caste.[45] When records begin, they constituted one or several, more or less contiguous, politically largely autonomous, Judaizing populations. Beginning in the fifteenth century, as a result of military defeats and a correlative loss of heritable land rights, they came to include a high proportion of artisans – initially often masons and carpenters, but, by the nineteenth century, mainly blacksmiths, numerous women being potters. By the nineteenth century also, the Falasha were becoming a minority in their home regions, where they were interspersed with Amhara-speaking colonists, while they left for other locations in pursuit of their craft vocations. There is no reason to believe that, prior to the downturn in their political and military fortunes, this once agriculturally orientated population included a high percentage of artisans.

The Falasha example suggests that (1) craft activities may become an identifying trait of groups for which they were once merely incidental; (2) the combined effects of assimilation and continued status loss may indeed transform a once large and prosperous population into a socially segregated, geographically dispersed minority – given the consequent decline of their religious institutions, and without outside assistance, over time the Falasha may well have become just another endogamous specialist group, and the question of their origins just another intractable puzzle; (3) their continued status loss is clearly linked to state intervention and manipulation; (4) while the Falasha do not claim to descend from kings, they affirm, like the Mbara and some other Chadian ironworkers, descent from a population that was once ruled by its own kings.

In summary, the scenario for the emergence and development of endogamous specialist groups in Ethiopia may yet prove to be very similar to the one outlined above for West Africa. Initially autonomous groups or populations (who, in Ethiopia, sometimes but not always had kingship) were whittled down and dispersed to form low status minorities. Once several such groups had formed, they then became a feature of the social structure of most of the peoples of the area, as a result of migratory movements – including both ones initiated by kings or chiefs, and ones undertaken by individual specialists and their families.

The Somali-speaking Peoples

The Somali-speaking peoples, who are located in Somalia, Djibouti, eastern Ethiopia and northern Kenya, distinguish at least four low-status minority groups, who have generally been labelled 'castes' or 'low castes'.[46] These are the *tumaal* blacksmiths and jewellers, *yibir* 'magicians', *midgaan* and *aweer* – both of which are associated with hunting; the fourth group is found exclusively in southern Somalia and northern Kenya. *Midgaan* are, additionally, leatherworkers, wood-workers, potters, hairdressers, circumcisers, healers, musicians, well diggers and sweepers. The *yibir* 'magicians' bless newlyweds and newlyborns, are musicians and entertainers and act as healers and diviners. Members of these groups are collectively known as *sab* or *bon* (depending on the region), and also (although this term may not have been used historically) as *nasab dhimaan* (lit. 'those without lineage'). Numerically, they constitute a minuscule proportion of Somali speakers. I. M. Lewis (1982 [1961]: 14) estimated that in the 1950s, British Somaliland included 9,000 *midgaan*, 2,250 *tumaal* and 1,300 *yibir* in a total population of 2,500,000. Mohamed Mohamed-Abdi (1998: 264) estimated that in 1989, just before the outbreak of the civil war, the *aweer* hunters numbered no more than 2,000, for a total Somali population of approximately 7,500,000. The majority of Somali are said to be 'noble', though different clans and lineages enjoy varying degrees of prestige. The Somali have traditionally also had some slaves, many of whom have been employed on plantations off the southern coast.

Members of the minority groups have traditionally been subject to very strong avoidance behaviour. Marriage with other Somali has been strictly prohibited; sexual relations have been punishable by death, mutilation, or relegation of the highborn partner to the lower-status group. Members of the minority groups have not been permitted to share meals with ordinary Somali or enter their homes. Majority Somali consider that *sab* or *bon* are in a permanent state of ritual impurity (*najaaso*)[47] which is linked to their dietary habits, falsely claiming that consumption of wild game and certain parts of domestic animals – habitually provided to the minorities by their majority patrons – are prohibited by Islam. One group of blacksmiths is believed to descend from a boy reared by hyenas. The *yibir* magicians are believed to have the ability to metamorphose into hyenas (and thus, presumably, consume corpses).

Geographical proximity suggests that there could be some connection between these endogamous specialists and those characteristic of Ethiopia and other parts of East Africa (and thus, indirectly, on the first hypothesis, to kingship). The Somali-speakers have been described as stateless, but they have powerful chiefs and at least one divine king, responsible for regulating the rain. It has often been hypothesized that *midgaan* and *aweer* developed from autonomous hunting and gathering populations, submerged by the Somali pastoralists. Oral traditions, and some peculiarities in language and custom, suggest that this is, to some extent, the case for the Aweer. However, the Aweer have elaborate induction rites that enable them to accept ordinary Somali into their groups, suggesting that there is also considerable demographic continuity between the Aweer and majority Somali populations. Some ordinary Somali, banished by their own clans in punishment of their heinous actions, have also joined the other minority groups. Christian Bader (2000: 167–71) has established a strong case for believing that the *yibir* derive from clans or lineages that, in pre-Islamic times, included highly regarded religious specialists. He compares them to the Iibir moiety of the Rendille of northern Kenya, a camel-herding people who speak a language closely related to Somali. Not only are the two groups similarly named, but the Iibir, like the *yibir*, have the power to bless and to curse, and manipulate special prayer-sticks, though they intermarry freely with most other sections of Rendille society.

The Masai and their Neighbours

Among most of the peoples of Kenya, ironworking (smithing and smelting) is hereditary, in the sense that, with few exceptions, only the son or another close relative of an ironworker may acquire this profession. Each ironworker transmits his skills to only one or a few persons, so that the supply of craftsmen does not outstrip demand. Individuals who have not learned the profession, and their descendants, are not considered 'ironworkers', and they and their ironworking relatives are subject to few, if any, peculiar restrictions in their choice of marriage partners. However, among the Nilotic-speaking Masai, Nandi, and Samburu and the Cushitic-speaking Rendille, ironworkers do form hereditary, endogamous groups that have been termed 'castes'. These have been described in most detail for the pastoral Masai, among whom members of this group have also been subject to the most severe social segregation. Among this people, all persons belonging to certain kinship groups have a special, hereditary status, whether or not they actually work iron. Commensality is forbidden. Masai 'blacksmiths' may own cattle, but must keep them separate, and pasture them away, from those of the pastoralists. Ordinary Masai may not immediately use an object manufactured by a smith, but must first oil it to remove 'pollution'.[48]

Several of the peoples of the region, including the Masai and the Nandi, maintain exchange relations with hunting groups, who have sometimes been labelled 'castes', though there is no absolute bar on liaisons, and members of each group may, under certain circumstances, forsake their birth identity for that of the other group.[49] Interestingly, in this area, where blacksmiths' wives are not necessarily potters and ordinary women may or may not be entitled to take up this activity, there is a craft connection, since the women of the hunter groups are the major producers of pottery.[50] Although some pastoralist communities (as well as individuals) have been assimilated by the hunters, and vice versa, and the two categories have maintained a symbiotic relationship for some time, oral traditions, as well as the persistence of distinctive customs, indicate that they were once culturally separate, politically fully autonomous populations.

I have been unable to uncover any particular relationship between the Masai 'blacksmiths', on the one hand, and their 'prophets' and 'diviners', on the other. This apparent lack of articulation, however, may be due to gaps in the ethnography. Also, the ironworkers do not seem to have any particular role in the initiation rites of the pastoral Masai, but organize their own separate initiations and age sets. The Dorobo hunters, on the other hand, act as circumcisers to the Masai.

These four examples of endogamous ironworkers are probably historically interrelated. Nandi smiths claim to be of Masai origin. The Samburu speak a dialect of the Maa (Masai) language and interact closely with the Rendille. At least one careful writer has posited the influence of the discriminatory practices of Cushitic-speaking peoples located further north (see Brown 1995: 137–8). On that hypothesis, there could be an indirect connection with kingship.

Conclusion

The above survey indicates that where the two institutions coexist, endogamous or quasi-endogamous groups of craft–musician or ritual specialists are systematically brought into relationship with kingship. Several groups of endogamous craft (primarily ironworking) specialists were also formed as the result of the transformation of the status of groups that once held royal power (for example, among the Sosso), or alternatively, of populations that were once ruled over by their own kings (for example, the Mbara and the Falasha). At least a portion of other endogamous groups, now associated with crafts and/or music, formed out of hunting and gathering populations that progressively lost their autonomy. Either way, both groups came to assume similar ceremonial – and supply – relationships with kings.

Thus, the above data suggest that there may be different pathways to the formation of very similar institutions, which may arise independently in very different cultures. However, within fairly large regions, diffusion may be the main factor explaining the resemblances among the institutions of neighbouring peoples. While in the present state of research there is little indication that the Western, Central and Ethiopian configurations of endogamous specialists significantly influenced each other, they do touch – or very nearly so – on a map. And there is every reason to believe that, were it not for European intrusion, a pan-African (or at least, pan-savannah, Sahelian and Saharan) caste system would have emerged.

Notes

1. See Tamari (1993). Eugenia Herbert (1993) provides by far the most comprehensive study of the symbolism of metalworking and pottery in sub-Saharan Africa. Peter Schmidt (1997) provides another significant recent statement concerning the ideology of ironworking in Africa and its political implications.

2. Certain aspects of this analysis of the relationships between structures and events were anticipated by Edwin Ardener (1978).

3. Delafosse (1894: 161, n.1); Haaland (1985: esp. 56–61; 70–2), Gosselain (1999). Gosselain has taken up these points again in a subsequent article (2001). All the 'caste systems' of sub-Saharan Africa were surveyed and compared in my doctoral thesis (1988: 591–655).

4. Hocart's position has been very extensively commented upon by Quigley (1993).

5. All statements made in this section, unless footnoted to more recent sources, can be documented through Tamari (1997), which provides a comprehensive bibliography up to 1992 on the endogamous specialists in the whole of this region. I have undertaken over three years' fieldwork in Mali, and visited several neighbouring countries. Information concerning all other areas is drawn exclusively from library research.

6. Delafosse (1912, vol. 3: 117–18); my translation.

7. Youssouf Cissé, personal communication (1990); confirmed by an informant in Segu, Mali (2002).

8. Granier-Duermaël (2003), esp. pp. 106, 117, 129, 132–3, 157, 161–2, 174–80, 192, 207–12, 254–6.

9. Fernandes (1951: 8–11); Alvares de Almada (1946: 24–5), English translation (1984: 34–5).

10. See, for example, the recent novel *Les Gardiens du temple* by the celebrated Senegalese writer, Cheick Hamidou Kane (1995).

11. See especially Mbow (2000: 83–90).

12. Conrad and Frank (1995: 7–13).

13. Including Ly (n.d., *c.* 1966: esp. 9–11), Silla (1966), Diagne (1967: esp. 61, 71, 188–97, 216–17), N'Diaye (1995 [1970]: 23–4, 38–43, 48, 62, 72, 74, 91–2), M. Diop (1971: esp. 42–67, 240, 248; 1972: esp. 32–52), C. A. Diop (1993 [1967]: 92–8; 1999 [1954]: esp. 533–5, 538–9, 542, 544), Camara (1992 [1976]: esp. 62–4, 67–8, 70–1,78–81, 92–9, 160, 189–91; 2001: 16–17), A.-B. Diop (1981 esp. 33–46, 59–64), Mbow (2000) and Béridogo (2002).

14. Al-ᶜUmari (*c.* 1337–8), English translation in Hopkins and Levtzion (1981: 265, 269); Ibn Battuta (travelled in the Mali empire in 1352–3) in Hopkins and Levtzion (1981: 288–93).

15. West Africa has, however, also known several states that have been compared to republics, though they might be better described as theocratic oligarchies, since the highest-placed political leaders usually had to be chosen from among the members of certain lineages. Like many contemporary writers, I believe that it is often meaningful to speak of kings and kingship even with respect to some small-scale societies that do not have the kinds of administrative structures usually associated with states. See, e.g., Simonse (1992: 1, 7–8, 429–30).

16. Fulani and Tukulor speak the same (highly dialectalised) language, Fulfulde.

17. For presentations of the linguistic data, see Tamari (1997: 157–214, 223–31, 239–54), summarized in Tamari (1991: 241–7), and Tamari (1995). George Brooks (1993, esp. 59–77, 97–119) has argued, on cultural, sociological and archaeological as well as linguistic grounds, for the spread of smiths preparatory to or concomitant with the expansion of Northern Mande-speaking peoples.

18. See Tamari (1997: 265–92), summarized in Tamari (1991: 236–41). See also Ivor Wilks (1999).

19. See Ibn Battuta in Hopkins and Levtzion (1981: 284, 290–1).

20. Stephen Belcher has written (1999: 229, n. 3) that I have 'documented the parallels among status groups in the region and suggested that the patterns may have been imposed from above, but the idea has met resistance'. This provides an opportunity to clarify a misunderstanding. Castes were not 'imposed' by an imperial power on hesitant or unwilling subjects. The institution caught on, not only because it benefited some populations, allowing local notables to imitate certain aspects of royal protocol and providing an increased or more varied supply of craft products, but also because it is grounded in deeply embedded representations concerning the activities in question.

21. There are descriptions of the Ghanaian court in: al-Bakri (*c.* 1068) in Hopkins and Levtzion (1981: 79–81) ; al-Idrisi (1154) in Hopkins (1981: 109–10).

22. For literature on the craftspersons of these two areas, see *inter alia*, Gardi (1954), Podlewski (1966), Vaughan (1970, 1973), Genest (1974), Barley (1983), van Beek (1991), Sterner and David (1991), Muller (2001).

23. See Podlewski (1966: 10, 36); Genest (1974: 496).

24. See Podlewski (1966: 12–13, 35); Vaughan (1970: 68–70, 77–8).

25. See Vaughan (1970: 85–9); (1973: 166–71).

26. The *Kitab ghazawat Barnu* (*Book of the War Expeditions of Bornu*), composed by Ahmad b. Furtu, a Bornu cleric and courtier, *c.* 1576, edited and translated by Dierk Lange (1987), particularly pp. 76–91, 99–100; Barth (1857), especially Chapter 33 of the English text (Vol. 2, Chapter 12 of the German text).

27. For studies of the specialists in this area, see *inter alia*, Carbou (1912, vol. 1: 49–72), Le Rouvreur (1989 [1962]: 375–85), Nicolaisen (1968), Brandily (1974: 18–21, 124–33, 144–58, 201–9), Conte (1983a: esp. 89–105, 167–74; 1983b), Tubiana (1985: esp. 37–49, 277, 309, 330–3; 1990), Tourneux, Seignobos and Lafarge (1986), Doutoum (1990) and Baroin (1991). Lange (1977: 151–4) is a commentary on the historical and archaeological sources.

28. See Conte (1983a: 167–9, 171–2; 1983b: 152).

29. See Conte (1983a: 93–4, 173–4; 1983b: 163).

30. See El-Tounsy (1851: 327, 367–8, 722), Nachtigal (1967 [1889], vol. 3: 70, 82, 234–5, 239), confirmed by Doutoum (1990: 150–1).

31. See Tubiana (1990: 335–6, 341–3).

32. See Tourneux, Seignobos and Lafarge (1986) and Pahai (1991).

33. However, Eugenia Herbert (1993) has argued for precisely such a relationship on the basis of analogous links to the symbolism of power, gender and repro-duction.

34. See Pâques (1977: 16–17, 121–3, 159).

35. Tourneux, Seignobos et Lafarge (1986: 105–6). (The section cited is by Christian Seignobos.)

36. Tourneux, Seignobos et Lafarge (1986: 93). See also Vaughan (1970: 87; 1973: 169) and above.

37. The most important discussions of this aspect of Bari social structure include: Whitehead (1929; 1953 (posthumous publication)), and Cooke (1939). See also Simonse (1992: esp. 243–4, 246–7, 252, 255, 266, 273–4, 299, 336n, 345, 361).

38. See A. Pankhurst (1999); Berhane-Selassie (1991). Among the most substan-tial and/or influential discussions, one may mention, in addition to the above two: Haberland (1962; 1964; 1993), Shack (1964), H. S. Lewis (1965: 53–7, 93–8, 121, 130), Hallpike (1968), Levine (1973: 45–6, 56–7, 62, 169–70, 195–7), Corlett (1974), W. Lange (1976, 1979, 1982), Todd (1977, 1978), Braukämper (1983: esp. 159–85), Donham (1985: 44–50, 107–13, 143–6, 162–3), Amborn (1990), Brandt, Weedman, and Hundie (1996), Silverman (ed.) 1999, esp. chapters by A. Pankhurst and Nida, and Berhane-Selassie.

39. See R. Pankhurst (1982: 48, 82n, 112, 155, 256, 269, 289–90, 293), (1985: 53, 102, 346), Silverman and Sobania (1999).

40. See Powne (1968) and Bolay (1998).

41. See W. J. Lange (1976: esp. 5–7, 9–10, 37–8).

42. See W. J. Lange (1979; 1982: 42–3, 134, 158–9, 261–3).

43. See H. S. Lewis (1965: 97–8, 119–20, 130).

44. See Haberland (1964) and W. Lange (1982: 158–62, 261–8).

45. See especially Quirin (1992); also Kaplan (1992: esp. 110–15).

46. This section is primarily based on the following sources: Paulitschke (1893:

29–35, 61, 111, 193, 231–8, 240–1), Cerulli (1957: 52–4), (1959: 24–9, 77–82, 95–113, 283–300), (1964: 90–1, 197–9, 213), I. M. Lewis (1982 [1961]: 14, 78–80, 187–8, 196, 212, 263–5), Bertin (1968; 1974), Mohamed-Abdi (1998: esp. 263–92), Bader (2000).

47. This term derives from the Arabic word *najasa*, which designates the ritual impurity which must be removed through ablutions or bathing prior to prayer.

48. Brown (1995) is a comprehensive study of metalworking in Kenya (through the early 1970s). The most significant discussions of the social status of Masai, Nandi, Samburu and Rendille ironworkers include: Merker (1904: 110–14), Hollis (1905: 330–331; 1909: 8, 36–38), Huntingford (1950: 82–86), Spencer (1973: 62–63, 118–119), Larick (1991), and Brown (1995: 119–148).

49. The most significant discussions of hunters include: Hollis (1971 [1905]: 296–9), Spencer (1973: 199–219), and Kratz (1994). Galaty (1979) analyses the status of ironworkers as well as hunters associated with the Masai.

50. See Barbour and Wandibba (eds) (1989).

References

Alvares de Almada, A. 1946 [*c.* 1594] *Tratado breve dos Rios de Guiné,* ed. by L. Silveira. Lisbon: Oficina Grafica.

—— 1984. 'An Interim and Makeshift Edition of André Alvares de Almada's Brief Treatise on the Rivers of Guinea.' Translation by P. E. H. Hair, notes by P. E. H. Hair and J. Boulègue. Department of History, University of Liverpool, unpublished typescript.

Amborn, H. 1990. *Differenzierung und Integration. Vergleichende Untersuchungen zu Specialisten und Handwerkern in südäthiopischen Agrargesellschaften.* Munich: Trickster.

Ardener, E. 1978. 'Some Outstanding Problems in the Analysis of Events', in E. Schwimmer (ed.) *Yearbook of Symbolic Anthropology*, London: C. Hurst, pp. 103–21; reprinted in M. Chapman (ed.) 1989. *The Voice of Prophecy and Other Essays* Oxford: Basil Blackwell, pp. 86–104.

Bader, C. 2000. *Les Yibro. Mages somali.* Paris: L'Harmattan.

Barbour, J. and Wandibba, S. eds. 1989. *Kenyan Pots and Potters.* Nairobi: Oxford University Press.

Barley, N. 1983. *Symbolic Structures. An Exploration of the Culture of the Dowayos.* Cambridge: Cambridge University Press.

Baroin, C. 1991. 'Dominant-dominé: complémentarité des roles et des attitudes entre les pasteurs teda-daza du Niger et leurs forgerons', in Y. Monino (ed.) *Forge et forgerons.* Paris: Editions de l'ORSTOM, pp. 329–81.

Barth, H. 1857–58. *Reisen und Entdeckungen in Nord- und Central-Afrika in den Jahren 1849 bis 1855,* 5 vols. Gotha: Justus Perthes.

—— 1965 [1857]. *Travels and Discoveries in North and Central Africa, Being a Journal of an Expedition Undertaken under the Auspices of H.B.M.'s Government in the Years 1849–1855*, 3 vols. London: Frank Cass. [First edition: London: Longmans Green, 1857, 5 vols.] There are some differences between the texts of the English and German versions, both penned by Barth.

Beek, W.E.A. van. 1991. 'Iron, Brass and Burial: The Kapsiki Blacksmith and His Many Crafts', in Y. Monino (ed.) *Forge et forgerons*. Paris: Editions de l'ORSTOM, pp. 281–310.

Belcher, S. 1999. *Epic Traditions of Africa*. Bloomington: Indiana University Press.

Béridogo, B. 2002. 'Le Régime des castes et leur dynamique au Mali', *Recherches africaines* (Bamako), January–June 2002: 3–27.

Berhane-Selassie, T. 1991. 'Gender and Occupational Potters in Wolayta: Imposed Femininity and "Mysterious Survival" in Ethiopia', in T. Berhane-Selassie (ed.) *Gender Issues in Ethiopia*. Addis Ababa: Institute of Ethiopian Studies, pp. 15–30.

Berhane-Selassie, T. 1999. 'Tabita Hatuti. Biography of a Woman Potter', in R. A. Silverman (ed.) *Ethiopia: Traditions of Creativity*. Seattle: University of Washington Press, pp. 217–39.

Bertin, F. 1968. 'L'Ougas des Issa', *Pount. Bulletin de la Société d'études de l'Afrique orientale* 5: 3–10.

—— 1974. 'L'Ougas des Issa', *Pount. Bulletin de la Société d'études de l'Afrique orientale* 13: 23–6.

Bolay, A. 1998. 'Musique et pouvoir royal. Le chant des *'azmari* en Ethiopie (xixe siècle – début xxe siècle)', *Cahiers du Centre de recherches africaines* 9: 7–37.

Brandily, M. 1974. *Instruments de musique et musiciens instrumentistes chez les Teda du Tibesti*. Tervuren: Musée royal de l'Afrique centrale.

Brandt, S. A., Weedman, K. J. and Hundie, G. 1996. 'Gurage Hide Working, Stone Tool Use and Social Identity in Ethnoarchaeological Perspective', in G. Hudson (ed.) *Essays on Gurage Language and Culture*. Wiesbaden: Otto Harrassowitz, pp. 35–51.

Braukämper, U. 1983. *Die Kambata. Geschichte und Gesellschaft eines südäthiopischen Bauernvolkes*. Wiesbaden: Franz Steiner.

Brooks, G. E. 1993. *Landlords and Strangers. Ecology, Society, and Trade in Western Africa, 1000–1630*. Boulder, Colorado: Westview Press.

Brown, J. 1995. *Traditional Metalworking in Kenya*. Oxford: Oxbow Books.

Camara, S. 1992 [1976]. *Gens de la parole. Essai sur la condition et le rôle des griots dans la société malinké*. Paris: Karthala.

—— 2001. *Vergers de l'aube. Paroles mandenka sur la Traversée du monde*. Bordeaux: Confluences.

Carbou, H. 1912. *La Région du Tchad et du Ouadaï*, 2 vols. Paris: Ernest Leroux.

Cerulli, E. 1964. *Somalia. Scritti vari editi ed inediti*, 3 vols. Rome: Amministrazione fiduciaria italiana della Somalia, 1957, 1959, Ministero degli affari esteri.

Conrad, D. C. and Frank, B. E. 1995. Introduction to D. C. Conrad and B. E. Frank, eds. *Status and Identity in West Africa. Nyamakalaw of Mande,* Bloomington: Indiana University Press, pp. 1–23.

Conte, E. 1983a. *Marriage Patterns, Political Change and the Perpetuation of Social Inequality in South Kanem, Chad*. Paris: ORSTOM.

—— 1983b. 'Castes, classes et alliance au sud-Kanem', *Journal des Africanistes* 53(1–2): 147–69.

Cooke, R. C. 1939. 'Bari Rain Cults', *Sudan Notes and Records* 22(2): 181–6.

Corlett, J. A. 1974. 'Despised Occupational Groups in Ethiopia.' B.Litt. thesis, Oxford University.

Delafosse, M. 1894. 'Les Hamites de l'Afrique orientale', *L'Anthropologie* 5: 157–72.

—— 1912. *Haut-Sénégal-Niger.* Paris: E. Larose; reprinted 1972, 3 vols. Paris: G. P. Maisonneuve et Larose.

Diagne, P. 1967. *Pouvoir politique traditionnel en Afrique occidentale*. Paris: Présence africaine.

Diop, A-B. 1981. *La Société wolof. Tradition et changement. Les systèmes d'iné-galité* et *de domination*. Paris: Karthala.

Diop, C. A. 1993 [1967]. *Antériorité des civilisations nègres: mythe ou vérité historique?* Paris: Présence africaine.

—— 1999 [1954]. *Nations nègres et cultures*, 4th edn [with addenda]. Paris: Présence africaine.

Diop, M. 1971. *Histoire des classes sociales dans l'Afrique de l'Ouest.* I: *Mali.* Paris: François Maspero.

—— 1972. *Histoire des classes sociales dans l'Afrique de l'Ouest.* II: *Sénégal.* Paris: François Maspero.

Donham, D. L. 1985. *Work and Power in Maale, Ethiopia*. Ann Arbor, MI: UMI Research Press.

Doutoum, M. A. 1990. 'Place et statut des forgerons dans la société maba du Tchad', *Journal des Africanistes* 60(2): 149–60.

El-Tounsy, M. 1851. *Voyage au Ouaday*. Translated from the Arabic by Dr Perron. Paris: Benjamin Duprat.

Fernandes, V. 1951 [*c*. 1506–1510] *Description de la Côte occidentale d'Afrique (Sénégal au Cap de Monte, Archipels)*. Critical edition of the Portuguese text and French translation by T. Monod, A. Teixeira da Mota, and R. Mauny. Bissau: Centro de Estudos da Guiné Portuguesa.

Galaty, J. G. 1979. 'Pollution and Pastoral Antipraxis: the Issue of Maasai Inequality', *American Ethnologist* 6(4): 803–16.

Gardi, R. 1954. *Der schwarze Hephästus. Ein Bilderbuch über die Schmiede der Matakam in den Mandara-Bergen Nordkameruns und ihre urtümliche Kunst, Eisen zu gewinnen.* Bern: Büchler.

Genest, S. 1974. 'Savoir traditionnel chez les forgerons mafa', *Canadian Journal of African Studies* 8(3): 495–516.

Gosselain, O. 1999. 'Castes, Pottery Technology and Historical Processes in the Mande Area, West Africa.' Paper presented at the Lampeter Workshop on 'Embedded Technologies. Reworking Technological Studies in Archaeology', coordinated by W. Sillar and B. Boyd, 24–27 September 1999.

—— 2001. 'Globalizing Local Pottery Studies', in S. Beyries and P. Pétrequin eds. *Ethno-Archaeology and Its Transfers.* Oxford: British Archaeological Reports, pp. 95–111.

Granier-Duermaël, A-L. 2003. 'Les Artisans-médiateurs en milieu dogon. Etude des groupes jan et gon.' Doctoral thesis, Ecole des Hautes Etudes en Sciences Sociales, Marseille.

Haaland, R. 1985. 'Iron Production, its Socio-cultural Context and Ecological Implications', in R. Haaland and P. Shinnie eds, *African Iron Working, Ancient and Traditional.* Oslo: Norwegian University Press, pp. 50–72.

Haberland, E. 1962. 'Zum Problem der Jäger und besonderen Kasten in Nordost- und Ost-Afrika', *Paideuma* 7(2): 136–55.

—— 1964. 'König und Paria in Afrika', in E. Haberland, M. Schuster and H. Straube eds. *Festschrift für Ad. E. Jensen*, 2 vols. Munich: Klaus Renner, vol. 1, pp. 155–66.

—— 1993. *Hierarchie und Kaste. Zur Geschichte und politischer Struktur der Dizi in südwest Athiopien.* Stuttgart: Franz Steiner.

Hallpike, C. R. 1968. 'The Status of Craftsmen among the Konso of South-West Ethiopia', *Africa* 38(3): 258–69.

Herbert, E. W. 1993. *Iron, Gender, and Power. Rituals of Transformation in African Societies.* Bloomington: Indiana University Press.

Hocart, A. M. 1950 [1938] *Caste: A Comparative Study.* London: Methuen. First published in French translation: *Les Castes*, Paris: Librairie orientaliste Paul Geuthner.

Hollis, A. C. 1971 [1905] *The Masai. Their Language and Folklore.* Freeport, NY: Books for Libraries Press.

—— 1969 [1909] *The Nandi. Their Language and Folklore.* Edited with a new introduction by G. W. B. Huntingford. Oxford: Clarendon Press.

Hopkins, J. F. P. and Levtzion, N. 1981. *Corpus of Early Arabic Sources for West African History.* Cambridge: Cambridge University Press.

Huntingford, G. W. B. 1950. *Nandi Work and Culture.* London: His Majesty's Stationery Office for the Colonial Office.

Kane, C.H. 1995. *Les Gardiens du temple.* Paris: Stock.

Kaplan, S. 1992. *The Beta Israel (Falasha) in Ethiopia. From Earliest Times to the Twentieth Century.* New York: New York University Press.

Kratz, C. A. 1994. *Affecting Performance. Meaning, Movement, and Experience in Okiek Women's Initiation.* Washington: Smithsonian Institution Press.

Lange, D. 1977. *Le Diwan des sultans du [Kanem-] Bornu. Chronologie et histoire d'un royaume africain (de la fin du Xe siècle jusqu'à 1808).* Wiesbaden: Franz Steiner.

—— 1987. *A Sudanic Chronicle: The Borno Expeditions of Idris Alauma (1564–1576) According to the Account of Ahmad b. Furtu.* Wiesbaden: Franz Steiner.

Lange, W. J. 1976. *Dialectics of Divine 'Kingship' in the Kafa Highlands.* African Studies Center, University of California at Los Angeles. (Occasional paper 15).

—— 1979. *Domination and Resistance. Narrative Songs of the Kafa Highlands.* East Lansing, MI: African Studies Center. (Ethiopian Series, Monograph no. 8).

—— 1982. *History of the Southern Gonga (Southwestern Ethiopia).* Wiesbaden: Franz Steiner.

Larick, R. 1991. 'Warriors and Blacksmiths: Mediating Ethnicity in East African Spears', *Journal of Anthropological Archaeology* 10: 299–331.

Le Rouvreur, A. 1989 [1962] *Sahéliens et Sahariens du Tchad*, 3rd edn, rev. Paris: L'Harmattan.

Levine, D. N. 1973. *Greater Ethiopia. The Evolution of a Multiethnic Society.* Chicago: University of Chicago Press.

Lewis, H. S. 1965. *Jimma Abba Jifar, Ethiopia, 1830–1932. A Galla Monarchy.* Madison: The University of Wisconsin Press.

Lewis, I. M. 1982 [1961]. *A Pastoral Democracy. A Study of Pastoralism and Politics among the Northern Somali of the Horn of Africa.* London: Oxford University Press.

Ly, B. n.d. [c. 1966] 'L'Honneur et les valeurs morales dans les sociétés wolof et toucouleur du Sénégal.' Doctoral thesis, University of Paris.

Mbow, P. 2000. 'Démocratie, droits humains et castes au Sénégal', *Journal des Africanistes* 70(1–2): 71–91.

Merker, M. 1904. *Die Masai. Ethnographische Monographie eines ostafrikanischen Semitenvolkes.* Berlin: Dietrich Reimer.

Mohamed-Abdi, M. 1998. 'Recherches sur une société riche d'une structure complexe: la société somalie.' Habilitation thesis, Université de Franche-Comté.

Muller, J-Cl. 2001. 'Le Foyer des métaphores mal soudées. Forgerons et potières chez les Dii de l'Adamaoua (Nord-Cameroun)', *Anthropologica* 43: 209–20.

Nachtigal, G. 1967 [1879–1889]. *Sahara und Sudan. Ergebnisse sechsjähriger reisen in Afrika*, 3 vols. Graz (Austria): Akademische Druck und Verlagsanstalt.

N'Diaye, B. 1995 [1970]. *Les Castes au Mali.* Paris: Présence africaine.

Nicolaisen, J. 1968. 'The Haddad, a Hunting People in Chad. Preliminary Report of an Ethnographical Reconnaissance', *Folk* 10: 91–109.

Pahai, J. 1991. 'Les Migrations des forgerons djorok chez les Massa du Cameroun', in Y. Monino (ed.) *Forge et forgerons*. Paris: Editions de l'ORSTOM, pp. 31–41.

Pankhurst, A. 1999. ' "Caste" in Africa: The Evidence from South-Western Ethiopia Reconsidered', *Africa* 69(4): 485–509.

Pankhurst, A. and Nida, W. 1999. 'Menjiye Tabeta – Artist and Actor. The Life and Work of a Fuga Woodworker', in R. A. Silverman (ed.) *Ethiopia: Traditions of Creativity*. Seattle: University of Washington Press, pp. 113–31.

Pankhurst, R. 1982, 1985. *History of Ethiopian Towns*, 2 vols. Wiesbaden: Franz Steiner.

Pâques, V. 1977. *Le Roi pêcheur et le roi chasseur*. Strasbourg: Institut d'anthropologie.

Paulitschke, P. 1893. *Ethnographie Nordost-Afrika. I: Die materielle Cultur der Danâkil, Galla und Somâl*. Berlin: Geographische Verlagshandlung Dietrich Reimer.

––––– 1896. *Ethnographie Nordost-Afrika. II: Die geistige Cultur der Danâkil, Galla und Somâl*. Berlin: Geographische Verlagshandlung Dietrich Reimer.

Podlewski, A-M. 1966. *Les Forgerons mafa. Description et evolution d'un groupe endogame*. Paris: ORSTOM.

Powne, M. 1968. *Ethiopian Music. An Introduction*. London: Oxford University Press.

Quigley, D. 1993. *The Interpretation of Caste*. Oxford: Clarendon Press.

Quirin, J. 1992. *The Evolution of the Ethiopian Jews. A History of the Beta Israel (Falasha) to 1920*. Philadelphia: University of Pennsylvania Press.

Schmidt, P. R. 1997. *Iron Technology in East Africa: Symbolism, Science, and Archaeology*. Bloomington: Indiana University Press.

Shack, W. A. 1964. 'Notes on Occupational Castes among the Gurage of South-West Ethiopia', *Man,* March–April 1964: 50–2.

Silla, O. 1966. 'Persistance des castes dans la société wolof contemporaine', *Bulletin de l'Institut français de l'Afrique noire* 28(3–4): 731–70.

Silverman, R. A. and Sobania, N. 1999. 'Silverwork in the Highlands', in Silverman, R. A. (ed.) *Ethiopia: Traditions of Creativity*. Seattle: University of Washington Press, pp. 183–99.

Simonse, S. 1992. *Kings of Disaster. Dualism, Centralism and the Scapegoat King in Southeastern Sudan*. Leiden: E. J. Brill.

Spencer, P. 1973. *Nomads in Alliance. Symbiosis and Growth among the Rendille and Samburu of Kenya*. London: Oxford University Press.

Sterner, J. and David, N. 1991. 'Gender and Caste in the Mandara Highlands: Northeastern Nigeria and Northern Cameroon', *Ethnology* 30(4): 355–69.

Tamari, T. 1988. 'Les Castes au Soudan occidental: étude anthropologique et historique.' Doctoral thesis, Université de Paris x.

—— 1991. 'The Development of Caste Systems in West Africa', *Journal of African History* 32(2): 221–50.

—— 1993. 'Relations symboliques de l'artisanat et de la musique', in M-J. Jolivet and D. Rey-Hulman eds. *Jeux d'identités. Etudes comparatives à partir de la Caraïbe*. Paris: L'Harmattan, pp. 217–34.

—— 1995. 'Linguistic Evidence for the History of West African Castes', in D. C. Conrad and B. E. Frank eds. *Status and Identity in West Africa: The Nyamakalaw of Mande*. Bloomington, IN: Indiana University Press, pp. 55–82.

—— 1997. *Les Castes de l'Afrique occidentale. Artisans et musiciens endogames*. Nanterre: Société d'ethnologie.

Tobert, N. 1988. *The Ethnoarchaeology of the Zaghawa of Darfur (Sudan)*. Oxford: British Archaeological Reports.

Todd, D. M. 1977. 'Caste in Africa?' *Africa* 47(4): 398–412.

—— 1978. 'Aspects of Chiefship in Dimam, South West Ethiopia', *Cahiers d'études africaines* 71, 18(3): 311–32.

Tourneux, H., Seignobos, C. and Lafarge, F. 1986. *Les Mbara et leur langue (Tchad)*. Paris: Société d'études linguistiques et anthropologiques de France.

Tubiana, M-J. 1985. *Des troupeaux et des femmes. Mariage et transferts de biens chez les Beri (Zaghawa et Bideyat) du Tchad et du Soudan*. Paris: L'Harmattan.

—— 1990. ' "Hommes sans voix." De l'image que les Beri donnent de leurs forgerons', *Paideuma* 36: 335–50.

Vaughan, J. H. Jr. 1970. 'Caste Systems in the Western Sudan', in A. Tuden and L. Plotnicov eds. *Social Stratification in Africa*. New York and London: The Free Press & Collier Macmillan, pp. 59–92.

—— 1973. 'Nkyagu as Artists in Marghi Society', in W. L. d'Azevedo (ed.) *The Traditional Artist in African Societies*. Bloomington, IN: Indiana University Press, pp. 162–93.

Whitehead, G. O. 1929. 'Social Change among the Bari', *Sudan Notes and Records* 12(1): 91–7.

—— 1953. 'Suppressed Classes among the Bari and Bari-Speaking Tribes', *Sudan Notes and Records* 34(2): 265–80.

Wilks, I. 1999. 'The History of the *Sunjata* Epic: A Review of the Evidence', in R. A. Austen, (ed.) *In Search of Sunjata. The Mande Oral Epic as History, Literature and Performance*. Bloomington, IN: Indiana University Press, pp. 25–57.

–9–

King House: The Mobile Polity in Northern Ghana

Susan Drucker-Brown

Introduction

This paper is about the immobile Mamprusi king, Nayiiri ('king house') and the movement of office-holders from the palace to the small, scattered villages of the former kingdom. Nayiiri embodies the element which Mamprusi call *naam*. It becomes a physical part of the king and chiefs at their installation to office and remains with them beyond their physical death. Analysis of kingship rituals suggests that the system of succession to royal office is conceived as a flow of *naam* from the king through his chiefs and back to the palace, which contains the source of *naam*. An independent 'filial' connection is established through ritual between the king and each of his chiefs. This connection of chiefs and king may be considered independent of the office-holders' location in a specific bounded territory. Villages and the capital are known to have moved over time and the entire polity might change its location while the relationship between king and chiefs persisted.

The presence of the physical body of the king defines the centre of the polity. Once installed, he is confined to his house in the capital village where he performs the rituals essential for the continuity of his kingdom. The significance of the building in which he resides is indicated by his title – 'King House'. The palace contains not only the living king, but also relics that are the embodiment of ancient kings. The living King House (Nayiiri) is said to be the owner of all things on earth. He controls the rain. His body is imbued with the transcendental power of kingship (*naam*). He allocates portions of *naam* to members of royal lineages during their installation to chiefly office, and this *naam* is returned to the palace when a chief dies. Whatever may be the genealogical connection between the two, installation makes Mamprusi chiefs 'king's children'. This conceptual extension of kinship by means of office is a mechanism that unifies the polity and underpins the judicial function of Mamprusi courts. In this non-literate society, the immobile king provides a fixed, central point where information is concentrated and used, particularly in the settlement of disputes.

171

Celebrating the King

In the annual festival of Damba, when chiefs from all over the former Mamprusi kingdom gather in the capital to greet the king, the origins of their kingship are celebrated. The story of Damba is simple. The first king arrived in Mamprusi country from the north-east on horseback, fleeing from his enemies. Some say he was offered water, the traditional welcome, by an indigenous woman whom he married. Others say that he was greeted by an earth-priest who offered him protection from his pursuers. Still others say he wandered through the country with an indigenous companion, creating mountains and rivers as they went. Flight on horseback, reception by an indigenous person and the king's decision to stay are the essential elements of the story.

Ritual adds another element. The culminating ceremony of Damba is the singing and drumming of kings' names, starting with those of ancient kings, ending with the names of the reigning king's own father. This long performance is followed by an earth-priest's dance. Three commoner-priests wield ancient spears and threaten the king with them. I was told that during this dance the king must weep: 'a single tear must come down from his eye'. I believe this tear symbolizes the king's power to control rain.[1]

Throughout the many hours of the Damba ceremony, while the king, chiefs and people watch and listen to the praise singer and the drumming, the king's horse, saddled and clad in leather armour, is held still by a palace servant outside the palace gate. The horse is there, I was told, so that the king may move on if he wishes to. Again explanations vary, but the king, as so often in the founding of kingdoms (de Heusch 1997), is said to have come from elsewhere and is here presented as one who may again disappear, abandoning his court and his people.[2]

The Mamprusi

The Mamprusi polity, now encompassed by the Ghanaian state, is the ritual senior in what was, prior to European conquest, a cluster of kingdoms that trace descent from a common founding ancestor. The people speak closely related Gur languages and share many cultural traditions. Scattered among that cluster of centralizing polities, which extends from northern Ghana into Burkina Faso and parts of Togo (Izard 1985, Kawada 1979, Staniland 1975), are numerous other Gur-speaking peoples. Although to an outsider these latter seem to share a common culture with members of the centralizing polities, they are traditionally organized into clans and lineages that recognize no single source of political or religious authority. The Tallensi (Fortes 1945) are typical of these and, like many sections of the non-centralizing, lineage-based polities, the Tallensi Namoos trace descent from Mamprusi forebears.

Ritual seniority is a feature of religious and political life as well as of domestic kinship among all these peoples and, more widely, throughout the savannah region of West Africa. The extended kin groups in this region, most commonly defined by patrilineal descent, distinguish the senior male sibling among the descendants of common ancestors in groups ranging from the sons of a single couple, to paternal half-siblings, through to classificatory siblings descended from common grandparents and more remote forebears. In those societies without kingship, inheritance of ancestor shrines by senior men is accompanied by the obligation to offer sacrifice to particular ancestors at those shrines. Diverse, politically significant congregations of kin are associated with different shrines (Fortes 1961; 1987).

The royals who belong to the related centralizing polities (Mossi, Dagomba, Wala, Nanumba) trace their descent from a common founding king. Mamprusi kings claim descent from the eldest son of that founder, which makes them senior in status to those kings descended from junior siblings. Thus it is the Mamprusi king, rather than a Dagomba or Mossi, who must send offerings for sacrifice at the founding king's gravesite. Such sacrifices are made at the beginning of a new reign as well as at other times. They manifest the attachment of the Mamprusi to the founder, as well as their connection to a territory where few Mamprusi now live. The sacrifice is made on the king's behalf, and in the presence of his representatives, by a priest who belongs to the neighbouring Kusase people, the present occupants of the surrounding territory. These people also speak a Gur language but regard themselves as having no original connection to kingship. As we shall see below, this type of sacrifice, connecting a living settlement with its prior location, is not unusual.

The ritual seniority of the Mamprusi, thought of as derived from ancestral kinship, is further expressed in spatial terms. The Mamprusi king's title, literally King (*na*) House (*yiiri*) is an assertion that their king is a place of origin. His title differs from that of all other chiefs and neighbouring kings in that it makes no reference to any specific location. 'King House' refers only to the place where *naam* is housed, while neighbouring chiefs and kings bear titles in which a reference to territory precedes the reference to chiefly office, as in 'Mogonaba' (Mossi king) or 'Yanaba' (Dagomba king). Mamprusi call themselves 'Dagbamba', a designation that locates them in a central position with respect to the inhabitants of the other kingdoms. They refer to their neighbours to the south, the 'Dagomba' of today, who live in more wooded land, as 'Yoba' – people of the forest (*yongo*). People of the various Mossi kingdoms to the north, where wooded hills give way to low scrub, are called 'Mossi' with reference to the bush (*mooni*). The title of the Dagomba king – Yanaba – is said to mean 'forest chief' while the Mossi king's title is said to mean 'chief of the bush'.

The centralizing polities of Mossi and Dagomba, like those of the Mamprusi, are characterized by a population containing a diversity of ethnic groups. The

Mamprusi region contains not only the descendants of Mamprusi kings and their followers, but also populations that predate their arrival and later immigrants (Drucker-Brown 1975). This ethnic heterogeneity in the former kingdom distinguishes Mamprusi settlements from those of neighbouring chiefless or non-centralizing peoples whose political organization rests on the assumption that residents of a common territory are kin (Fortes 1945). Mamprusi occupying a single settlement are linked as 'townspeople' (*tingwa-dima*) through recognition of a common chief (*naba*) rather than by virtue of common origins.

Characteristics of the Kingdom

Elsewhere I have suggested that the installation rituals which link the king to chiefs throughout the Mamprusi kingdom could be considered analogous to the cells formed in the physical process of convection. In order for a medium to become heated, it must move from the source of heat to a cold place, circulating to and from the source (Drucker-Brown 1989). In this paper I want to focus on the implications of spatial mobility as emphasized in ritual and as it operates in the connections between Mamprusi royal chiefs and the king that are established through installation. Mamprusi settlements are typically small. The mean population size of settlements in 1960 was 500 (Ghana Population Census 1960). Population in the region may have tripled since then, but Mamprusi settlements are still notably small and congregated rather than dispersed among cultivated fields like those of neighbouring peoples.

I will argue here that the basic element that creates the Mamprusi polity is the dyadic ritual connection between the king at the centre and the royal chiefs who are located in small, scattered settlements. The installation ritual, as well as certain prohibitions surrounding the kingship that are discussed below, are more than symbols of the divinity inherent in office. They establish and maintain connections between those with specific roles in a political/religious system: office-holders with rights and duties that must be performed. In respect of the imperative obligation attached to office, ritual has effects which are similar to those produced by physical force. Given this argument, it is important to ask if physical force rather than ritual might have been used to maintain connections between villages and the capital.

In 1965 there was no evidence of any large-scale, polity-wide military organization, such as is found in the forest kingdoms of the Ashanti peoples to the south (McKaskie 1995). Battles or conquests associated with named Mamprusi kings seem to have occurred prior to their accession, as part of the competition among rival princes rather than as elements of attempts to expand the king's domain. Contemporary evidence suggests that Mamprusi chiefs and the king had at their disposal only limited military force provided by small groups of their armed followers. The elders reported conventions that encouraged ceremonially sanctioned battles for kingship (Drucker-Brown 1975). However these were the exception rather than the rule. The king had the largest group of armed men, and stores of powder larger than those of any chief. It seems likely that the Mamprusi kingdom was never more than a loosely centralized structure with relatively little specialized governmental machinery of either a military or administrative nature.

The Capital

Mamprusi believe that the founding king established himself at a site called 'Pusiga' some forty miles north-east of the present capital. Evidence of settlement can be found in the remains of a large circular room, the walls of which are visible, buried just below the ground. At this site the king is said to have disappeared into the earth on hearing that his favourite son, and chosen successor, had been killed by a rival son. Note that in this foundation legend fratricidal violence attends the initial succession. Competition among siblings is characteristic of succession disputes. When the name of the chosen prince is announced, the priest-elder who makes the announcement adds: 'And if you do not agree (directed to the gathering of princes) go to some uninhabited place and play, and then bring me my husband'. 'Play' here, is a euphemism for battle.

Other sites are mentioned as later Mamprusi capitals. One of these is said to be located at Tamalerigu, an uninhabited place in the bush near the market town of Gambaga. The priest-chief of Gambaga claims that his ancestor gave the Mamprusi king that place to settle when he arrived on horseback, fleeing his enemies, like his ancestor the founding king. A later king moved from Tamalerigu into the market town of Gambaga, displacing his former host. From Gambaga the capital moved to its present site at Nalerigu. This move was associated with the death of Na Atabia, recorded in an Arabic chronicle as occurring in 1741/2 (see Wilks 1989: 89).

Seen as part of the wider kingdom, the Mamprusi capital is like the hub of a wheel to which the diverse settlements of the kingdom are attached by the myriad of chiefly installations. In 1965 there were roughly seventy chiefs installed directly by the Mamprusi king. By means of the installation ritual, *naam* – which is embodied in the king at his own installation (see Drucker-Brown 1989) – is transmitted to each chief. *Naam* enters the body of the new chief from the gown and hat in which he is dressed at his public investiture by priest-elders. Later and in private, the king himself sacrifices a sheep that has been provided by the new chief to the royal ancestors. He returns the animal's skin to the new chief with a blessing and the chief then carries it to his village. He will sit on it when he meets with the village elders. Once established, the chief will sacrifice to the royal ancestors on behalf of his village. In this way the ancestors of the royal lineages are believed to operate on behalf of the entire population and chiefly office is referred to by Mamprusi as 'skins'.

When a chief dies, an effigy is prepared and sent to the palace so that the vacant chiefship may be reallocated. This circulatory movement of living royals through the capital, leaving after investiture and returning at death so that *naam* may be re-embodied in a new chief, is the process which creates a connection between king and chief analogous to the convection cell carrying heat from a single source to a surrounding region. In this metaphor *naam* is the analogue to heat, having its source in the kingship and being suffused through the polity by means of the bodies of the royal chiefs.

Royal chiefs include both distant and close kin of kings. However it is from among the sons of kings that the elders should choose a new king when the reigning king dies. There is no automatic rule of succession. There are simply a series of prohibitions. No king should be directly succeeded by his own son. Sons of kings who have recently reigned should not be chosen. No royal who has not held chiefly office should be eligible. The chosen king must not be missing an eye, an ear, or a nostril. The choice is made by a group of elders who are not themselves eligible to succeed. The king is chosen from a group of competing princes and the elders try to maintain as wide a pool of eligible candidates as possible while taking into account their genealogies, their characters, their performance as chiefs, the contemporary political situation of the former kingdom in relation to the national government and the gifts the candidates have made to the court while seeking preferment. Kings have many sons. Posthumously born sons may also receive office, and it is common for the sons of kings whose reigns are long past to compete against the sons of more recent kings.

The King's Person and the King's Names

Mamprusi concern that the physical body of the prince who embodies *naam* should be intact seems to express the conception of his body as a vessel. *Naam* is concentrated in the king's physical body in ways that make him powerful, but also vulnerable. He lives constrained by a host of prohibitions and it is not entirely clear if the prohibitions are to protect him, or to protect others. Thus, the king may not move quickly. He may not step barefoot on the ground, or endanger his body by holding any sharp instrument such as those used in farming or warfare. For him to shed blood on the earth would bring disaster. He may not see certain parts of his palace or certain ritual specialists who reside in his kingdom. He may not hear certain words. He may not cross either of the two streams that traverse his village east and west of the palace. He sits only on the skins of animals that have been sacrificed to his ancestors, or those – such as the lion and leopard – which are embodiments of ancient kings. He is surrounded by titled elders who attend his physical person, one is responsible for carrying the skins, another for holding the bowl into which he might spit, yet another for carrying the kettle with the kola nuts he distributes. All of the senior elders also have priestly functions and special shrines to attend on behalf of the king.

Another important section of the court is formed by the gun bearers (*kambonsi*). They own ancient front-loading muskets that are regarded as their shrines. Gunpowder was provided by the king. Though clearly weapons of war, the muskets carried by the gun bearers were used in conjunction with cutlasses, spears, bows and arrows, all regarded as more effective weapons than the gun.

A final section of the court is made up of praise singers and drummers. In this non-literate society, the musicians are a particularly important group. They preserve the names and genealogies of princes who themselves are often ignorant of all but their own immediate kin. Royal chiefs in outlying villages also have praise singers who similarly conserve and exchange local genealogies. Groups of musicians pool their knowledge during calendrical festivals such as Damba, at installations when village royals gather in the capital, or during funeral performances attended by village chiefs and the king's representatives.

The performance of kings' names accompanies all public royal ritual and though the names are seen as praise – they glorify the living and please the dead – they are more than entertainment. In a sense the court exists to perpetuate itself, and the performance of the names of kings and chiefs is an expression of this exigency. While praising the dead, the performance of names simultaneously asserts the claims to office of living royals. It is significant that any royal who hears his father's name performed must pay the drummer. Royals may choose not to attend public celebrations in order to avoid the expense. However, the fact that musicians must be paid suggests that the names of royals with no descendants, or descendants who cannot afford to pay, will sooner or later be dropped from the lists. While they have other functions, the names are essential to preserve succession claims, not only to kingship but also to village chiefship.

During my longest period of residence in the Mamprusi capital (1963–5) it was noteworthy that the Mamprusi king and court spent far more time and effort in dealing with competitions for chiefship than they did in any other activity. The principal activity of the court can be said to be the settlement of disputes (Drucker-Brown 1993). Succession is normally contested, and entails both dispute settlement and adjudication by the king's court. The king's court also acts to settle other disputes. Some of these originate in the capital though more are sent from village courts where they could not be settled.

Royal village chiefs hear disputes in their houses. They may also patrol their villages, or be called to the spot where a quarrel is taking place. While the king should not physically move much beyond his palace forecourt, he has control of special oracles as well as the power to move invisibly and thus discover the knowledge he needs in order to 'disentangle truth from falsehood'. This ability is regarded as one of the king's most important powers. Given his privileged access to information, his omniscience is not entirely mythical.

Kingship and the Concentration of Information

The pooling of genealogical information by musicians at the king's court is only one of the ways in which the king's presence facilitates the concentration of information. The competition among Mamprusi royals for chiefly office is another. Acquisition of royal chiefship entails long periods, often many years, of competition during which the rival candidates regularly come from all parts of the kingdom to the capital bringing gifts to the king and elders. This process is part of 'greeting' (see Goody 1972). Gifts are made both in kind and in cash but an essential part of greeting is conversation. Mamprusi value the spoken word; clever conversation is highly prized and they revel in word play and subtle verbal wit. Mamprusi kings and chiefs are often witty though they tend to be men of few words, highly skilled at eliciting information while giving very little away.

Messengers sent from the king on any errand are expected to return directly to the palace and under no circumstance to stop elsewhere before reporting to the king. My experience accompanying such persons is that they were able to report extensive verbatim speech and detailed observation of such things as the size of a village, the number of gun bearers at a funeral and the conditions of agriculture and of markets. In view of the development of memory which must be associated with such skill, it is interesting that the musicians' mistrust of writing led them to assure me that if I were to write down the words of their drummed genealogies the names would surely be forgotten.

In general, strangers are sent immediately to the king. After I had spent more than a month in the vicinity of his village, a chief told me that he and the people of his village would only agree to talk to me after they had seen that the king approved of me. They had been polite in their treatment of me, but very guarded in conversation. The village in question was more than thirty miles from the capital. The king's court also draws information from most of the cities in Ghana where Mamprusi are living.

Agriculture and the Imagery of Chiefly Installation

At chiefly installation the king names the new chief and charges him with the task of guarding a portion of his estate. The portion is a named village but it usually is spoken of metaphorically as a farm, and the new chief is told to scare off the birds, or perform some other light agricultural task such as is assigned to young boys.

The new chief accepts his charge with a promise that if he is called by day or by night he will come. This promise – to come if called – emphasizes the filial role of the chief. Although chiefs normally only visit the king's court on festival occasions, the oath makes explicit the continuing obligation of the chief to maintain communication with the king.

When a royal chief dies and is returned in effigy to the capital, the effigy is accompanied by a token payment to the king, referred to as 'profit' (gained from the dead chief's stewardship of his father's farm). The profit takes the form of a live sheep. The effigy also contains among its parts the basic farming instruments – hoe, knife, scythe and a flint for making fire. The retention of the flint is particularly interesting: since it has been replaced by matches in the everyday world, it is unequivocally of symbolic importance. These symbolic references to the agriculture and livestock on which Mamprusi village economy is based are part of a representation of the physical person of the deceased chief which also includes clothing he has worn. Thus the constituent elements of the effigy indicate the profound association of *naam* (kingship/chiefship) with fertility in its widest sense – the successful outcome of basic life-sustaining activities.

Belief that the king has ultimate control of rain is an expression of this same association. However, it is in the nature of shifting hoe cultivation such as that practised in the Mamprusi region that the land around long-settled villages tends to become exhausted. Farmers open new farmland in the bush, leaving cultivated land to recover its fertility. Several chiefly titles testify to the fact that a village was once located at a considerable distance from its present site. Where this fact is preserved in the title of a chiefship, the incumbent chief is often obliged to provide a sacrifice to his predecessors on the graves located at the former site of the village, much in the manner that the Mamprusi king sends sacrifices to the grave of the founding king. Chiefly titles and rituals of sacrifice thus record the movement of villages and document what must be a widely occurring phenomenon. The gradual movement of farming through an essentially unbounded territory suggests that as the villages move, so also the territory of the king's domain changes.

The King's House

As noted above, the unique title of the Mamprusi king is literally, 'King (*na*) House (*yiiri*)'. One might say that a Mamprusi king is totally identified with the house/palace he inhabits. Each king is buried in the sleeping room of his palace and his movement both within and outside of the house is strictly curtailed. The king's title – Nayiiri – is nearly identical to the words used for a royal chief's house *na yiiri*. This suggests the presence of the kingship in those houses. The palace, by contrast, is referred to as *nayiini*, which could be translated as 'innermost king's house' – king (*na*), house (*yii*), inside (*ni*).

When the king's death is announced in the capital, hordes of adult grandchildren invade the palace and may loot it with impunity (Drucker-Brown 1999). The powerful relics that embody deceased kings are removed from the palace by the appropriate elders in order to be hidden outside the village. They are returned for use in the secret phase of the new king's installation. When those secret rites are done, the palace will be dismantled. The structural wooden supports will be removed, and the mud walls left to collapse in the rains. Thus a living king's house is surrounded by an uninhabited area containing the graves of his most recent predecessors and the remains of their palaces.

Mamprusi say that a new king must build his house on the site of his father's grave. This may be done simply by taking earth from a father's gravesite and incorporating it into the new building. Since no king should be immediately succeeded by his own son or by a close patrikinsman, the succeeding king must move the site of his house well away from the tomb of his predecessor. The location of kings' gravesites in the capital constitutes a map of recent succession but it is a map that is intelligible only to senior elders. Though some of the more recent gravesites are marked by remnants of the original construction and some older sites are marked by large trees, others must have disappeared completely.

If the construction of the new palace recalls the death of the new king's father, the manner in which the palace is constructed suggests the announcement of the new king's death. The palace is identical in most respects to a normal Mamprusi house. However, in ordinary houses the circular walls of the rooms are built by raising layer upon layer of mud, as though building up the sides of an enormous pot. The palace is constructed differently. A series of woven grass huts are constructed, one for each room of the new palace. These are called *suga* and they form a grass replica of the palace. Once the king takes up residence there with his wives and children, the huts are gradually replaced by the normal mud-walled rooms. However, at least one *suga* must be retained for an entire year and any child born during that first year of the king's reign will be called 'Suguri'.

This distinctive name for children born during the king's first year in the palace provides a means of dating the reign and, if the child survives to adulthood, also of calculating its length. A similar practice is followed in the construction of royal chiefs' houses except that for the new chief only one *suga* is constructed, rather than an entire house. Similarly, the *suga* must be retained for an entire year and children born during that year will also be named 'Suguri'.

The *suga* prefigures the king's death because it is formally referred to in the announcement of that event. It is forbidden to say 'the king is dead'. The news is carried from the capital to villages throughout the kingdom by palace servants. As I was told by the king's elders in 1965: 'Arriving in a settlement the messenger will cry out the words: "Fire has swallowed the huts (*Bugum-ma voli suga*)". Then the messenger must flee, for if he were to be caught, he could be killed'. A mission doctor who was present at the death of Na Saa in 1985 confirmed that he heard the announcement made in those words. The conventional words are pure metaphor. At the time of the king's death there are no huts in the capital and there is no fire. The reference is to the initial construction that becomes the palace. Yet the phrase 'Fire has swallowed the huts' conjures up a vision of disaster that draws power from many different sources. The looting grandchildren who consume property in the palace might be likened to fire. Throughout Africa new kings often introduce new fires. Recall the flint among the chief's tools. The construction of a new palace does, of course, imply a new fire.

On the other hand, in ordinary Mamprusi houses fire is often a source of domestic tragedy. Thatch and wood are dangerously close to cooking fires. To live in a house, or even a room of grass, in the presence of normal domestic activities is to be extremely vulnerable, particularly to fire. The grass palace of a new king is clearly an insecure environment. Even a single grass hut attached to a normal house increases the danger of fire. To live in such a construction for the first year of his reign is to place the king in what is, realistically, an unsafe environment – one that must make him aware of his dependence on those who serve him. Thus the announcement of a king's death with an image of the grass huts burning can only emphasize the vulnerability of the new king.

The word I have translated as 'hut' (*suga*) is used in ordinary speech to refer to a rustic construction of woven grass routinely built on 'bush' farms for refuge during inclement weather, or as a place to sleep when the farm is distant from the farmer's village. Mamprusi settlements are nucleated, and cultivation and the pasturing of animals take place outside of the residential areas. Farms thus become further removed from the residential areas as cultivated land is left to fallow. Typically, the *suga* is built on a farm that has been recently cleared for cultivation. Thus it is a symbol of colonizing the bush, converting it from wild into fertile land. The imagery of farming used in chiefly installation resonates with an image of the king's huts. Together they seem to identify the whole Mamprusi polity as the king's bush farm.

The King's Body

My own first contact with African kingship was through reading the ethnography of the Ashanti. I was particularly struck by Rattray's description of the Asantahene's person, so weighted with gold objects that courtiers needed to help him move his body (Rattray 1929). That image recalled to me fieldwork I had done in an Amerindian village in Brazil, where I spent several months living with an elder in the remnant of a Caraja settlement. The elder was referred to as an 'Iyolo' by local Brazilians, but he himself told me that the Iyolo no longer existed. In former times, he said, a child – the most beautiful of the youngest un-initiated boys

– was chosen to be the Iyolo. He was kept in seclusion until his initiation, at which time a new Iyolo would be chosen. The Iyolo served to keep the peace. His body was decorated with the white down feathers of young birds and his excrement was distributed over the ground so that it became invisible. If there were quarrels in a settlement, the Iyolo emerged from his seclusion. He was lifted onto the shoulders of his mother's brother and carried to the place where a dispute was in progress. Once the Iyolo arrived, peace would have to be made because there could be no fighting in his presence (Drucker-Brown 1962).

These two disparate cases exemplify the concern with the physical body of the king that is a universal thread in what has become known as 'divine', or 'sacred' kingship. Another thread, illustrated by the Caraja example, is the task of peace-keeping associated with the kingly figure. What might be the relationship between these two apparently unrelated elements of kingship?

Far from associating kingship with peace, it has more often in recent writings, been seen as linked to violence. Valeri (1985) has argued that sacred kingship is the first stage in the emergence of a type of polity antithetical to kinship; one in which exploitation and violence replace peace and amity. The argument is most forcefully put by Sagan (1985) who sees sacred kingship as a stage that was essential in order that individualism, a kind of driving force in the make-up of the human species, might emerge from the cosy shackles of corporate lineage society.

While Simonse (1992) rejects the evolutionary frame, he too sees kingship as inextricably tied to violence though he sees this violence as directed against the 'scapegoat king' in a displacement that enables a polity to sustain more pacific interaction. If we look at those attributes of sacred kingship proposed in the definitions of an earlier generation of anthropologists (Hocart 1927, Seligman 1934, Frazer 1911) we find that they all emphasize the importance of the physical body of the sacred king. But they do not ask why the mystical powers so commonly found in kings should be vested in the physical body of a human being. For Mamprusi these mystical qualities include the ability to transform himself into any animal or object; the destructive power of his gaze; the ability to curse his people by stepping barefoot on the earth; the ability to bring and to withhold rain; and, in the contemporary situation, the power to cause or miraculously rescue people from road disasters.

Conclusion

I would argue that the segregation of the king's person and his dependence on others for the satisfaction of his simplest needs is a direct consequence of the extraordinary powers he is believed to embody. Among the powers associated with the king, Hocart (1927) emphasized as most important his removal from the environment over which he acted. Indeed, Hocart regarded 'the invention of a person who does no work with his hands but acts on the environment at a distance' as 'nothing less than the invention of government' (Hocart 1927: 45–6).

I would like to suggest that this invention of a figure with transcendental powers, removed from the environment on which he acts, requires as a precondition that he be dependent on others. At least in part as a consequence of that dependence, those who serve him constitute the court that inevitably accompanies a king.

A second precondition of kingship might be a degree of demographic diversity in the population which provides that surrounding support. By demographic diversity I mean the coexistence in a single territory of people who regard themselves as having distinct origins, but who need to maintain peace in a shared territory. The institution of kingship does seem to be associated with confrontations of diverse people, whether the encounter is depicted as one between conquerors and conquered, refugees and host, or simply between the bearers of a particular social artefact – such as the powers inherent in the king – and a set of curious and covetous neighbours. Legends recounting the origin of kingship in Africa describe all these situations.

Fortes (1975) has suggested that underlying kinship is the axiom of 'prescriptive amity' – an obligation to share, and a prohibition on the more violent expressions of hostility. Kinship amity stands in contrast to the ever-present potential for open hostilities among non-kin. Kinship relations, in other words, ideally stand in direct contrast with those of warfare, though the dividing line is by no means always clear. However, data from peoples as far removed from one another as the Yanamamo (Chagnon 1983) and the Nuer (Evans-Pritchard 1940) indicate that even where aggressiveness and the capacity for violence are highly valued, such behaviour is modified by kinship. In particular, control over weaponry, which in turn means control over how lethal fighting may be, varies directly with the closeness of kin as defined by the actors.

Kingship introduces a new principle. Through the presence of a king it is possible to establish solidarity among people unrelated to one another, but related to the king. The presence of the king may be used to evoke and intensify reciprocities modelled on *kin*ship. In the Mamprusi case, the interdependence of successive generations is clearly highlighted. The distant figure of an all-powerful yet dependent human being provides an image that may evoke simultaneously sentiments of awe and protectiveness. This combination emerges very clearly at the installation of the Mamprusi king, when he is symbolically supported by his people while he eats and drinks at the shrines of the commoner-priests (see Drucker-Brown 1992). This is followed by the final phase of the ceremonies in which the Mamprusi king literally feeds his people, beginning with those royals who were among his own rivals for the kingship. The 'father–son' connection that is established at chiefly installation between king and chiefs becomes the basis for an extension of kinship amity. The king appears at his installation as both child and father of his people.

This common recognition of the king as a figure to whom a kin-like status is extended may in turn be an aspect of his position that enables conflicts to be resolved in his presence without recourse to violence. No ordinary person, embedded in the normal network of kinship ties, could perform this function. Kingship universally demands that distancing which Hocart notes, and the mystical powers of the king are a product of his transformation and objectification. His very dependence on others is perceived as power, but there is a real power associated with the immobility and social distance that creates dependence. That is to say, he becomes a unique witness to the central accumulation of information at his court.

In this chapter I have tried to support and amplify with ethnographic evidence what I have elsewhere called a convection model of the Mamprusi kingship. To the analysis of installation ritual from which that model was derived, I have added evidence that the agricultural technology of the Mamprusi is consistent with spatial movement of both the capital and the villages that make up the former kingdom. The political imagery of installation refers to that agricultural technology, as do the ritual construction of huts at the beginning of a king's reign, and the imagery of the burning huts that announces a king's death. I have also suggested that the mystical powers associated with the king's person might facilitate the co-existence of diverse populations in a shared territory by extending the amity of kinship through his powerful presence. The immobility and central position of the king make it possible to accumulate, verify and disseminate information, and this function of kingship can be used to provide effective dispute settlement and peace-keeping within the range of chiefly courts dependent on the kingship.

Notes

1. This was not told to me by any Mamprusi person. I only thought of the association later in remembering fieldwork done in the coastal Mixtec region of Mexico. There I was told that, in case of drought, children might be brought out in procession and beaten so that they would weep and their tears would bring the rain.
2. A ritual with a similar message was performed daily at the court of the Mossi King (Izard 1985).

References

Chagnon, N. 1983. *Yanamamo: The Fierce People*. 3rd edn. New York: Holt, Rhinehart & Winston.
Evans-Pritchard: E. E. 1940. *The Nuer*. Oxford: Oxford University Press.

Drucker-Brown, S. 1962. Unpublished fieldnotes.

—— 1975. *Ritual Aspects of Mamprusi Kingship*. Cambridge–Leiden African Social Research Documents. Cambridge: African Studies Centre.

—— 1989. 'Mamprusi Installation Ritual and Centralization: A Convection Model', *Man* 24: 485–501.

—— 1992. 'Horse, Dog and Donkey: The Making of a Mamprusi King', *Man* (N.S.) 27: 71–90.

—— 1993. 'The Divorce of Zanjiili's Daughter', *Droits et cultures* 27: 225–49.

—— 1999. 'The Grandchildren's Play at the Mamprusi King's Funeral: Ritual Rebellion Revisited in Northern Ghana', *Journal of the Royal Anthropological Institute* 5(2): 181–92.

Fortes, M. 1945. *The Dynamics of Clanship among the Tallensi: Being the First Part of an Analysis of the Social Structure of a Trans-Volta Tribe*. London: Oxford University Press.

—— 1961. 'Pietas in Ancestor Worship. The Henry Meyers Lecture, 1960', *Journal of the Royal Anthropological Institute* 91: 5–49.

—— 1975. *Kinship and the Social Order*. Cambridge: Cambridge University Press.

—— 1987. 'Ancestor Worship in Africa', in J. R. Goody (ed.) *Religion, Morality and the Person*, pp. 66–83. Cambridge: Cambridge University Press.

Frazer J. G. 1911. *The Golden Bough, I: The Magic Art and the Evolution of Kings*. London: Macmillan.

Goody, E. N. 1972. 'Greeting, Begging and the Presentation of Respect', in J. S. Lafontaine (ed.) *The Interpretation of Ritual: Essays in Honour of A. I. Richards*, pp. 39–72. London: Tavistock.

Heusch, L. de 1997. 'The Symbolic Mechanisms of Sacred Kingship: Rediscovering Frazer', *Journal of the Royal Anthropological Institute* 3: 213–32.

Hocart, A. M. 1927. *Kingship*. Oxford: Oxford University Press.

Izard, M. 1985. *Gens du pouvoir, gens de la terre. Les institutions politiques de l'ancien royaume du Yatenga (Bassin de la volta Blanche)*. Cambridge: Cambridge University Press; Paris: Editions de la Maison des Sciences de l'Homme.

Kawada, J. 1979. *Genèse et évolution du système politique des Mosi méridionaux (Haute Volta)*. Tokyo: Institute for the Study of Languages and Cultures of Asia and Africa. Monograph Series 12.

McKaskie, T. 1995. *State and Society in Pre-colonial Ashanti*. Cambridge: Cambridge University Press.

Rattray R. S. 1929. *Ashanti Law and Constitution*. Oxford: Oxford University Press.

Sagan, E. 1985. *At the Dawn of Tyranny. The Origins of Individualism, Political Oppression and the State*. New York: Random House.

Seligman, C. G. 1934. *Egypt and Negro Africa: A Study of Divine Kingship.* London: Routledge.

Simonse, S. 1992. *Kings of Disaster. Centralism and the Scapegoat King in Southern Sudan.* Leiden: E. J. Brill

Staniland, M. 1975. *The Lions of Dagbon: Political Change in Northern Ghana.* Cambridge: Cambridge University Press. African Studies Series.

Valeri, V. 1985. *Kingship and Sacrifice.* Chicago: Chicago University Press.

Wilks I. 1989. *Wa and the Wala. Islam and Polity in Northwestern Ghana.* Cambridge: Cambridge University Press. African Studies Series.

–10–

Kings and Tribes in East India: The Internal Political Dimension

Burkhard Schnepel

Introduction

Before Independence, traditional Indian political systems were not mono-archies with fixed territories, but multi-centred, multi-levelled conglomerates of little kingdoms, hierarchically and dynamically organized around the shifting centres of great kingdoms.[1] In order to understand the nature of Indian kingdoms properly, I therefore suggest that we look more carefully at little kingdoms as objects of study in their own right. In this chapter I shall do just this by presenting and discussing ethnohistorical material which relates to the little kingdoms of Orissa in the east of the Indian subcontinent. Furthermore, I shall focus on an important sub-category of the unit of the little kingdom, namely the 'jungle kingdom'. This type of little kingdom is characterized by two features. First, the territories of jungle kingdoms are situated in remote or inaccessible forest, hill or desert areas. Secondly, their populations contain a high percentage of tribal groups, also known as *adivasis*.[2]

Examining jungle kingdoms poses, as we shall see, a challenge to some long-established paradigms in political anthropology. To pinpoint these, we have to go back to the heyday of British social anthropology, that is to the 1940s and 1950s, and consider the theory of segmentary lineage societies that was developed at that time, mainly on the basis of African material. Particularly after the publication of *African Political Systems* (Evans-Pritchard and Fortes (eds) 1940), it became apparent that political systems of occasionally quite large size could be formed without kings or other forms of central government, and the mechanisms that made this possible became understood. Ethnic groups like the Nuer, Tiv or Dinka were described as 'tribes without rulers', or, to put it more scientifically, acephalous segmentary political systems. The main constituent of these systems, in both a social and political sense, was the lineage.

These discoveries still count as some of the most important contributions to social anthropology. Yet with hindsight, the dichotomy that was thus established, both implicitly and explicitly, between states and stateless societies must be questioned. Where exactly did an acephalous society end and a state begin? Was the Dinka 'Master of the Fishing Spear' more like the Nuer 'Leopard-skin Priest' or the Shilluk divine king? Did the Nuer prophets not rally great numbers of Nuer from different lineages and clans behind them? Was the Shilluk king really the head of a kingdom, or only the figurehead of a number of loosely connected clans? While pursuing such questions, considerations concerning the borders between states and stateless societies were often phrased in evolutionary terms: Nuer, Dinka, Anuak, Shilluk, Bantu kingdoms and the Zulu state, for example, were then presented as paradigms of different evolutionary stages from 'no state' to a 'fully developed state'. Mixed forms were regarded as the result of conquests, mainly those of pastoralists over agriculturalists.

Moreover, in these debates the identification of two different political systems was often connected with two different kinds of approach. This was especially the case when, in the late 1960s and 1970s, the 'old' ethnographies of Evans-Pritchard and others were rediscovered by young anthropologists, who, in line with the spirit of their time, looked for alternative models of society with which to formulate criticisms of their own society and, possibly, develop alternatives for it. The Nuer and others of their kind became exemplars of third-world freedom fighters and proponents of a mentality commonly denoted by the umbrella term 'egalitarian'. The political systems of these groups were seen as a species of 'anarchy', albeit 'ordered' anarchy. They were, as Clastres (1974) put it succinctly, not just societies *without* a state, but societies *against* the state.

An early alternative to such schemes of interpretation was posed by Leach (1970 [1954]) in his study *Political Systems of Highland Burma*. For him the question was not state or no state. Rather, he drew attention to the fact that these kinds of political systems are not always and necessarily diametrically opposed to one another. Instead they merely represent different developmental stages in one and the same society. To this insight one could add another: the question of whether or not there was a state might also be differently assessed and/or stressed by different members or sections of the societies concerned depending on the social situations, events or issues they confronted at different times. The distinction between tribe and kingdom reifies what are in essence dynamically changing identities. As a consequence, in African anthropology the dichotomy between states and segmentary lineage societies was thought to have been overcome by Southall (1953), among others, when he coined the term 'segmentary state'. His concept was later applied to India by Fox (ed.) (1977) and Stein (1980). As far as north India is concerned, Fox (1971) stressed that lineage-controlled estates or *taluks* could turn into local kingdoms ruled by monarchs or vice versa, if and when the constellation of power between the lineages of an area changed or the respective position in the 'developmental cycle' of a given dominant lineage favoured the formation of one or other organizational form. Chattopadhyaya (1976; 1995 [1983]: 213–21) and Thapar (1984) have also stressed, from a historical perspective, the fact that lineages have often formed the starting point for state formation in India.

Six Dimensions in the Study of Jungle Kingdoms

There are at least six dimensions to the study of jungle kingdoms. These can be separated analytically, although they are all closely linked:

1. *The historical-developmental dimension*. Frequently jungle kingdoms were not only important components of larger state formations, but were even themselves the nuclei and initiators of processes that led to the formation of larger political systems and states. For example, the dynasty of the Late Eastern Gangas, which established a regional empire during the twelfth century, had as its initial basis a little kingdom in a marginal area south of their later central Orissan stronghold. This kingdom and others extended their initial nuclear areas step by step in concentric extensions of their initial domains and nuclear areas, from the periphery into the centre.[3]

2. *The external political dimension*. Great kings, like the Gajapatis of Orissa or the Vijayanagara Empire in south India, needed jungle kingdoms at the borders of their realms as buffer zones and allies, and to safeguard trade and military routes.[4] Jungle kingdoms were often also places of retreat for rebellious or aspiring kings. Their remote locations and inhospitable natural environments allowed their inhabitants to use guerrilla tactics successfully. As a result, most Indian jungle kingdoms could act relatively autonomously.

3. *The internal social and politico-economic dimension*. The study of jungle kingdoms allows us to see in some detail how kingdoms in India were organized in practice on the ground. In particular, focusing on jungle kingdoms brings to light considerable information on two issues: the much discussed question of the relationship between kings and castes and the seldom studied, but equally significant, relationship between kings and tribes.

4. *The (external) religious dimension*. To some extent, jungle kingdoms copied the cults of the great kings. For example, the jungle kingdoms within the Vijayanagara Empire all celebrated Dasara as their main festival of the year, following the imperial model.[5] In Orissa, the main state ritual of the centre focused on Jagannath in Puri, especially on his 'Car Festival' (Ratha Yatra), held in July. The jungle kingdoms of central Orissa were closely involved in the cult of this deity and in this particular celebration, for with regard to Jagannath there existed an elaborate division of ritual labour.[6] But jungle kings could also use ritual matters to express dissent, for example, by failing to attend central festivals and instead celebrating their own versions of these festivals.[7]

5. *The (internal) religious dimension.* Studying the religious life of jungle king-doms provides great insights into what in Indian studies has come to be termed 'Hinduization', 'brahmanization' or 'Sanskritization'. For example, in the absorption of the hinterland in the state of Orissa, we find that the jungle kings often established and maintained their rule by patronizing local goddesses. Bit by bit, these autochthonous goddesses became 'Hinduized' in iconography, cult and mythology and thus associated with fully established Hindu goddesses like Durga or Kali. But in turn, the life of jungle kings and their courts was also quite strongly determined by the tribalization of Hindu modes of worship and belief.[8]

6. *The ideological dimension.* In Hindu thought the jungle possesses a great imaginary force. Many narratives and epics, such as the *Ramayana*, suggest that one can only become a legitimate Hindu king after spending, and sur-viving, some time in a jungle exile.[9]

All of these dimensions, except the last one, can be further subdivided into two parts, one ideological, the other actual.

In this chapter I want to address these issues by drawing attention away from 'great' kingdoms towards what, in recent years, have come to be termed 'little kingdoms'. My ethnohistorical material relates to India, in particular Orissa in the east of the Indian subcontinent.

The Jungle Kingdoms of South Orissa

The one dimension that I would like to place in the centre of my discussion here is the internal political dimension, especially its ideological aspect. To provide the necessary background information for this discussion, let me first give a general overview of the little kingdoms of southern Orissa.[10] I will provide statistical and historical data of some of the more important of these kingdoms and this will give some idea of the others.[11]

1. The kingdom of Khallikot is recorded as having had an area of 238 square miles and containing around 350 villages. The yearly tributary payments owed by the Khallikot kings to the British amounted to 18,482 rupees. In their family chronicle, the royal family traces its origins back to a certain Rama Buya, who is said to have cleared and settled the jungle. In recognition of this feat the ruling 'great king' of the region and the time, Gajapati Purushottama Deo, appointed him governor of the area.[12]

2. The kingdom of Bodogoda, at the foot of the Eastern Ghats, was mostly hilly and covered with jungle. It occupied 167 square miles and had 143 villages. Taxes amounted to 3,770 rupees. Attached to the kingdom were the roughly 300 square miles of the Bodogoda *maliahs* or hill territories.[13]

3. Chikiti had an area of 110 square miles consisting of open, well-watered country with 151 villages. The yearly taxes came to 30,045 rupees. According to tradition, one of the Gajapatis granted the territory to a *sirdar* named Kasano after he had conquered it from the *adivasis*, settled there and erected a fort.[14]

4. Parlakimedi, the second largest little kingdom in the south of Orissa, had over 639 square miles of territory with more than 500 villages. Attached to the kingdom were the Parlakimedi *maliahs*, with an area of 354 square miles. The Parlakimedi kings still regard themselves as the descendants of the imperial Gangas.[15]

5. Butrasingi, a little kingdom at the foot of Mount Mahendra, south of Jalantra, extended over about 22 square miles. It was hilly territory, known to be unhealthy. Yearly taxes amounted to 525 rupees. The founder of the Butrasingi ruling family is said to have been a Sora chief named Damodra Nissunko.[16]

6. With an area of about 10,000 square miles, Jeypore was the largest of all the little kingdoms of southern Orissa, and it was only matched by Parlakimedi in political significance. In the 'permanent settlement' of 1803, Jeypore's tribute was set at 16,000 rupees. The Jeypore Suryavamshis traced their origin back to a prince by the name of Vinayaka Deo who, according to local tradition, came from a branch of a Rajput family from Jammu and took over the kingdom in 1453. Of all the kingdoms of southern Orissa, Jeypore was the only one whose core area lay exclusively in the mountainous region of the Eastern Ghats.[17]

The data presented so far allow some generalizations.[18] To start with, some of the ruling houses mentioned here trace their origins back to the middle or end of the fifteenth century. According to local traditions, their founders were military officers in the armies of the first two imperial Gajapatis of the Suryavamsha dynasty, Kapilendra (1434–67) and Purushottama (1467–97), who appointed them as local governors during or after a military campaign.[19] The initial military function of these individuals also finds expression in the fact that the names of many of these kingdoms end in 'fortress' or 'fort' (*gada, garh, goda, kot*),[20] and that they were often located at strategically important points such as a river crossing, a pass through the Ghats or an isthmus.[21] The Gajapatis expected these kings to be loyal and to ensure access routes to and through their territories. In many cases they also had to participate in the Gajapatis' military campaigns, and to provide soldiers, provisions and equipment. Moreover, the emphasis laid in many chronicles on the heroic clearing of the jungle by the founders of these dynasties indicates that these military vassals and their little king successors were expected to develop agriculture and trade, as well as ensure the internal pacification and colonization of their realms.

Among the royal houses of southern Orissa, there are also many whose origins are not explicitly linked with the Suryavamsha Gajapatis. This group includes those dynasties whose territories lay, at least in part, in the mountainous, jungle-covered hinterland of the Eastern Ghats: Athgarh, Ghumsur, Dharakot, Bodogoda, Sheragada, Sanakimedi, Badakimedi, Surangi, Jarada, Parlakimedi, Butrasingi and Mandasa. Both in their origin and in their day-to-day affairs these jungle kingdoms were more independent of the great kings or Gajapatis than the little kingdoms on the coast.

In Orissa as a whole, tribals, or *adivasis*, constitute around 25 per cent of the total population. This percentage increases significantly the further one moves away from the coast and fertile river valleys into the hills. Here, up to 70, even 75, per cent of the population belongs to the category of 'Scheduled Tribes'. Most of the tribes are based on exogamous, totemic patriclans, which frequently combine into larger, equally exogamous clan groups. In addition, many of these ethnic groups are divided into endogamous halves, or moieties. Generally, the most important corporate group is the village, governed in a form of dual authority by a headman (*naik*) responsible for 'wordly' affairs and a priest (*pujari, disari, jani*). In many tribes today there is a superordinate corporation (*desh, muttha*) consisting of several villages whose assemblies or *panchayats* are governed by a common headman (*patnaik, bhatanaik*). However, there are no organs or institutions at a higher level of organization that would endow these ethnic groups with a corporate character in politico-jural affairs. As far as *political* unity is concerned, these ethnic groups seldom have a common head,[22] and politically, any degree of corporate organization rarely transcends the level of the village or the village group. Given the demographic situation in the region, therefore, studying Orissa's jungle kingdoms ultimately means studying a particular relationship that has so far attracted relatively little scholarly attention, namely the relationship between kings and tribes.[23]

In order to address this relationship more thoroughly, three further points must be emphasized. First, the politico-territorial units of Orissan jungle kingdoms were seldom coterminous with clear-cut social or ethnic units. In other words, we seldom find that there was *one* dominant ethnic group within a given little kingdom's territory: usually several vied for predominance. And these competing groups, in their turn, were not confined to one kingdom. Instead, their respective ethnic boundaries usually ran through a number of kingdoms. Secondly, the kings and royal dynasties who are reported to have founded the Orissan jungle kingdoms usually did not originate within their realms. As far as we can discern from family chronicles and similar documents, in most cases they were outsiders, not local tribal chiefs turned kings. Thirdly, in establishing and consolidating kingly authority in the mountainous hinterland of Orissa, any contender for royal status had to gain legitimacy in the eyes of the indigenous tribal population. Kingly rule could not be built up or maintained on a long-term basis without the loyalty and military support of a king's tribal subjects. Most important, however, was the fact that the king was only in a position to defend his kingdom against the outside attacks of competing kings and even colonial powers if he had the active help of indigenous warriors who were familiar with the rigours and characteristics of their difficult natural environment.

Foundation Stories

How was the relationship between royal principles of rule and authority on the one hand and tribal principles of rule and authority on the other viewed by the actors themselves? Can we discern an antagonism between two starkly different mentalities and ideals of organization? Or was there rather some mutual understanding and even elective affinity between the two sides? In order to answer these questions, let us now consider a number of emic points of view regarding the foundations of some Orissan jungle kingdoms within an area traditionally dominated by acephalous, lineage-based *adivasi* societies.

To start with, we have the following report of the founding of Bissamcuttack. This was an estate or 'little little kingdom' within the little kingdom of Jeypore in the southwest of Orissa:[24]

> The original founder ... was one Mallu Mahunty, by caste a Srishti Kurnam (a highly warlike race in those days), who emigrated from Parlakimidi in the early part of the 17th century ... Mallu Mahunty started his life as a trader in Bissemkatak and a few of its surrounding villages, and in a couple of years or so completely gained the confidence of the Khonds who, being impressed with his assiduity and prepossessing appearance and manners, elected him as their headman. He was therefore no longer a bustling trader going from door to door and from village to village, but a man of some rank and influence, to whom people from all parts of the neighbourhood poured in with petty presents in the shape of grain and other articles of produce, with a view to obtaining good advice and for settlement of disputes among themselves. These presents gradually took the shape of occasional nuzzars [gifts of homage] signifying a silent acknowledgement of the superiority and authority of the recipient. (Koraput District Records [KDR] 2168, para. 3, in the Orissa State Archives)

This report was prepared by the descendants of Mahunty some three hundred years after the events being reported, at a time when the last estate holder had to support his claim against both the little king of Jeypore and the British colonial authorities during a long-running court case. As such its content is legitimatory in character. In other petitions, statements like the one above are embellished in various ways, e.g. when it is remarked that, before Mahunty's arrival, Bissamcuttack was 'inhabited by a mountainous race of Khonds', who had a 'notoriously inborn nature of turbulence and lawlessness' (KDR 2168, para. 2).

If we take these statements at their face value (without forgetting the politico-legitimatory texts and contexts in which they are embedded), we are presented with the image of one tribe, the Kondhs, whose life is disrupted by internal anarchy and strife among the clans, and which willingly accepts the rule of an outsider. It does so voluntarily, but only after being 'impressed with his assiduity and prepossessing appearance and manners'. It is even stated that the Kondhs elected him and that they showered him with presents (a common way of showing allegiance). Thus, Mahunty's quasi-royal status gradually developed out of the actions of men who would later become his subjects. Initially he was a trader, and therefore began by acting mainly in the economic domain. Once elevated to the position of ruler, however, he ceased to trade in commodities, but instead began to receive (and redistribute) gifts. In this capacity his actions acquire a politico-ritual character; they are no longer narrowly economic. The gifts, which are initially given voluntarily, gradually become *nazar*s. That is to say they are still gifts, but they are provided regularly and take on more of the character of feudal tax payments.

Apart from being a merchant-turned-king, Mahunty was also a military man:

> The sphere of his influence and authority having thus expanded, Mallu Mahunty left no stone unturned to maintain his position by all means possible. He being by virtue of his birth a man of enterprising character, thoroughly initiated into the tactics of the martial science, at once formed a well organised force of armed men in order to protect himself and his newly formed dominion which he was master of without the knowledge of any one to whom it might have rightly or wrongly belonged. In the course of a few years he could command a militia consisting of no less than one thousand men and managed to continue in unmolested possession of his self-acquired estate till his death. (KDR 2168, para. 4)

Thus, the founder of the Bissamcuttack estate did not trust in his 'inborn' abilities as a charismatic entrepreneur and peacemaker alone. Instead he supplemented them with his own martial skills, and by setting up a powerful military force within his new realm.[25]

Let us now examine another report of the foundation of a jungle kingdom, namely Parlakimedi. According to this report or legend, a prince called Bhima Deo went into the hinterland of south Orissa in search of a kingdom of his own. A 'local man' recognized the prince's noble birth and inquired as to the reason for his journey:

> Bhima Deo was walking along in his journey towards a second home, when a crow followed him flying around his head, and uttering certain auspicious words. A man was drawing toddy from a tree, and hearing these words, came to the conclusion that a person of rank must be in the neighbourhood. Seeing the prince approach he recognized him to be such from his demeanour, saluted him, and inquired the cause of his being alone. The prince replied that he was in distress, and in quest of some country

over which he might become ruler. The man carried him on his shoulders until they came to a place where eight chieftains, desirous of a prince to rule over them, were assembled in council. He was gladly received and became the head of a small tract in Kimedi, designated the country of the 'Eight Mallikas' ... While being carried on the man's shoulders, *he made an inward vow to sacrifice him to some chosen goddess*, if he obtained his wishes. The votary on being informed of his fate, cheerfully offered himself for immolation. (Carmichael 1869: 88; his emphasis)

The local man and the eight chiefs were undoubtedly *adivasis*. Thus in this case too, a man (here a prince and not just a trader) was made into a king and equipped with a kingdom in a tribal surrounding. This happened not only with the consent of the local inhabitants but in conformity with their express wishes and with their active help; one of them even offered his life. It is notable that the prince did not end his quest after being offered the kingship by the eight tribal chiefs, although this might have been sufficient to establish his kingdom in a purely political sense. Instead, he continued to search for a goddess to whom he could sacrifice and who would be his and the kingdom's tutelary deity. Only after stealing the image of a goddess – in this case Manikeshvari – and only after fulfilling his vow to make a human sacrifice was his royal authority fully established.[26]

The report expressly links the foundation of a jungle kingdom with the ritual killing of a tribal chief in front of a goddess. This motif is so common all over Orissa that Kulke sees it as having a basis in reality, interpreting the ritual killings of tribal chiefs as a 'primordial violent force to establish power' (Kulke 1976: 10). For him, killing a tribal chief was an important means of establishing kingdoms since it brought about the subordination of tribal chiefs to the newly arriving kings. However, some questions arise if we take seriously the fact that, as reported in this story and in numerous others, the tribal chiefs *voluntarily* submit to their fate. What is the meaning of these voluntary submissions? Kulke argues that these legends record the literal subjugation and killing of tribal chiefs. He suggests that these aggressive acts were subsequently reinterpreted, depicted as glorious sacrifices in order to transform the subjugated tribes into allies. I would suggest an alternative interpretation. Perhaps the motif of the chief who 'cheerfully' offers himself for immolation rather expresses a complex and fragile juxtaposition of tribal and royal principles of authority and power. The Parlakimedi legend certainly expresses hierarchy, as is strikingly manifested by the image of the tribal man carrying his future king on his shoulders. But it also expresses consensus, manifested in the common veneration of a goddess, the motif of the eight chiefs 'desirous of a prince to rule over them', and the tribal chief's consent to being killed. Goddess, king and tribal chief act as three interdependent actors in a single politico-ritual complex.

Another foundation story refers to Durgi, an estate in Bissamcuttack. Local people reported to me that one family of *ksatriyas* or warriors came from Puri (the abode of Jagannath) to Durgi some 400 to 500 years ago. They are said to have had tantric knowledge and weapons, like the thunderbolt. After establishing a settlement at Durgi, the brothers spread out in all directions. They managed to control the *adivasis* of the area by giving them knowledge and training them in martial skills. The Durgi rulers are also said to have gained the confidence of the local *adivasis* by giving them sacred food or *mahaprasad* from Puri. Thus they established ritual friendship with the indigenous population, even addressing them as 'blood brothers' (*soi-sangho-to*). The Durgi rulers also impressed the *adivasis* through miracles, such as being able to hold glimmering charcoals without getting burnt. When the *adivasis* revolted, they are said to have worn magic charms around their arms which prevented the arrows from hitting them.

Various elements are stressed in the emic narratives that explain why *adivasis* accepted newly arriving outsiders as kings to 'rule' over them. First, there is the trade factor: it seems that many jungle kings started their careers as merchants, trading jungle products for products from the coast and the valleys, or traversing the jungle areas of the macro-region to carry commodities from the Deccan to the east Indian coast.[27] Next there is the ability of outsiders to use their charisma and power to settle conflicts within a tribe, especially if these involved prolonged violent feuds between clans or lineages that could not be reconciled by the indigenous leaders alone.[28] Often the outsiders' superior military power allowed them to establish their rule. This could be done either by using sheer force or by impressing the tribals with their skills in combat, thereby stimulating their desire to partake in this power. In this context, it should be mentioned that *shakti*, a life-giving and life-taking semi-divine power, was the one element that also attracted the *adivasis* most in their worship of local deities. The outsiders, so it seemed to them, had their share of *shakti*, not only in a military but also in a religious sense. The significance of the latter is also emphasized by the fact that most outside rulers soon established themselves as the patrons of the cult of these tribal/local goddesses.

The Adivasis' Points of View and Their Expressions of Loyalty to 'Their' Kings

So far we have looked at how the foundation of jungle kingdoms was conceived by the jungle kings and their scribes. Let us now consider tribal points of view concerning royalty and the *adivasis'* expressions of loyalty to their kings. Was their acceptance of kings and the principle of Hindu kingship only claimed by the kings themselves, thus making it a mere rhetorical device on the part of the latter with which to legitimate their rule? Or do tribal sources and data also convey a positive evaluation of royal modes of authority and rule? In what follows I shall continue to examine indigenous points of view, but this time with a focus on the tribal side of the king–*adivasi* relationship.

My first data in this connection come from a sub-section of the Kondh ethnic group, namely the Dongria Kondhs, who live in the remote Niam Hills, adjacent to the high plateau occupied by Bissamcuttack estate. The Dongria Kondhs trace their origins back to a mythical ancestor named Niamraja, or the 'King of the Niam Hills'. Today, Niamraja is worshipped in a temple that lies on the northern edge of Bissamcuttack town. However, this temple is merely an offspring of a more ancient cave temple up in the hills which is dedicated to Niamraja. I was told that in earlier times the Kondhs living on the plateau of the Bissamcuttack estate were forced to make pilgrimages into the hills at festival time in order to pay homage there to Niamraja, who took the form of a footprint. When the pilgrims saw the god one day in his full form, he is said to have called out in anger, 'Why do these people keep coming up the mountain to worship me?' whereupon he threw an earthenware water jug into the valley. The current temple is located where the water jug fell. This temple therefore embodies the movement of a tribal deity into the area of influence of Hindu culture and power. Niamraja's coming down into the valley does not simply mean that the plateau Kondhs are now spared the difficult passage into the hills. More important is the fact that, for the Hill Kondhs, the temple in Bissamcuttack represents a point of entry and integration into the valley whenever they descend into the high plateau with their jungle produce to trade, or for festivals, elections and other reasons. Through this temple the Kondhs are also incorporated into a system of ritual relationships with other deities in the town, and through it they also enter into ritual, socio-economic and political relationships with the devotees of these other deities and ultimately with the *thatraja* and the non-*adivasi* inhabitants of Bissamcuttack.

One deity that is of the greatest importance for the relationship of Niamraja and his people is Markama, the tutelary deity of Bissamcuttack and its kings. This goddess is regarded by the Kondh as Niamraja's consort:

> In ancient times Niam Raja kidnapped a Dongria girl named Markama from Tanda village in the Niam hills. But at night the girl fled away and later on it was reported that she repented. Hearing the news, the king suddenly realized his fault. He built a temple near Bissamcuttack in the name of Markama. After this the king died. His grandson Gaising came to the throne. One night he dreamt that the apparition of his grandfather, Niam Raja, was telling him something. It told him to tell the Dongria to worship him in the Markama temple. (Nayak 1989: 39)

From the tribal point of view, therefore, the origin of Markama's cult, the central cult of the kings and inhabitants of Bissamcuttack town and its surroundings, is traced directly back to the actions of the ancestor of all Donghria Kondh, and the royally patronized Markama herself is of tribal origin.

Thus, even though nowadays the Donghria Kondhs are divided into numerous clans and do not have a head, they acknowledge a common ancestor. Moreover they see this ancestor in the guise of a king. It is this Niamraja who allows the Donghria Kondhs to envisage and, in practice, to establish links with Bissamcuttack's tutelary deity Markama, a partially Hinduized local goddess, and thus with the king and subjects of this estate.[29]

Let us now look at one further example that refers to another section of the Kondhs, those who live near Narayanapatna. This town, located in the centre of the former Jeypore little kingdom, served as the royal capital for several Jeypore kings, of whom Viswambhara Deo II (1713–52) was the most prominent. Viswambhara is said to have been a great follower of the teachings of Chaitanya, the founder of a Vaishnava *bhakti* sect that continues to be very popular in Orissa and beyond. Singh Deo, the son-in-law of a later Jeypore king and panegyrist of this dynasty, reports:

> The said cult was preached to the people of Jeypore Agency without any distinction of caste or creed through the native dances here ... Viswambhara retired from the worldly affairs and entered into a cave in a neighbouring hill called Atmaparvata. The cave in the said hill is still pointed out to the spectators by the Khonds of the locality who believe that Raja Viswambhara is still alive in the said cave and meditating on the almighty. (Singh Deo 1939: 80–1)

These pieces of information reveal another point of contact and mutual attraction between kings and *adivasis* in addition to the tantric cults of local goddesses. This was a shared adherence to *bhakti* forms of religion, where it is less brahmanic ritualism than mere devotion that promises rewards and blessings for the adherents of a deity. In *bhaktism*, deities can be approached without brahmanical mediation and regardless of one's standing in the hierarchical caste system. Even being outside the caste system is no bar. *Bhaktism* thus offers scope for the integration of tribal strata of society into the Hindu fold, and it provides a platform for *adivasis* to identify themselves with Hindu modes of worship and forms of authority. Tantrism, in the form of the worship of local goddesses who were revered and feared on account of their *shakti*, and *bhakti*, an egalitarian path to salvation, were thus two religious domains in which royal and tribal modes of ideology and worship could and did meet. Both evince a certain tribal sympathy with royal claims to authority.

However, it was not just in the 'misty' domain of religious beliefs, mythology and ritual where kings and tribals shared common ideals and found a platform to meet, nor was it simply a matter of the rather passive consent and acceptance of royal principles by the *adivasis*. Rather, this consent stretched into the realm of everyday action and *realpolitik*. It could even go as far as the *adivasis'* actively and forcefully defending 'their' king, and even installing a king when one was absent or 'wrong'.

The *Koraput District Gazetteer* reported the following events in the quasi-royal estate of Kalyansingpur, an estate or 'little little kingdom' which, like Bissamcuttack, was located within the little kingdom of Jeypore:

Krishna Deo, king of Kalyansingpur, died in 1884 leaving behind his widow Neela Devi: She had been authorised by her husband to adopt an illegitimate son of 12 years, named Gopinath Deo. But the Ranee [queen] disputed his right of succession and put forward her own claim with the support of the manager Sripati Dalapati. The Maharaja [king of Jeypore] also sent his men to take possession of the property as Krishna Deo had no legitimate heir. The zamindar [estate-holder, king] was, however, warmly supported by the subjects, the local Khonds. Thus a triangular struggle ensued for the possession of Kalyansingpur. On the next Dashara celebration, the Khonds congregated at Singpur and declared Gopinath Deo as the Raja. The widow queen refused to recognise this demand whereupon the Khonds entered into the palace and carried off Gopinath Deo to Jeypore with an escort of 300 men. A temporary settlement was subsequently made according to which the minor received an allowance and was sent to prosecute his studies in the College at Vizianagram [on the coast]. (Senapati 1966: 416)

The struggle continued, with agents of the Jeypore king finally taking charge of the estate. However, in 1823, two sons of Gopinath Deo returned to Kalyansingpur and settled there: 'The faithful Khonds, once again, supported them and the elder brother, resuming the title of zamindar began to collect rents and issue receipts. The Deo brothers gained the ready support of the people everywhere which caused great apprehension in the Royal court of Jeypore.' (ibid.) The Kondhs of Kalyansingpur wanted a king. Certainly, they could have settled for the Jeypore king, but they wanted a local king, one from a dynasty living close by whose members could be approached in face-to-face contacts rather than through representatives alone. Kings? Yes! But not a far away king who was merely interested in creaming off the agricultural surplus without establishing a personal relationship with the local subjects or attending personally to their needs and petitions.

Another historical incident of a similar nature occurred in the little kingdom of Golgondah in the south of Orissa. During the mid nineteenth century the reigning king, Ananta Bhupati, was deposed by the British after he had repeatedly failed to pay the annual tax of 1,000 rupees. The widow of a predecessor king was installed:

This election was highly distasteful to the hill sirdars [local chiefs]: firstly, because they were not consulted; and secondly, because the succession in former times was always through male heirs. Troubles of all kinds thickened around the unfortunate Ranee, and it was not long that she was carried off to the jungles by a party of hill peons and there barbarously murdered. (Carmichael 1869: 236)

As a consequence, the deposed king, who was believed by the British to have been behind these events, was placed in jail, where he subsequently died. His estate was then placed under government control.

The hill sirdars were not disturbed in their tenures by the officers of Government, but they were not long in discovering that the extinction of their ancient Chiefs had seriously lowered their own status. They were now directly subject to the surveillance of the Collector's native Amin: and some slight show of inconsideration to one of their party brought about a hostile confederation. They united to raise an insurrection against the Government for the restoration of the Bhupati family ... Chinna Bhupati, a lad of nineteen ... was set up by the insurgents as their 'Rajah', and for three years, or from 1845 to 1848, they successfully held their jungles against the military force employed against them. (ibid.: 237)

Chinna Bhupati was finally accepted by the British as estate holder.

Thus, tribals and local chiefs wanted a king nearby with whom face-to-face interaction could be established. Three further observations can be deduced from these examples. First, seemingly paradoxically, the *adivasis* regarded their own dignity and sovereignty as being enhanced by their deference to the dignity and sovereignty of 'their' king. A relationship with a royal official or government representative did not equate to partaking in royalty; indeed, it even rendered it impossible. And this participation in the sovereignty of one's own king concerned both power (the hill chiefs were angered at not being consulted when a new king was appointed) and status ('the extinction of their ancient Chiefs had seriously lowered their own status'). Secondly, the *adivasis* and their chiefs wanted a male ruler, not a woman or widow-queen. Thirdly, they wanted a king with an established dynastic link ('the succession in former times was always through heirs male'). These two latter preferences clearly relate to the important tribal principles of agnation and male political supremacy. In other words, the *adivasis* only accepted men as 'players' in the public political domain, and the status of those men was largely defined and legitimized by the hereditary charisma of the male line.

Let us add further examples of tribes' active support for their kings. The first concerns what came to be known as the 'Ghumsur Wars'. In 1836, the Raja of Ghumsur, of the ancient royal house of the Bhanjas, refused to pay his tribute. When other forms of 'insurrection' occurred, the British sent an army into his kingdom. But before it could reach the royal capital of Bhanjanagar, the *raja* fled into the so-called *maliahs* or hill region, where the local Kondhs were extremely loyal to him and supported him in all ways, even sacrificing numerous lives for his military cause. For several years, the king could not be captured. There were heavy losses on both sides before he was killed, together with a great number of tribal chiefs and foot soldiers. In the neighbouring kingdom of Mohuri, similar events occurred at the end of the eighteenth century. The Mohuri king, Gana Deo, refused to pay tribute, and government soldiers were killed when they came to punish him. Like the *raja* of Ghumsar, he too disappeared into the nearby jungles, where he obtained the support of a branch of the Kondhs who lived in the Kerandi Hills. The royal dynasty of the Kingdom of Jeypore also repeatedly obtained military support from tribal warriors. 'Our enemies knew that the next battle will be in the jungle', I was told by Shakti Vikram Deo, the eldest son of the last king. He also explained that, in the case of war, the king sent a messenger into the tribal regions. As symbols of an ensuing or ongoing war for which the king needed tribal support, the messenger threw a red pepper in the air and drums were beaten. The *adivasis* then prepared for war and came down to Jeypore. If the fight was successful, they were allowed to keep a part of the war booty. Among the ethnic groups living in Jeypore kingdom, the Bonda, who live in the inaccessible Bonda Hills, are said to have been especially loyal soldiers, even forming a sort of suicide squad for the Jeypore king. The close association between the Bonda and the King of Jeypore was also manifested in the fact that the *adivasis* regarded the latter as their elder brother. Something similar is reported with regard to another tribe, the Paroja, literally 'common people' or 'subjects' (Sanskrit *praja*). One legend of this tribe states that the kings of Jeypore and the Parojas formerly lived together like brothers, but the former adopted luxurious habits like riding horses, while the latter accepted the hardship of carrying burdens.[30]

Another prominent ethnic group living in the hinterland of south Orissa, the Sora, were very much attracted by *ksatriya* values, that is those associated with the (royal) warrior *varna*. This sympathy is expressed, among other things, by the fact that Sora shamans (usually women) marry *ksatriya sonums* or 'warrior spirits' in the underworld (when travelling there during their trances) and that they themselves become ksatriyas after death.[31] Thus the Sora and most other tribal communities of Orissa were attracted less by brahmanical values of purity and impurity than by manifestations and forms of power typically associated with the *ksatriyas*. It is 'ksatriya-ization' rather than brahmanization or Sanskritization that they strove for. The *adivasis* were prepared to fight – to fight for their own cause, of course – but also, if necessary, for that of their own king, with whom they often conceived a close, sometimes 'brotherly' relationship.

Conclusions

All in all, then, it appears to me that studying jungle kingdoms is important, not *despite* their being little and at the margins of the greater power centres, but exactly *because* this is so. Typically, before Independence Indian political systems were not unitary constructs with just one centre and rigid territorial boundaries. Rather, they represented multi-centred, multi-layered networks of politico-ritual relationships stretching out in many directions, becoming fuzzy at the edges, and overlapping into neighbouring kingdoms. The little kingdoms lying at the peripheries of these systems, that is the kingdoms here called 'jungle kingdoms', were in many respects as important as the centres of politico-religious power. The borders between kingdoms and acephalous segmentary lineage societies were fluid, and their respective members partook of a similar kind of mentality that allowed interaction at all levels, whether political, social, cultural, religious or economic.

Notes

1. I have presented this argument in greater detail elsewhere (Schnepel 2002: Chapter 1). See also Berkemer (1993).
2. All diacritical marks have been deleted from the transcription of words from Indian languages, including from passages in quotation, for the benefit of the reader unfamiliar with these languages.
3. See Kulke (1993), (1995a), (1995b) and Kulke (ed.) (1995).
4. This capacity of jungle kingdoms is an important characteristic for Dirks (1987).
5. For accounts of Dasara celebrations in Orissan kingdoms, see Schnepel (1996).
6. See especially Kulke (1978a, b, c, d), (1979a), (1987) and (1992), as well as Schnepel (1995a).
7. This aspect is especially stressed in Schnepel (2001) and (2002: Chapter 4).
8. On the internal religious dimension of Orissa's jungle kingdoms, see Kulke (1980) and Schnepel (1993), (1995b) and (2002: Chapters 5 and 6).
9. See, among others, Heesterman (1985) and Schnepel (2002 Chapter 2, Section 5).
10. For a more detailed account of the kingdoms of southern Orissa, see Schnepel (2002: Chapter 2, Section 4).
11. The historical frame of reference is the period from the 'permanent settlement' of 1802 to the absorption of the kingdoms into the state of Orissa around 1950.
12. On Khallikot, see Behuria (ed.) (1964: 74) and Maclean (ed.) (1982: 246).
13. See Behuria (ed.) (1964: 78) and Maclean (ed.) (1982: 99–100).
14. See Behuria (ed.) (1964: 80) and Maclean (ed.) (1982: 161).
15. See Behuria (ed.) (1964: 81–2), Berkemer (1993: 200–2) and Maclean (ed.) (1982: 417).
16. See Maclean (ed.) (1982: 101).
17. See Behuria (ed.) (1965: 1), Schnepel (1992), (2002: Chapter 3) and Senapati (1966: 2).
18. In making these generalizations, I have also taken into account the other little kingdoms of south Orissa that can be found on Map 1, although they are not mentioned specifically in the passage above.
19. For example, the founders of the little kingdoms of Khallikot, Biridi, Palur, Humma, Mohuri, Chikiti, Jalantra and Tarla.
20. For example, Khallikot, Athgarh, Dharakot, Bodogoda, Shergada.
21. For example, in the south the kingdoms of Jalantra, Butrasingi and Mandasa were located on the Mahendragiri isthmus, while in the north Khallikot, Biridi, Palur and Humma were located at Lake Chilika and on the Khallikot Ghat, which separates south from central Orissa.

22. Occasionally a mythological ancestor may be believed to be the head of a clan or even of the whole ethnic group, but no living person represents and acts for a tribe in its entirety.

23. This lack of academic interest is quite surprising, especially given that another significant relationship – that between kings and castes – has become one of the most controversial and hotly debated issues in research on India. Some exceptions pertaining to Orissa should be mentioned. On the relationship between the kings of the Orissan plains and the tribes of the hinterland, see especially Kulke (1978a), (1979a, 17–26), (1980) and (1984). The ritual policy of the little kings of the hinterland of central Orissa in establishing and consolidating their rule is discussed in Kulke (1979b). The structural characteristics of the early development of state forms out of egalitarian tribal societies are also discussed by Bailey (1957; 1960), Biller (1986, 61–123) and Schnepel (2002: Chapter 2, Section 2). Other studies on the relationship between tribes and kings or on the development of tribal societies into little kingdoms outside Orissa are Chaudhuri (1993) and Sinha (1962).

24. I speak of 'kingdom/estate' in order to capture the fact that from the Jeypore kings' point of view Bissamcuttack was a tributary estate, while the 'estate holders', the Bissamcuttack *thatrajas*, considered themselves royal, as did their immediate subjects.

25. On the *thatrajas* of Bissamcuttack, see also Schnepel (2002: Chapter 5).

26. On stealing goddesses, see Schnepel (1995b).

27. For example, the Jeypore kings probably originated from traders traversing the area from central India to the east Indian coast, as argued in Schnepel (1992) and (2002: Chapter 3).

28. See Nayak (1989).

29. See Nayak (1989: 123). Markama and the role of the Dongria Kondh in the Dasara festival in Bissamcuttack is discussed in Schnepel (2002: Chapter 6, Section 4).

30. See Elwin (1950), Senapati (1990: 221) and Marglin (1985: 245–6).

31. See Vitebsky (1993: 29–33).

References

Bailey, F. G. 1957. *Caste and the Economic Frontier: A Village in Highland Orissa*. Manchester: Manchester University Press.

—— 1960. *Tribe, Caste and Nation: A Study of Political Activity and Political Change in Highland Orissa*. Bombay: Oxford University Press.

Bakker, H. T. (ed.) 1992. *The Sacred Centre as the Focus of Political Interest*. Groningen: Egbert Forsten.

Behuria, N. C. (ed.) 1964. *Final Report on the Major Settlement Operation in Ganjam Ex-Estate Areas, 1938–1962.* Cuttack: Orissa Government Press.

—— 1965, *Final Report on the Major Settlement Operations (Koraput District), 1938–64.* Cuttack: Orissa Government Press.

Berkemer, G. 1993. *Little Kingdoms in Kalinga: Ideologie, Legitimation und Politik Regionaler Eliten.* Stuttgart: Franz Steiner Verlag.

Biller, J. 1986. *Zur Entstehung von Herrschaft und Staat: das Beispiel des indischen Regionalreiches von Orissa.* Freiburg: Hochschul Verlag.

Boholm, Å (ed.) 1996. *Political Rituals.* Gothenburg: Institute for Advanced Studies in Social Anthropology.

Carmichael, D. F. 1869. *Manual of the District of Vizagapatam in the Madras Presidency.* Madras: Asylum Press.

Chattopadhyaya, B. D. 1976. 'Origin of the Rajputs: The Political, Economic and Social Processes in Early Medieval Rajasthan', *Indian Historical Review* 3: 59–82.

—— 1995 [1983]. 'Political Processes and the Structure of Polity in Early Medieval India', in Kulke (ed.) *The State in India, 1000–1700.* Delhi: Oxford University Press, pp. 195–232.

Chauduri, A. B. 1993. *State Formation among Tribals: A Quest for Santal Identity.* New Delhi: Gyan Publishing House.

Clastres, P. 1974. *La Société contre l'état.* Paris: Les Editions de Minuit.

Dirks, N. B. 1987. *The Hollow Crown: Ethnohistory of an Indian Kingdom.* Cambridge: Cambridge University Press.

Elwin, V. 1950. *Bondo Highlander.* Bombay: Oxford University Press.

Eschmann, A., Kulke, H. and Tripathi, G. C. (eds) 1978. *The Cult of Jagannath and the Regional Tradition of Orissa.* Delhi: Manohar.

Evans-Pritchard, E. E. and M. Fortes (eds) 1940. *African Political Systems.* Oxford: Oxford University Press.

Fox, R. G. 1971. *Kin, Clan, Raja and Rule: State-hinterland Relations in Pre-industrial India.* Berkeley: University of California Press.

—— (ed.) 1977. *Realm and Region in Traditional India.* Durham: Duke University Press.

Heesterman, J. C. 1985. *The Inner Conflict of Tradition: Essays on Indian Ritual, Kingship, and Society.* Chicago: Chicago University Press.

Kulke, H. 1976. 'Kshatriyaization and Social Change: A Study in Orissa Setting', in S. Pillai (ed.) *Aspects of Changing India, Studies in Honour of G.S. Ghurye.* Bombay: Popular Prakashaan, pp. 398–409.

—— 1978a. 'Early Royal Patronage of the Jagannatha Cult', in A. Eschmann, H. Kulke and G. C. Tripathi (eds) *The Cult of Jagannath and the Regional Tradition of Orissa.* Delhi: Monohar, pp. 139–55.

—— 1978b. 'Jagannatha as the State Deity under the Gajapatis of Orissa', in A.

Eschmann, H. Kulke and G. C. Tripathi (eds) *The Cult of Jagannath and the Regional Tradition of Orissa*. Delhi: Monohar, pp. 199–208.

—— 1978c. 'The Struggle between the Rajas of Khurda and the Muslim Subahdars of Cuttack for Dominance of the Jagannatha Cult', in A. Eschmann, H. Kulke and G. C. Tripathi (eds) *The Cult of Jagannath and the Regional Tradition of Orissa*. Delhi: Monohar, pp. 321–42.

—— 1978d. '"Juggernaut" under British Supremacy and the Resurgence of the Khurda-Rajas as 'Rajas of Puri', in A. Eschmann, H. Kulke and G. C. Tripathi (eds) *The Cult of Jagannath and the Regional Tradition of Orissa*. Delhi: Monohar, pp. 345–57.

—— 1979a. *Jagannatha-Kult und Gajapati-Königtum: Ein Beitrag zur Geschichte religiöser Legitimation hinduistischer Herrscher*. Wiesbaden: Franz Steiner Verlag.

—— 1979b. 'Early State Formation and Royal Legitimation in Tribal Areas of Eastern India', in R. R. Moser and M. K. Gautana (eds) *Aspects of Tribal Life in South Asia*, vol. 1, *Strategy and Survival*. Studia Ethnological Bernensia 1. Bern: University of Bern. pp. 29–37.

—— 1980. 'Legitimation and Town-Planning in the Feudatory States of Central Orissa', in J. Pieper (ed.) *Ritual Space in India. Studies in Architectual Anthropology*. London: Art and Anthropological Research Papers 17, pp. 30–40. Reprinted in Kulke 1993, pp. 93–113.

—— 1984. 'Tribal Deities at Princely Courts: The Feudatory Rajas of Central Orissa and Their Tutelary Deities (*Istadevatas*)', in S. Mahapatra (ed). *Folk Ways in Religion: Gods, Spirits and Men*. Cuttack: Institute of Oriental and Orissan Studies, pp. 13–24. Reprinted in and cited from Kulke 1993, pp. 114–36.

—— 1987. 'The Chronicles and the Temple Records of the Madala Panji of Puri: A Reassessment of the Evidence', in *Indian Archives*, vol. 36: 1–24. Reprinted in and cited from Kulke 1993, pp. 137–58.

—— 1992. 'Ksatra and Ksetra: The Cult of Jagannatha of Puri and the "Royal Letters" (*Chamu Citaus*) of the Rajas of Khurda', in Bakker, H. T. (ed.) *The Sacred Centre as the Focus of Political Interest*. Groningen: Egbert Forsten, pp. 131–42. Reprinted in and cited from Kulke 1993, pp. 51–65.

—— 1993. *Kings and Cults: State Formation and Legitimation in India and Southeast Asia*. Delhi: Manohar.

—— 1995a. 'Introduction: The Study of the State in Pre-modern India', in Kulke (ed.) *The State in India, 1000–1700*. Delhi: Oxford University Press, pp. 1–47.

—— 1995b. 'The Early and the Imperial Kingdom: A Processural Model of Integrative State Formation in Early Medieval India', in Kulke (ed.) *The State in India, 1000–1700*. Delhi: Oxford University Press, pp. 233–62.

—— (ed.) 1995. *The State in India, 1000–1700*. Delhi: Oxford University Press.

Kulke, H. and B. Schnepel (eds) 2001. *Jagannath Revisited: Studying Society,*

Religion and the State in Orissa. Delhi: Manohar.

Leach, E. R. 1970 [1954]. *Political Systems of Highland Burma: A Study of Kachin Social Structure*. London: Athlone Press.

Maclean, C. D. (ed.) 1982 [1893]. *Glossary of the Madras Presidency*. New Delhi: Asian Educational Services.

Mahapatra, S. (ed.) 1984. *Folk Ways in Religion: Gods, Spirits and Men*. Cuttack: Institute of Oriental and Orissan Studies.

Marglin, F. A. 1985. *Wives of the God–King: The Rituals of the Devadasis of Puri*. New Delhi: Oxford University Press.

Moser, R. R. and Gautan (eds) 1979. *Aspects of Tribal Life in South Asia I. Strategy and Survival*. Studia Ethnologica Bernensia 1. Bern: University of Bern.

Nayak, P. K. 1989. *Blood, Women and Territory: An Analysis of Clan Feuds of the Dongria Kondhs*. New Delhi: Reliance Publishing House.

Pieper. J. (ed.) 1980. *Ritual Space in India. Studies in Architectural Anthropology*. London: Art and Anthropological Research Papers 17.

Pillai, S. (ed.) 1976. *Aspects of Changing India. Studies in Honour of G. S. Ghuyre*. Bombay: Popular Prakashan.

Schnepel, B. 1992. 'The Nandapur Suryavamshis: Origin and Consolidation of a South Orissan Kingdom', *Orissa Historical Research Journal* 38: 170–99.

—— 1993. 'Die Schutzgöttinnen: Tribale Gottheiten in Südorissa (Indien) und ihre Patronage durch hinduistische Kleinkönige', *Anthropos* 88: 337–50.

—— 1995a. *Twinned Beings: Kings and Effigies in Southern Sudan, East India and Renaissance France*. Gothenburg: Institute for Advanced Studies in Social Anthropology.

—— 1995b. 'Durga and the King: Ethnohistorical Aspects of the Politico-Ritual Life in a South Orissan Jungle Kingdom', *Journal of the Royal Anthropological Institute* 1: 145–66.

—— 1996. 'The Hindu King's Authority Reconsidered: Durga-puja and Dasara in a South Orissan Jungle Kingdom', in Å Boholm (ed.) *Political Rituals*. Gothenberg: Institute for Advanced Studies in Anthropology, pp. 126–57.

—— 2001. 'Kings and Rebel Kings. Rituals of Incorporation and Dissent in South Orissa', in Kulke and Schnepel (eds) *Jagannath Revisited: Studying Society, Religion and the State in Orissa*. Delhi: Monohar, pp. 271–96.

—— 2002. *The Jungle Kings: Politics and Ritual in South Orissa*. Delhi: Manohar Publishers.

Senapati, N. 1966. *Orissa District Gazetteers: Koraput*. Cuttack: Orissa Government Press.

Senapati, R. M. (ed.) 1990. *Tribes of Orissa*. Bhubaneswar: Harijan and Tribal Welfare Department.

Singh Deo, K. B. 1939. *Nandapur: A Forsaken Kingdom*. Cuttack: Utkal Sahitya Press.

Sinha, S. 1962. 'State Formation and Rajput Myth in Tribal Central India', *Man in India* 42: 35–88.

Southall, A. W. 1953. *Alur Society. A Study in Processes and Types of Domination.* Nairobi: Oxford University Press.

Stein, B. 1980. *Peasant State and Society in Medieval South India.* Delhi: Oxford University Press.

Thapar, R. 1984. *From Lineage to State: Social Formations in the Mid-First Millennium BC in the Ganges Valley.* Bombay: Oxford University Press.

Vitebsky, P. 1993. *Dialogues with the Dead. The Discussion of Mortality among the Sora of Eastern India.* Delhi: Cambridge University Press.

–11–

Japanese Monarchy in Historical and Comparative Perspective

Emiko Ohnuki-Tierney

Introduction

There have been at least four different monarchical systems in Japanese history. The purpose of this chapter is to discuss these systems briefly from a comparative perspective, using the conceptual apparatus that arose from the discussion of divine kingship in anthropology. In order to do so, I distinguish between kingship as polity and kingship as an ideological/symbolic system. For the interpretation of Japanese kingship as a symbolic system, the imperial accession ritual is crucial. Throughout history it has retained some continuity and has been performed despite drastic changes in Japanese kingship as well as in the broader sociopolitical context. I interpret the ritual against a broader context of Japanese cosmology.

Ancient Kingship (*Kodaiōchō*)

Japanese kingship was established on the basis of the political economy and agrarian cosmology of wet-rice agriculture. Yet almost six centuries elapsed between the introduction of rice agriculture and the emergence of Japanese kingship at the end of the fourth century AD. when the Ōjin Emperor established his Yamato state near present-day Ōsaka (Waida 1975: 319–20). During its early stages 'ancient kingship' (*kodaiōchō*) went through significant developments until its political, economic and symbolic bases became firmly established.[1]

The early agrarian leaders, including the early emperors, were magico-religious leaders, i.e. shamans *qua* political leaders whose political power rested on an ability to solicit supernatural power to ensure a good rice crop. The annual harvest ritual thus served to legitimate a local political leader, ensure the leader's symbolic rebirth, and strengthen his political power (see Murakami 1977: 4–6). For this reason, many scholars consider the emperor first and foremost as the officiant in rituals for the soul of rice (*inadama no shusaisha*) who ensures the blessings of the deities for the new rice crop on behalf of the people.[2] The importance of the religious–ritual character of Japanese kingship, agreed upon even by Marxist scholars like Murakami, de-emphasizes it as being strictly political.

On the question of kingship as ideology and as polity, during the ancient period symbolic power was coterminous with political power. By this I do not propose that polity (or economic structure etc.) is a simple permutation of the symbolic structure. Marshalling extensive historical and ethnographic evidence for what he labelled the 'galactic polity', which emerged during the second half of the nineteenth century in Thailand and persisted as a 'pulsating' or 'radial polity', Tambiah (1976; 1985: 252–86) argues against Eliade and others. He insists that 'a cosmological mode of thought' should not be given 'an ontological priority', nor constitute 'a sociological anteriority'. The symbolic power of the emperor was a very pragmatic capacity to communicate with the deities in order to bring about human production and reproduction. Because the emperor's 'symbolic power' had vital economic consequences, when the shoguns took political and military control, they could not dispense with rice rituals. Nor did they dare to take over the role of officiant in these rituals.

As the heads of the nascent Yamato state, the emperors were military leaders. However, their military role was a far cry from the warrior kings of medieval Europe. At that time the emperor was safe in Yamato and a few hundred soldiers were sent to the western frontiers of Japan to guard the border (for details, see Ohnuki-Tierney 2002a).

The religious *qua* political *qua* economic nature of the agrarian rituals of these early leaders, including emperors, is clearly expressed in the concept *matsurigoto*, which was the conceptual basis of the political system, called *ritsuryō-sei*, at that time (cf. Kitagawa 1990: 138–89). Advancing the interpretation of Mitsuya Shigematsu and Andō Seiji, Orikuchi (1975a [1928]: 160–1; 1975b [1928]: 175–7; 1983 [1947]: 275–7) proposes that the early use of the term *matsuri*, which in contemporary Japanese means festivals or ceremonies, was contained in the expression *osukuni no matsurigoto*. Written in three characters representing 'to eat', 'country' and 'polity', it denotes the country where food for the deities is made. In other words, food and food consumption were an essential aspect of the polity at the time, and rice already stood for food in general.[3]

Although other rituals were added in different historical periods, the core imperial rituals officiated over by the emperor were established during the ancient period. They all relate to rice harvesting: *niinamesai, ōnamesai (daijōsai)*, and *kannamesai*.[4] The annual harvest ritual of *niinamesai* becomes the *ōnamesai* at the time of the accession of a new emperor, although another accession ritual, introduced from China and independent of the *ōnamesai*, was performed early on. At the accession of Emperor Kanmu (r. 781–806) in the eighth century, this installation ritual of Chinese origin was formalized as the imperial accession ceremony

(Murakami 1977: 21). Consequently, the *ōnamesai* has come to be seen as a ceremony (*saiten*) rather than a political event. The earliest form of the *ōnamesai* included the rite of *senso* (*kenji togyo*) during which the three imperial treasures – the mirror, the sword and the *magatama* jewel – were handed to the new emperor. These three items have been found in tombs of what appear to be aristocrats of the Yayoi period, indicating that they were symbols for royalty or political leaders. This rite, called *senso* (*kenji togyo*), became independent of the *ōnamesai*. Thus, from the beginning of the Heian period the imperial accession has involved three separate rituals: *senso* (*kenji togyo*); *sokui no rei*; and *ōnamesai*. Of these, the *senso* is held immediately after the death of an emperor so that the three symbols of kingship are handed to the new emperor without any lapse of time. In China and Korea the new emperor's accession took place right after the death of an emperor. By contrast, the timing of *senso* is related to the Japanese aversion to the impurity associated with death. This required that the accession ritual be held after the imperial funeral, at which the impurity created by the previous emperor's death was ritually removed. Only then could a new emperor be enthroned (M. Inoue 1984). Despite these changes, since the time of the Emperor Tenmu in the mid seventh century, the *ōnamesai* has been essential for the accession of a new emperor (Murakami 1977: 21–2).

Since the imperial rituals are all rice harvest rituals and share many essential elements, I will confine my discussion to the *ōnamesai*, which, as part of the imperial accession ritual, is the most important of all rituals and is observed even today.[5]

Ōnamesai: The Imperial Accession Ritual

The imperial harvest ritual of the *ōnamesai*, modelled after the folk harvest ritual in ancient Japan (Yanagita 1982 [1949]: 133–4), evolved over time. The earliest reference to it occurs during the reign of Seinei (AD 480–4)[6] (Miura 1988: 143). Before the imperial system became established various deities of production and reproduction were addressed in the ritual (*saishin*) (cf. Orikuchi 1975b [1928]: 236–7).[7] After its establishment the sun goddess (Amaterasu) became the focus.

Preparation for the *ōnamesai* starts in the spring (February-April) preceding the major ceremony which takes place in the autumn (Kōshitsu Bunka Kenkyūkai, ed. 1988) when the locations of two fields – *yuki* and *suki* – are chosen by divination. Rice for offering during the *ōnamesai* is grown in these fields with great care to prevent contamination by impurities. Situated southeast and northwest of Kyoto, respectively, these two fields symbolically represent the Japanese nation. A series of purification rituals used to be performed by the emperor and Japanese people in preparation for the November ceremony. The entire process of the *ōnamesai* in November lasted four days during the Heian Period (794–1185) and consisted of eleven segments (Hida 1988: 214; Kurabayashi 1988: 37). Although the duration and details of the ritual have changed over time, basically it consists of the same elements: the *mitamashizume*, the rejuvenation of the soul; *shinsen* (or *kyōsen*), offering of the new crop of rice by the new emperor to the deity; *naorai*, commensality between the emperor and the deity; and *utage*, commensality among humans, signalled by a feast hosted by the emperor (Orikuchi 1975b [1928]: 239; Yoshino 1986: 13–20).

Of these rituals, the most difficult to interpret is the *mitamashizume* (the rejuvenation of the soul), which takes place the night before the public ceremony and continues until dawn. It is a strictly private ritual during which the emperor lies in a sacred bed (*ohusuma*) that is placed on a sacred seat (*madoko*). Meanwhile, a court lady, sometimes two ladies (Miyata in Amino, Ueno and Miyata 1988: 52), performs a ritual to receive and rejuvenate the emperor's soul, which is departing from his body. Since the *mitamashizume* is a private (secret) ritual, there is little information about what took place during the ritual in different historical periods. Even today some refrain from discussing it openly.

The ritual's secrecy has given rise to controversy over its interpretation. Three types of explanation for it have been offered. One holds that the ritual rejuvenates the emperor's soul, thus enabling him to perform the *ōnamesai* the following day at the height of his spiritual powers (Murakami 1977: 15–16). The presence of a court lady leads to an alternative interpretation: that the emperor engages in sexual intercourse with her. The third interpretation pertains to the *ōnamesai* held at the time of the previous emperor's death, when, according to some scholars, the deceased emperor's corpse is placed on the sacred seat. His soul enters the new emperor's body during the *mitamashizume*.

It is essential to understand the notion of 'soul' in ancient Japan in order to appreciate the *mitamashizume* fully. According to Orikuchi (1975b [1928]: 189–90), the Japanese believed that the soul of a person or an object waxed in the winter and waned in the spring. It splits and is easily detached from the body. Once it becomes detached, another soul must enter the body if the person is to continue to live. The attachment of this new soul occurs in an act called *tamafuri*. Alternatively, as conceptualized later in history, the soul must be recaptured, an act called *tamashizume*. The *mitamashizume* (*mi* = a prefix indicating the polite form) ritual thus first of all rejuvenates the emperor's soul which might have waned or been ready to leave his body.

The sexual act thesis is not incompatible with the soul rejuvenation theory if we take into account that in ancient Japan production and reproduction were seen as identical processes and both were conceptualized in terms of a soul. The term *musubi* meant, on the one hand, encapsulation of a soul in a knot, and, on the other hand, production and reproduction. Thus, the act of making a knot (*musubi*) with a string, twig, or piece of grass, as described in the *Manyōshū* and other literature of the time, was a ritual act to encapsulate a soul in a knot. During the *mita-mashizume*, a cotton knot is tied as a ritual act of capturing the soul of the emperor, which is ready to depart from his body (Matsumae 1977: 96–7). But the term *musubi* also meant reproduction and production: *musu* meant reproduction and *bi* (=*hi*) meant production or growth with the aid of the sun (Ebersole 1989: 42, 56; Matsumae 1977: 96–7; Orikuchi 1976c [1953]: 253–60). If the emperor had sexual relations with the court lady *cum* sacred lady, this had very different meanings from what we might assume today. In ancient Japan sexual intercourse was coterminous with soul rejuvenation and this, in turn, was a necessary condition for agricultural reproduction.

The third proposition was originally advanced by Orikuchi (1975b [1928]: 194). He argues that the Japanese emperor is uniquely characterized by the possession of what he calls an imperial soul. According to him, the *ōnamesai* ritually enables the imperial soul that is leaving the previous emperor's body to enter the new emperor's body, thereby assuring the lineal transmission of the imperial soul, which is crucial to the Japanese imperial system. He is said to have remarked that a new emperor used to bite into the corpse of the deceased emperor in order for the latter's soul to enter him (Miyata: personal communication). Orikuchi's interpretation opens up an important problem in comparative kingship – the continuity of kingship or the imperial system irrespective of individual emperors. This is what Kantorowicz (1981) [1957] referred to as the problem of the 'king's two bodies'.

Nonetheless, Orikuchi offers no evidence for his proposition and, given his propensity to be nationalistic, it is difficult to accept it without reservation. In fact, some scholars have interpreted the Japanese imperial system as a form of divine kingship. Orikuchi sees the foundation of the imperial system as being laid by myth-histories and ritual that enabled the imperial system to transcend the problem of the emperor as a person and his/her biological mortality – the problem of the 'king's two bodies'. Contemporary followers of Orikuchi's interpretation include Ebersole (1989) and Yamaori (1990a, 1990b). Like Orikuchi, Ebersole believes that the imperial soul is transmitted from one emperor to the next, guaranteeing the continuation of the imperial system regardless of individual emperors, and he specifically links 'the descent of the heavenly grandson' episode to the problem of 'king (emperor)' v. 'kingship (imperial system)' (Ebersole 1989: 96).

Following this private ritual, the emperor offers various foods to the deity (the *shinsen*). The most important offerings are products of the new rice crop grown in the two fields described above: cooked rice gruel, white *sake* (*shiroki*), and black *sake* (made from *sake* coloured with plant ashes, or, in later periods, black sesame). Other food offerings include cooked Italian millet (*awa*) that has been freshly harvested, fresh fish, dried fish, fruits, soup and stew (*oatsumono*) (Kōshitsu Bunka Kenkyūkai, ed. 1988: 104–5; Murakami 1977: 18). These foods are offered during the ritual, which lasts more than two hours, and are then consumed by the deity and the emperor together (the *naorai*). The *ōnamesai* concludes with an elaborate banquet in which the emperor and the guests feast together (the *utage*). At the time of the *ōnamesai* for Shōwa Emperor, the feast lasted for two days.

The *Ōnamesai* and the Myth-histories

Unlike the Malinowskian claim that myths and ritual provide a charter for action, Saigō (1984) and others argue that the two earliest writings of Japan – the *Kojiki* and the *Nihonshoki* – represent attempts to validate the existing harvest rituals at the court *ex post facto*. A systematic comparison is difficult since these oral myth-histories were set down in writing over a long period of time and contain many different versions of apparently similar episodes and themes. Nevertheless, the two episodes are seen to parallel the imperial harvest ritual and a brief discussion will further illuminate the meaning of the accession ritual.

In what is popularly referred to as 'the heavenly cave' (*ameno iwaya*) episode, the sun goddess, Amaterasu Ōmikami, isolates herself in a building (cave) because her younger brother has offended her by his defiling behaviour.[8] Myriad deities gather noisily in front of the building, laughing and engaging in merrymaking. A shaman deity, Ameno Uzume no Mikoto, dances semi-nude in front of the building, causing uproarious laughter. The deities hang a long octagonal mirror from a branch in front of the building and tell Amaterasu that there is a deity superior to her in front of the building. Curious, she peeks and mistakes her own image in the mirror for the superior deity. With her emergence from seclusion, the universe is again bright with the sun (Kurano and Takeda, eds 1958: 81–3).

This episode is often interpreted as a symbolic enactment of the death and rebirth of the Sun Goddess (Saigō 1984 [1967]: 78–87; Orikuchi 1975b [1928]: 198), which in turn is seen to correspond to what happens to the emperor's soul during the *mitamashizume*. Like Amaterasu in the myth, the emperor in the ritual goes into seclusion while his soul, 'split' and ready to depart from his body, returns and is rejuvenated. Likewise, the behaviour of the court lady during the *mitamashizume* is seen to parallel the dancing by Ameno Uzume mo Mikoto in front of the building where Amaterasu is isolated (Matsumae 1977: 119; Murakami 1977: 15–16).

The second episode from the myth-histories that is seen to correspond to the imperial harvest ritual is the *tenson kōrin* – the descent of the heavenly grandson, Ninigi no Mikoto, who, wrapped in the *madoko ohusuma*, the sacred bedding, is sent by the sun goddess to earth to govern.[9] This episode is seen to correspond to the scene during the *mitamashizume* when the emperor wraps himself in bedding.

In the version in the *Kojiki* written after the sun goddess was established as the ancestral deity to the imperial family, she is the mother of a grain soul called

'Masakatsu Akatsu Kachihaya Hiame no Oshihomimi no Mikoto' (Kurano and Takeda, eds 1958: 111, 125). Thus the Jinmu Emperor, the legendary 'first' emperor, is the son of the grain soul and, therefore, the great grandson of the sun goddess who sent him to rule the earth. Another name for this grandson-cum-first emperor portrays rice stalks with succulent grains: Amatsu Hiko Hiko Ho no Ninigi no Mikoto (Kurano and Takeda, eds 1958: 125). At the time of his descent Amaterasu gives her grandson the original rice grains that she had grown in the two fields in heaven (Takamagahara) from the seeds of the five types of grains (*gokoku*) given to her by Ukemochi no Kami, the deity in charge of food (Kurano and Takeda, eds 1958; see also Murakami 1977: 13). The grandson of Amaterasu transforms a wilderness into a country of rice stalks with succulent ears of rice (*mizuho*) and abundant grains of five types (*gokoku*), thanks to the original seeds given to him by Amaterasu.

Although there are a number of different versions of these myth-histories, those introduced here, which are both well known, are *not* about the creation of the universe. Rather, they are about the transformation of wilderness (*ashihara no nakatsu no kuni*) into a land of abundant rice at the command of the sun goddess, whose descendants, the emperors, rule the country by officiating at the rice harvest rituals (Saigō 1984: 15–29; Kawasoe 1980: 86).

Imperial Accession Ritual and Japanese Cosmology: An Interpretation

In order to further understand the symbolic meaning of the imperial accession ritual in comparative perspective, I turn now to the agrarian cosmology.

Deities and the Reflexive Structure

A predominant interpretation of Japanese deities among contemporary scholars is that from the earliest times they have been characterized by a dual nature and power: a peaceful soul (*nigimitama*), which is good and creative, coexists with a violent soul (*aramitama*), which is evil and destructive. Orikuchi (1965a [1924]: 78–82; 1965b [1925]: 33–5; 1976a [1947]: 303–17) first drew attention to this aspect of the deities, known as *marebito*.[10] According to Orikuchi, the *marebito* was a god in ancient Japan who periodically visited the villages from a world located on the other side of the sea where aging and death were unknown. The god visited villagers to bring good luck, although he was also potentially dangerous. Because deities are natural beings for the Japanese, the dual character ascribed to deities extends to other natural beings and phenomena as well.

I would suggest that from the perspective of reflexivity, the *marebito*, or stranger–outsider deities who come from outside a settlement or outside of Japan,

constitute the semiotic 'other' for the Japanese. This Other is symbolically equivalent to a transcendent self, that is to say the self perceived at a higher level of
abstraction than a reflective self. The dual nature of *marebito* deities is therefore a
projection of the dual qualities that the Japanese see in themselves. The Japanese,
who ritually harness the positive power (*nigitama*) of the deities, do so because of
their awareness of the deities' negative side (*aratama*), just as they are aware of
their own negative qualities. Given the structure of self and other, to remain pure,
humans must either fetch purity and energy – the *nigitama* – from the deities, or
remove impurity from their own lives by creating scapegoats (see Ohnuki-Tierney
1987). The purpose of ritual for the Japanese, then, is to harness the energy of the
deities in order to rejuvenate their lives, which would otherwise wither into a state
of impurity.

That the *marebito* deities provide the basic model of the reflexive other is
evident when we explore further the symbolic relationships among purification,
the rebirth of the self and the reflexive process with reference to the metaphor of
the mirror in Japanese culture. In the *Kojiki* and the *Nihonshoki*, a mirror plays a
significant role. We recall an episode in which Amaterasu Ōmikami (sun goddess
or 'the Heaven Illuminating God'), ancestress of the Japanese in creation myth,
emerged from seclusion (that is was reborn) thanks to a mirror and the Japanese
universe was reborn with her light. If she took her own image to be that of a deity
superior to her, the mirror represents, I think, her transcendent self. In other words,
the rebirth of the sun goddess and the Japanese universe was facilitated by a
mirror, which in turn symbolizes a self perceived at a higher level. The *Nihonshoki*
also contains many passages that symbolically equate a mirror with a deity
(Sakamoto *et al*. 1967: 88, 146; see also 555, 570–1). For example, two deities are
described as being born from white-copper mirrors (Sakamoto *et al*. 1967: 88).

Other ethnographic data describe mirrors or reflections in water as the embodiment of deities. The belief that supernatural power can be harnessed by a mirror is
illustrated by the figurines found in ancient tombs who hold mirrors on their
chests. These figurines, called *haniwa*, are considered to represent ancient
shamans (Yanagita, ed. 1951: 94). Even today mirrors are installed in many shrines
as the embodiment (*goshintai*) of the deity enshrined there. Throughout Japan, a
number of valleys, ponds, mountains, hills and rocks bear the term *kagami*
(mirror) in their designations; these are sacred places where supernatural powers
are thought to reside (Yanagita, ed. 1951: 94).

A Few Ounces of Divinity: Rice as Deities

The notions that each rice grain has a soul and that rice is alive in the husk are fundamental to the meanings assigned to rice in Japanese culture and in most other
cultures that use rice as a 'staple food'. Husking, for example, was traditionally

done a short while before consumption to prevent rice from losing its soul; husked rice soon becomes lifeless rice, i.e. 'old rice' (*komai*). The belief in the soul of rice was further developed in the agrarian cosmogony and cosmology, expressed in the well-known versions of the myth-histories, as we saw. It was the mission of the grandson of the sun goddess to transform the wilderness into a land with succulent rice stalks. Rice constitutes Japanese deities whose names carry references to rice or to a bountiful rice crop. I suggest that the soul of rice grain is not simply equivalent to deities but is identified more specifically as the *nigimitama*, the positive power of divine purity. It is relevant to note here that while most deities have dual qualities and powers, the deity of the rice paddy has only the *nigimitama* or peaceful soul. In fact, drought or flood, which destroys rice paddies, is an act of the *Mizu no Kami* (water deity) rather than an expression of the *aramitama* (violent spirit) of the deity of the rice paddy.[11]

I therefore see the following symbolic equivalents as being crucial to an understanding of the cosmological significance of rice:

[rice = soul = deity = the *nigitama* (peaceful/positive power of the deity)]

Production, Reproduction, Consumption, Ritual and Polity

Since human lives wane unless the positive principle replenishes their energy, humans and their communities must rejuvenate themselves by harnessing the positive (*nigitama*) power of the deities. This can be accomplished in two ways: by performing a ritual or through the consumption of food. Through the consumption of rice, the Japanese internalize the divine power of being, which then becomes part of the human body and its growth.

The divine souls objectified in rice grains do not stand for static objects. They symbolize 'growth' – the dynamic energy for transforming the Japanese universe – and are the moving force in the dualistic universe. More concretely, they represent agricultural growth as well as growth of the human body that consumes them. Thus, the rituals of the common people and the imperial court which involve rice mark the growth cycle: planting of rice seeds, planting of seedlings and harvesting.

We have seen that in ancient Japan the term *musu* meant both reproduction and growth stimulated by the sun. Note that in Japanese cosmology the sun – the source of agricultural growth – is female, unlike the male sun god in many other cultures of the world. Thus, the rejuvenation of the soul is equated with sexual intercourse, and production and reproduction are symbolically synonymous. Other evidence also illustrates the close association between rice and reproduction. As with a number of other deities identified as *kokurei* (souls of grains, not exclusively rice), this deity is female. Yanagita (1981 [1953]) sees a parallel between the gender of grain deities and a ritual first recorded during the tenth century and still observed today in some parts of Japan in which rice grains are scattered in the parturition hut. The parallel led to Yanagita's well-known statement that the birth of grains and the birth of humans were once thought to be identical. Again production is equated with reproduction.

From the emperor's perspective, the harvest ritual is an important personal and political rite of passage that ensures the renewal of his soul and his political power, as expressed in the notion of *matsurigoto* in which polity is defined as an act of producing the food for deities. From the perspective of the structure of the Japanese self, rice consumption, polity, rice production, the harvest ritual and human reproduction are all equivalent in meaning. They facilitate the rejuvenation of the Japanese collective self through the incorporation of the divine power of *nigitama*. These activities then are coterminous with ritual. The above interpretation can be summarized in the following symbolic equations:

[food consumption = ritual = agricultural production = human reproduction = polity]

The Harvest Ritual as the Exchange of Self

If rice is a deity, however, rice production and consumption are not merely mundane activities. Rice consumption is a religious act and thus requires a proper ceremony in order to appropriate rice for human consumption. We recall that the basic theme of the imperial harvest ritual and the myth-histories is the re-enactment of the way the original seeds of rice were given to humans – represented by the emperor-shaman – by the deities. In turn humans offer the new crop of rice at harvest time and share it through an act of commensality not only between the emperor-shaman and the deities, but also with the guests present at the feast.

On one level, the harvest ritual is a cosmic gift exchange in which a new crop of rice – a few grains of divinity – is offered to the deities in return for the original seeds given by the deities to the first emperor. The mode of exchange takes the form of commensality between deities and humans, including the emperor. On another level, the harvest ritual constitutes a cosmological exchange of the soul and the body. Since rice embodies the peaceful soul of the deities, by offering rice grains to humans, the deities offer a part of themselves – and not just any part, but their souls. Rice production, therefore, is not an economic activity as such, but a system of gift exchange. It is the original gift of rice seeds from the deities and the counter-gift of the new rice crop at harvest. Ultimately, the soul and the body that are embodied in rice are exchanged in this cosmological system of exchange.

The gift exchange, then, is not a gift exchange in the ordinary sense. No separate gift is being exchanged. It is not a sacrificial ritual since no sacrificial victim is involved. Instead of a gift of a sacrificial animal, Japanese deities initiate the gift exchange cycle by offering themselves to humans, who return their trust by growing the seeds to full maturity, *nurturing* the deities, as it were. This exchange is therefore not a simple 'generalized exchange', an exchange 'on credit' based on trust (Lévi-Strauss 1969 [1949]: 265); it is a generalized exchange of souls and bodies between the deities and humans. They give their selves as an expression of their trust, just as in the classical Maussian sense 'a man gives himself' (Mauss 1966 [1950]: 45).[12]

Yet on another level, given the symbolic equivalence of agricultural production and human reproduction, the harvest ritual enacts the cosmic cycle of production and reproduction, facilitated by the flow of rice seeds, the soul and semen. Semen is involved here because of the symbolic equation of production and reproduction, regardless of whether or not the shaman-emperor in fact engages in sexual intercourse during the harvest ritual.

Rice as the Food for Commensality

The cosmological exchange of the divine soul and power embodied in rice does not exist in the abstract in myths and the private ritual of the emperor. In fact, it is enacted by the people in their daily lives as well as during their folk festivals. Rice and rice products, such as rice cakes and rice wine, have historically been the food for commensality between humans and deities, on the one hand, and among humans, on the other (Yanagita 1982 [1940]). The three essential components of most Japanese rituals and festivals, whether folk or imperial, are: *shinsen* (or *kyōsen*), offerings to the deities; *naorai*, commensality between the officiant of the ritual and the deities; and *utage*, the feast with the host and the guests. While other food items are also used, rice and rice products are indispensable for all three types of commensality.

Japanese Kingship during Subsequent Periods

After reaching its zenith during the eighth century, Japanese 'ancient kingship' soon lost its power, and never regained it (Kitagawa 1990: 140). With the rise of the warrior class, political and military power were transferred to the shoguns and their courts, leaving to the emperors only the symbolic power of officiating at rice harvest rituals.

After the shogunate government was overthrown in 1868, it took twenty-one years before the Constitution of Imperial Japan was promulgated on 11 February 1889. After lengthy consultation with German scholars, they chose the Prussian constitution as a blueprint, with some articles being almost verbatim reproductions of the German scholars' draft (for details of the constitution, see Ohnuki-Tierney 2002a). That said, the Meiji oligarchs inserted Article 1 against strong and unanimous opposition from their foreign scholar-consultants. Three articles described the new emperor:

- Article 1: The emperor belongs to one line for eternity *(bansei ikkei)* and he governs Imperial Japan.
- Article 3: The emperor is sacred *(shinsei nishite)* and may not be violated *(okasu bekarazu)*.
- Article 11: The emperor shall command the Army and the Navy.

(Emura ed. 1996: 430–4).

The political significance of the two key terms *shinsei* ('sacred', 'divine') and *okasubekarazu* ('inviolable') in Article 3 was fairly clear. They were intended to relieve the emperor of any political responsibility. But their religious meaning is far from clear, with many different scholarly interpretations in the past and more recently (Satomi 1972: 652).[13] What is clear is that in religious terms, the Pledge, a prayer read by the emperor to his 'ancestors' before the promulgation of the constitution, as well as Articles 1 and 3, assigned the emperor a divinity which surpassed that of European monarchs. European monarchs, including Louis XIV, were never divine themselves. Rather, they were only a conduit for divine power, always serving 'by the Grace/Will of God'. In contrast, the Japanese emperor became God by possessing *the* divine soul. The emperor was officially transformed from *a* deity *(kami)* in the pantheon whom people had traditionally manipulated, into *the* Deity, endowed with sacredness and inviolability – a notion that was hitherto completely alien to the Japanese.

The Meiji architects of the constitution thus ascribed an unprecedented 'divinity' to the emperor. Furthermore, through the assignment of the divine soul, the oligarchs solved the problem of the king's two bodies by guaranteeing the eternity of both the individual emperor and the imperial system, regardless of the death of individual emperors. The divine emperor was, however, bound to Japan, a political unit, unlike the Christian God, who transcends political boundaries. While the first three parts of the accession ritual (the transference of the three imperial jewels, the soul rejuvenation and the offerings by the emperor to the deities) have never become public rituals, the last element of the accession ritual – commensality between deities and humans – became ever more public and international, with dignitaries from around the world being invited to take part. Nonetheless the major emphasis by the Meiji government was on an elaborate series of rituals instituted in order to bolster the notion that the Japanese imperial system has been in place from time immemorial and is eternal (for further details, see Ohnuki-Tierney 2002a and 2002b).

Article 11 put the emperor directly in charge of the military. Japan's modernization was conterminous with the country's intense militarization and its colonial and imperial ambition. The military took advantage of this article to bypass any other governmental checkpoints and approach the emperor directly. Nevertheless, he was far from being the European model of 'warrior king'. The concept of the militarized and sacralized emperor remained throughout Japan's military period. However, it was thoroughly revised by yet another foreign power at the end of World War II, when the idea of the 'symbolic emperor' (*shōchō tennō*) took its place.

Conclusion

The concept of divine kingship, as originally proposed by Frazer (1911–15) and elaborated by Hocart (1969 [1927]; 1970 [1936]), remains a perennial concern in anthropology, with neo-Frazerians, neo-Hocartians and neo-Dumontians all contributing to this debate. Spirited charges against Frazer in recent years include that by Feeley-Harnik (1985: 276), who tells us that divine kingship has existed mostly in the imagination of anthropologists, and not in African and other kingships. Ray (1991: 22–53) strongly criticizes Frazer's original formulation, arguing that it was based only on the classical example of the slaying of the priest-king of Diana at Nemi but was used by Frazer and others to develop a universal model.[14]

In order to understand the Japanese emperorship in comparative perspective, I will briefly discuss some of the key concepts that have been proposed as characteristics of divine kingship in anthropological literature. My discussion begins by placing the emperor in the broader context of Japanese society in order to compare it with kingship elsewhere. The ancient emperor system was founded on the basis of the political economy of wet-rice agriculture and its concomitant cosmology. Those who held non-agrarian occupations, including funeral attendants, traders, entertainers, and so on, never held politically central positions. The symbolic opposition of purity and impurity has always been, I dare say, the most important principle in Japanese culture, from ancient times to the twenty-first century. It was of paramount importance in native folk shintoism, which abhorred human deaths and manifested this by assigning impurity to corpses and activities related to human deaths. Buddhism, introduced from India via China, extended the notion of impurity to the deaths of all animals and all activities related to them. Yet it was only around the twelfth century that the notion of impurity became radically negative. While the non-agrarian people who engaged in occupations with culturally defined impurity had been associated with impurity, they did not constitute a cloistered social group or a unilinear descent group. In the late sixteenth century, however, they were placed in two caste groups and became stigmatized (Ohnuki-Tierney 1987; 1998).

Although, like India and neighbouring societies, the Japanese created scapegoats to carry the burden of impurity, at no point in history was there a social group of ritual specialists, equivalent to *brahmans*, in Japanese society. Instead, unlike Frazer's divine king, the emperor represented the principle of purity. The dual quality – purity and impurity – assigned to the king in the Frazerian model was assigned to 'strangers,' or a 'sacred monster' (see de Heusch in this volume). These stranger-deities came from outside the village and possessed both the positive/peaceful soul (*nigimitama*) and the negative/destructive soul (*aramitama*). The emperor as a shaman draws only the positive power from them for the benefit of the people. The Japanese emperor represents reproductive and productive power, just like the king of the Upper Nile whose power is positive, and relates to rain making and fertility, that is productive and reproductive capacities (see Simonse in this volume).

The Japanese emperors have never been 'divine' as in the Frazerian model. Briefly put, the God of the orthodox Judeo-Christian tradition, which provided the model for Frazer, is, in comparative perspective, uniquely sacred, as Redfield (1959 [1953]: 102) points out (for a detailed discussion of this point, see Ohnuki-Tierney 1991: 108–11). The imposition of the model of divine kingship on other societies therefore conceals, rather than elucidates, the nature of kingship in relation to the conception of the sacred in different cultures.

Despite radical transformations of the imperial system through time, what has remained constant, at least until recently, is the emperor's identity as a deity (*kami*), but only in a Japanese sense. The *kami* is radically different from the God of the ancient Hebrews. One example of this can be seen in relation to the warriors who stripped the emperors of their political power at the end of the ancient period, and demanded their own apotheosis. Thus, Toyotomi Hideyoshi, the military leader who succeeded in uniting Japan for the first time in 1590, asked the imperial court to deify him as Toyokuni Daimyōjin. His life as a deity was short-lived, however, and his descendants were unable to enjoy his divine status. Upon his death, his rival, Tokugawa Ieyasu, the most powerful of all shoguns, defeated the Toyotomi clan and ordered the imperial court to deny the divinity previously granted to Hideyoshi. In his will Ieyasu requested the imperial court to deify him as Tōshō Daigongen and his divinity became the bulwark of Shogunate power for the next 250 years (Inoue 1967: 258–9). Napoleon's self-glorification sounds quite innocent in contrast.

From the perspective of power, the hierarchy of beings in the universe consists of humans, shaman-emperors, and deities in ascending order. If we assume this hierarchy to be permanent and linear, then the orders by Hideyoshi and Ieyasu to the emperors to deify them constitute an inversion of this hierarchy. This means that these humans bestowed upon the emperor the extraordinary power to create deities out of mere humans. Likewise, the human architects of the imperial system during the Meiji period assigned themselves the power to create a bona fide deity out of an emperor. On the other hand, such inversions of the hierarchy are embedded in Japanese religions where the hierarchy of supernatural beings is neither fixed nor linear. Thus, in Japanese religion, an ordinary human can assign divinity even to a toothpick (Miyata 1975).

These individual instances expressing the dynamic characterization of the *kami* in Japanese religion are paralleled by the fluidity with which the Japanese adopted various foreign religions. When Buddhism was introduced from India via China and Korea, it was embraced eagerly by the elites, including the imperial family. But 'most people in Japan at that time [the sixth and the seventh centuries] probably thought of the Buddha as just another *kami*' (Kitagawa 1990: 136). Officially, the Japanese tried to reconcile the two religions by claiming that the *kami* are manifestations of the buddhas and bodhisattvas, a theory known as *honji suijaku*. With equal ease, the Tokugawa Japanese, especially the elites, adopted Neo-Confucianism with its emphasis on natural law and the Way of Heaven (Kitagawa 1990). Astonishing as it may be from the perspective of Western religions, the Meiji government concocted what Kitagawa (1990) has called 'non-religious Shintō' which was to be adhered to by every Japanese subject, regardless of his or her personal ' "religious" affiliation' (Kitagawa 1990: 161). Most Japanese today are at least nominally both Buddhist and Shintoist simultaneously, and usually without personal conviction (Ohnuki-Tierney 1984; 1991).[15] To understand Japanese religiosity is to abandon the false dichotomies of magic/religion, and primitive/civilized (modern). How else could one explain the profusion of what I call 'urban magic' among educated Japanese today?

If the Japanese have shown a fluid attitude towards individual deities as well as towards particular religious systems, they also did so in relation to both individual emperors and the imperial system. From the perspective of the Japanese common people, neither the emperor nor the imperial system is divine, if the term implies an ascription of absolute divinity to kingship.

The trials and tribulations of the Japanese imperial system since the end of the ancient period certainly do not indicate the presence of divine kingship in Frazer's sense. From the perspective of the people, individual emperors have always been *kami*. As with all other deities, they do not have almighty power, and are thus susceptible to human manipulation. Yet they are also capable of exercising power over humans (for historical and ethnographic details, see Ohnuki-Tierney 1991).

With the coming of the Meiji period and Japan's modernity, the emperor, a mere shaman in origin and one deity in a vast pantheon, acquired the status of Almighty God and warrior king. The Meiji oligarchs inverted de Maistre's famous proclamation 'Dieu fait les rois' (God makes kings) by making their emperor into God Almighty. But these changes only took place on paper, in the Constitution of Imperial Japan. Japanese 'secular religiosity' remained unchanged and the emperor on a white horse remained human.

Turning to the question of regicide and sacrifice, the classical model of sacrificial ritual developed by Robertson Smith (1972 [1889]) and Hubert and Mauss (1964 [1898]) – seen by some to be integral to kingly accession and divine kingship – has similar problems in cross-cultural perspective. In both the harvest ritual-cum-imperial accession ritual of *ōnamesai* and sacrifice, one sees the same basic theme of the exchange of the self. Purification and commensality are other common elements. On the other hand, the Japanese case does not involve atonement and other features found in the classical model of sacrifice. Most importantly, it differs radically in that animal sacrifice and violent death, either of the king himself or the sacrificial animal, are absent.

In order to provide a critique of the classical model and to place the Japanese case in comparative perspective, let me briefly discuss one major point, the use of plant food rather than animals in offerings. In the original model of sacrifice, an exclusive emphasis is placed on animals for two main reasons: the necessity of violent death and the provision of food for commensality. In the model of divine kingship (Frazer 1911: 15; Hubert and Mauss 1964 [1898]), a violent death, either of the sacrificial animal or in the form of regicide, is the most critical element since it is identified as the precondition of the rebirth of the divine king. Furthermore, animal food is considered as the only food appropriate for commensality following the sacrifice. Robertson Smith, a major architect of the theory of sacrifice, makes a critical distinction between animal sacrifice and an oblation consisting of cereals. Animal sacrifice, according to him, is essentially an act of communion between the god and his worshippers, whereas a cereal oblation is a tribute paid to the god. The animal victim thus becomes holy, requiring its parts to be consumed only by ceremonially clean individuals. The cereal oblation, on the other hand, makes the entire crop 'lawful', but not holy, thereby enabling anyone, clean or unclean, to freely consume it (Robertson Smith 1972 [1889]: 236–43). In fact, Robertson Smith (1972 [1889]: 242–3) relegates to a footnote a reference to Wilken who, on the basis of information provided by his friend Frazer states that: 'a true sacrificial feast is made of the first-fruits of rice' and the act is called 'eating the soul of rice' – which may imply 'killing' but not an act of 'blood sacrifice'.

In the Japanese case, instead of animals or the king himself being 'violently' sacrificed, rice – as the gift of self – occupies the central role and there is no concept of killing involved. Rice serves as the food for commensality. Far from being insignificant, among the Japanese rice is not just an offering to the gods for consecration; rather, every grain of rice *is* a deity. Rice consumption is not seen as violent death or killing the deities.[16] Thus the rebirth of the Japanese emperors is not predicated upon his violent death.

As with the rainmaker king of the Upper Nile (see Simonse in this volume), there was little reason for regicide. Why kill a king whose role is to guarantee good crops of rice and who is not a repository of impurity? Moreover, one of the most important principles concerning death among the Japanese, even in the twenty-first century, is that death should be natural, with the body intact (Ohnuki-Tierney 1994). They had no reason to kill the king if they wished for his rebirth in order to bless the rice crop.

At any rate, I think there are a range of interpretations about the animal and plant offerings, and 'killing' and 'violent death' are only some of them. What is most important is that violent death as the precondition of the rebirth of a new king cannot be seen as a universal theme.

To conclude, the key concepts proposed in the scholarly discussion of divine kingship help us understand the Japanese emperorship. Nonetheless, they do not come in a neat bundle. As Simonse argues in this volume, kingship covers a wide range of institutions and our deliberations must illuminate each case through the use of the concepts associated with divine kingship, rather than reducing every case to a single model.

Notes

1. For example, according to Macé (1985), there was a sharp break in the funeral ritual for emperors during the early eighth century. When the Empress Genmei (r. 707–15) died in 721, her body was cremated and buried one week after the funeral. This contrasts sharply with the funeral for the previous emperor, the Emperor Monmu (r. 697–707), after which the *mogari* ritual for mourning was performed for six months before his body was buried. The *mogari* was an elaborate mourning practice that lasted often several months to several years (Macé 1985: 58) during which a special hut was built in which to place the corpse, where funeral attendants (*asobibe*) – antecedent of the later 'outcaste' – entered with weapons to symbolically fight against the death. There is virtually no description of how the corpse was kept, but it seems to have been left to decay (Macé 1985: 58). The *mogari* mourning involved the sacrifice of horses and, possibly, of humans.

2. E.g. Akasaka 1988; Hora 1979, 1984; M. Inoue 1984; Miyata 1988: 190–4, 1989; Murakami 1977, 1986; Okada 1970; Yamaori 1978.

3. Clearly rice occupies a special place in the Japanese diet (Ohnuki-Tierney 1995). Although rice has never been the staple food in a quantitative sense for all Japanese, it has always been the food for ritual occasions. Yanagita (1982: 159–60) points out that of all grains rice alone is believed to have a soul and it alone requires ritual performances. In contrast, non-rice grains are called *zakkoku* (miscellaneous grains), a label that places them in a residual category.

4. While the *niinamesai* and the *ōnamesai* are almost identical, the *kannamesai* is a ritual in which a new crop of rice is offered to the Ise Shrine, rather than

at the Imperial Palace itself (Orikuchi 1975b: 183). For details of these imperial harvest rituals, see Miura 1988: 143; Murakami 1977: 13; Nihiname
Kenkyūkai, (ed.) 1955; Ohnuki-Tierney 1993: 44–98, 2002b; Orikuchi
1975b: 180–1; Sakurai 1988: 33; Tanaka (1988: 29); Ueda (1988: 32);
Yamamoto, Satō and staff, (eds) 1988: 224–31; Yokota 1988. For descriptions
of the imperial rituals in English, see Bock 1990, Ebersole 1989, Ellwood
1973, Holtom 1972, and Mayer 1991.

5. It is more common to refer to this ritual as *daijōsai* at present, although I use
   ōnamesai, which was the customary pronunciation for the same characters
   until recently. Its full name was *ōname matsuri* (reading all the characters in
   kun) or *ōnie matsuri* (see Bock 1990: 27). For the timing of this ritual, see
   Hida 1988: 214).

6. Historically, Seinei's existence has not been verified.

7. For interpretations of to whom the ritual was addressed, see Matsumae 1977:
   90–137; Murakami 1977: 19; Orikuchi 1975b: 178, 194; Saigō 1984: 87–90;
   Sakamoto *et al.* 1967: 554; Shimonaka 1941: 426; 1941b: 290, 332–3.

8. Saigō (1984: 78–80) stresses that Amaterasu is not 'hiding' in the 'cave', but
   that the act represents her ritual seclusion from the world in the *'iwaya'*,
   which means a building or structure, not a cave.

9. In the main text (*honbun*) and Sections 4 and 6 of Book 1 of the *Nihonshoki*,
   it is Takami Musubi, rather than Amaterasu, who sends the heavenly grandson
   Ho no Ninigi (Ninigi no Mikoto), to earth, wrapped in the *madoko ohusuma*
   (sacred bedding) (Matsumae 1977: 95–6).

10. For further discussions of the *marebito*, see Higo 1942: 103–4; Matsudaira
    1977; Ouwehand 1958–9; Suzuki 1974, 1979; Yamaguchi 1977; Yoshida
    1981. For the continuation of the *marebito* concept into the present day, see
    the incisive analyses of folk festivals in contemporary Japan by Higo (1942)
    and Matsudaira (1977).

11. Yanagita (1964 [1945]: 123–4) equates the *inadama* with the *soshin*
    (Ancestral Deity) who in turn is the *Ta no Kami* (Deity of the Rice Paddy).

12. Mauss's position on the nature of gift is not consistent, however, and vacillates
    between 'pure gifts' and quasi commodity.

13. The term *shinsei* consists of two characters: *shin* (deity) and *sei* (sacred). The
    kan (Chinese) pronunciation of these characters indicates that it is a relatively
    new term. Importantly, other than in the constitution, it is most often used in
    reference to events in the West that are 'holy,' such as the Holy War of ancient
    Greece, Holy Roman Empire, and the Holy Alliance of 1815 in Austria. The
    term *okasubekarazu* is also a relatively new term and remains somewhat alien
    to the Japanese even in the twenty-first century.

14. For a recent review of divine kingship and the related concepts of priestly king
    and magical king, see Feeley-Harnik (1985). See also de Heusch (1985);

Dumont (1970); Geertz (1980: 121–46); Sahlins (1985), and Tambiah (1976). Valeri (1985) uses the term 'diarchic kingship'.

15. Eisenstadt (1996) explains this phenomenon in terms of his scheme of Axial v. non-Axial religions; Kitagawa (1990) describes it as 'eclectic', others as 'multilayered', while still others see that various religions have been 'fused' (for details, see Ohnuki-Tierney 1984: 145–9).

16. In some agrarian societies, such as among the Balinese and Javanese, rice is reported to 'suffer the pain of severance' (van der Meer and van Stetten 1979: 111) when it is harvested. Whether this act is seen as an act of violence is not clear. The Javanese harvest ritual enacts the marriage of a daughter of the king of gods and her husband, both transformed into rice stalks (Geertz 1960: 81), but it is not connected with the kingly accession.

References

Akasaka, N. 1988. *Ōto Tennō* (King and emperor). Tokyo: Chikuma Shobō.

Amino, Y., Ueno C. and Miyata N. 1988. *Nihon Ōkenron* (Japanese kingship). Tokyo: Shunjūsha.

Bock, F. G. 1990. 'The Great Feast of the Enthronement', *Monumenta Nipponica* 45(1): 27–38.

Dumont, L. 1970 [1966]. *Homo Hierachicus*. Translated by M. Sainsbury from the original French. Chicago: University of Chicago Press.

Ebersole, G. L. 1989. *Ritual Poetry and the Politics of Death in Early Japan*. Princeton: Princeton University Press.

Ellwood, R. S. 1973. *The Feast of Kingship: Accession Ceremonies in Ancient Japan*. Tokyo: Sophia University Press.

Eisenstadt, S. N. 1996. *Japanese Civilization*. Chicago: University of Chicago Press.

Emura, E. ed. 1996. *Kenpō Kōsō* (Drafts for the constitution). *Nihon Kindai Shisō Taikei,* vol. 9. Iwanami Shoten.

Feeley-Harnik, G. 1985. 'Issues in Divine Kingship', *Annual Review of Anthropology* 14: 273–313.

Frazer, J. G. 1911–15. *The Golden Bough: A Study in Comparative Religion.* 12 vols. London: Macmillan.

Geertz, Clifford 1960. *The Religion of Java*. New York: Free Press.

—— 1980. *Negara: The Theatre State in Nineteenth-Century Bali*. Princeton: Princeton University Press.

Heusch, L. de 1985. *Sacrifice in Africa*. Bloomington, IN: Indiana University Press.

Hida, Y. 1988. 'Sokuirei to Ōnamesai no Kiso Chishiki' (Basic knowledge of the accession ritual and the *Ōnamesai*) in H. Yamamoto, M. Satō, and staff (eds),

Zusetsu Tennō no Sokuirei to Ōnamesai, pp. 212–23. Tokyo: Shinjinbutsu Ōraisha.

Higo, K. 1942. *Nihon Shinwa Kenkyū* (Research on Japanese myths). Tokyo: Kawade Shobō.

Hocart, A. M. 1969 [1927]. *Kingship.* Oxford: Oxford University Press.

—— 1970 [1936]. *Kings and Councilors: An Essay in the Comparative Anatomy of Human Society.* Chicago: University of Chicago Press.

Holtom, D. C. 1972 [1928]. *The Japanese Enthronement Ceremonies.* Tokyo: Monumenta Nipponica.

Hora, T. 1979. *Tennō Fushinsei no Kigen* (The origin of the apolitical nature of the emperor system). Tokyo: Azekura Shobō.

—— 1984. *Tennō Fushinsei no Dentō* (The tradition of the apolitical nature of the emperor system). Tokyo: Shinjusha.

Hubert, H. & Mauss, M. 1964 [1898]. *Sacrifice: Its Nature and Function.* Chicago: University of Chicago Press.

Inoue, K. 1967 [1963]. *Nihon no Rekishi* (History of Japan) vol. 1 (Jō). Tokyo: Iwanami Shoten.

Inoue, M. 1984. *Nihon Kodai Ōken to Saishi* (Kingship and ritual in ancient Japan). Tokyo: Tōkyō Daigaku Shuppankai.

Kantorowicz, E. H. 1981 [1957]. *The King's Two Bodies: A Study in Medieval Political Theology.* Princeton: Princeton University Press.

Kawasoe, Taketane. 1980. *Kojiki no Sekai* (The world of Kojiki). Tokyo: Kyō ikusha.

Kitagawa, J. M. 1990. 'Some Reflections on Japanese Religion and its Relationship to the Imperial System', *Japanese Journal of Religious Studies* 17(2–3): 129–78.

Kōshitsu Bunka Kenkyūkai (ed.) 1988. 'Ōnamesai – Yuki Sukiden no Shogi' (*Ōnamesai* – various rituals for the *Yuki* and *Suki* fields), in H. Yamamoto, M. Satō and staff (eds), *Zusetsu Tennō no Sokuirei to Ōnamesai,* pp. 88–95. Tokyo: Shinjinbutsu Ōraisha.

Kurabayashi, S. 1988. 'Ōnamesai no Henkaku' (Changes in the *Ōnamesai*), in H. Yamamoto, M. Satō and staff (eds), *Zusetsu Tennō no Sokuirei to Ōnamesai,* pp. 36–37. Tokyo: Shinjinbutsu Ōraisha.

Kurano, K. and Takeda. Y. 1958. *Kojiki Norito* (*Kojiki* and *Norito*). Tokyo: Iwanami Shoten.

Lévi-Strauss, C. 1969 [1949]. *The Elementary Structures of Kinship.* London: Eyre and Spottiswoode.

Macé, F. 1985. 'Genmei Dajō Tennō no Sōgi ga Imisuru Maisō Gireishijō no Damzetsuten' (A break in the history of funeral rituals as indicated by the funeral for the Empress Gemmej). *Shūkyō Kenkyū* 266: 55–77.

Matsudaira, N. 1977. *Matsuri: Honshitsu to Shosō – Kodaijin no Uchū* (Festivals:

Their Essence and Dimensions – The universe of the ancient Japanese). Tokyo: Asahi Shinbun.

Matsumae, T. 1977. *Nihon no Kamigami* (Japanese deities). Tokyo: Chūōkōronsha.

Mauss, M. 1966 [1950]. *The Gift: Forms and Functions of Exchange in Archaic Societies*. London: Cohen & West.

Mayes, A. C. 1991. 'Recent Succession Ceremonies of the Emperor of Japan', *Japan Review* 2: 35–61.

Meer, N. C. van der, van Setten 1979. *Sawah Cultivation in Ancient Java: Aspects of Development During the Indo-Javanese Period, 5th to 15th Century*. Canberra: Australian National University Press.

Miura, S. 1988. 'Tairei Seido no Enkaku' (Outline of the *Tairei* (imperial ritual) system). In Yamamoto, M. Satō and staff (eds), *Zusetsu Tennō no Sokurei to Ōnamesia*, pp. 142–6. Tokyo: Shinjinbutsu Ōraisha.

Miyata, N. 1975. *Kinsei no Hayarigami* (Popular deities during the early modern period). Tokyo: Hyōronsha.

—— 1988. *Rēkon no Minzokugaku* (Folklore of the soul). Tokyo: Nihon Editā Sukūru Shuppan.

—— 1989. 'Nihon Ōken no Minzokuteki Kiso' (The ethnographic basis of Japanese kingship). *Shikyō* 18: 25–30.

Murakami, S. 1977. *Tennō no Saishi* (Imperial rituals). Tokyo: Iwanami Shoten.

—— 1986. *Tennō to Nihon Bunka* (The emperor and Japanese culture). Tokyo: Kō dansha.

Nihiname Kenkyūkai (ed.) 1955. *Nihiname no Kenkyū* (Research on the *Nihiname*). Tokyo: Yoshikawa Kōbunkan.

Ohnuki-Tierney, E. 1984. *Illness and Culture in Contemporary Japan: An Anthropological View*. Cambridge: Cambridge University Press.

—— 1987. *The Monkey as Mirror: Symbolic Transformations in Japanese History and Ritual*. Princeton: Princeton University Press.

—— 1991. 'The Emperor of Japan as Deity (*Kami*): An Anthropology of the Imperial System in Historical Perspective', *Ethnology* xxx (3): 1–17.

—— 1993. *Rice as Self: Japanese Identities Through Time*. Princeton: Princeton University Press.

—— 1994. 'Brain Death and Organ Transplantation: Cultural Bases of Medical Technology', *Current Anthropology* 35(3): 233–54.

—— 1995. 'Structure, Event and Historical Metaphor: Rice and Identities in Japanese History. *Journal of the Royal Anthropological Institute* 30(2): 1–27.

—— 1998. 'A Conceptual Model for the Historical Relationship between the Self, and the Internal and External Others: The Agrarian Japanese, the Ainu, and the Special Status People', in D. Gladney (ed.) *Making Majorities*, pp. 31–51. Stanford: Stanford University Press.

—— 2002a. *Kamikaze, Cherry Blossoms, and Nationalisms: The Militarization of Aesthetics in Japanese History.* Chicago: University of Chicago Press.

—— 2002b. 'Ōnamesai to Ōken '(The Imperial accession ritual and kingship)', in Y. Amino, C. Ueno and N. Miyata (eds) *Ten'nō to Ōken wo Kangaeru* (The emperor and kingship), vol. 5, *Ōken to Girei* (Kingship and ritual), pp. 41–67. Tokyo: Iwanami Shoten.

Okada, S. 1970. *Kodai Ōken no Saishi to Shinwa* (The ritual and myth of the ancient emperor system). Tokyo: Hanawa Shōbō.

Orikuchi, S. 1965a [1924]. 'Marebito' ('Stranger'). *Orikuchi Shinobu Zenshū* (Collected works of Orikuchi Shinobu), vol. 1, pp. 78–82. Tokyo: Chūōkōronsha.

—— 1965b [1925]. '*Marebito* no Otozure' (Visits by Marebito). *Orikuchi Shinobu Zenshū* (Collected works of Orikuchi Shinobu), vol. 2, pp. 33–5. Tokyo: Chūōkōronsha.

—— 1975a [1928]. 'Shindō ni Arawareta Minzoku Ronri' (Ethnographic interpretation of Shintoism). *Orikuchi Shinobu Zenshū* (Collected work of Orikuchi Shinobu), vol. 3, pp. 145–73. Tokyo: Chūōkōronsha.

—— 1975b [1928]. 'Ōnamesai no Hongi' (The meaning of the *Ōnamesai*). *Orikuchi Shinobu Zenshū* (Collected work of Orikuchi Shinobu), vol. 3, pp. 174–240. Tokyo: Chūōkōronsha.

—— 1976a [1947]. 'Ijin to Bungaku' (The stranger and literature). *Orikuchi Shinobu Zenshū* (Collected Work of Orikuchi Shinobu), vol. 7, pp. 303–17. Tokyo: Chūōkōronsha.

—— 1976b [1933]. 'Kakinomoto Hitomaro' (Kakinomoto Hitomaro). *Orikuchi Shinobu Zenshū* (Collected work of Orikuchi Shinobu), vol. 9, pp. 461–93. Tokyo: Chūōkōronsha.

—— 1976c [1953]. 'Sanrei no Shinkō' (The belief in the deities of reproduction). *Orikuchi Shinobu Zenshū* (Collected work of Orikuchi Shinobu), vol. 20, pp. 253–60. Tokyo: Chūōkōronsha.

—— 1983 [1947]. 'Matsuri no Hanashi.' *Orikuchi Shinobu Zenshū* (Collected work of Orikuchi Shinobu), vol. 15, pp. 271–80. Tokyo: Chūōkōronsha.

Ouwehand, C. 1958–9. 'Some Notes on the God Susano-o', *Monumenta Nipponica* 14 (3–4): 138–61.

Ray, B. C. 1991. *Myth, Ritual, and Kingship in Buganda.* Oxford: Oxford University Press.

Redfield, R. 1959 [1953]. *The Primitive World and Its Transformations.* Ithaca, NY: Cornell University Press.

Robertson Smith, W. 1972 [1889]. *The Religion of the Semites.* New York: Schoken Books.

Sahlins, M. 1985. *Islands of History.* Chicago: University of Chicago Press.

Saigō, N. 1984 [1967]. *Kojiki no Sekai* (The world of the *Kojiki*). Tokyo: Iwanami Shoten.

Sakamoto, T. Ienaga, S., Inoue, M. and Ōno, S. 1967. '*Nihonshoki* (Jō)'. Vol. 1 of *Nihonshoki*, Tokyo: Iwanamai Shoten.

Sakurai, K. 1988. 'Ōnamesai to Kannamesai' (*Ōnamesai* and *Kannamesai*), in H. Yamamoto, M. Satō and staff (eds) *Zesetsu Tennō no Sokwirei to Ōnamesai*, pp. 32–4. Tokyo: Shinjinbutsu Ōraisha.

Satomi, K. 1972. *Tennō-hō no Kenkyū* (Research on the laws of the emperor system). Tokyo: Kinseisha.

Shimonaka, Y. 1941. *Shindō Daijiten* (Comprehensive dictionary of Shintoism), vol. 3. Tokyo: Heibonsha.

Smith, T. C. 1959. *The Agrarian Origins of Modern Japan*. Stanford: Stanford University Press.

Suzuki, M. 1974. *Marebito no Kōzō* (The structure of the 'Stranger'). Tokyo: Sanichi Shobō.

—— 1979. *Marebito* (The stranger), in Saurai Tokutarō, ed. *Kōza Nihon no Minzoku* (Folk cultures of Japan), vol. 7, *Shinkō* (Belief systems), pp. 211–39. Tokyo: Yūseidō Shuppan.

Tambiah, S. J. 1976. *World Conqueror and World Renouncer: A Study of Buddhism and Polity in Thailand Against a Historical Background*. Cambridge: Cambridge University Press.

—— 1985. *Culture, Thought and Social Action: An Anthropological Perspective*. Cambridge, MA: Harvard University Press.

Tanaka, T. 1988. 'Niiname' kara 'Ōname' e (From the *Niiname* to the *Ōname*), in H. Yamamoto, M. Satō and staff (eds), *Zesetsu Tennō no Sokuirei to Ōnamesai*, pp. 28–30. Tokyo: Shinjinbutsu Ōraisha.

Ueda, K. 1988. Ōnamesai Seiritsu no Haikei (The background of the establishment of the *Ōnamesai*), in H. Yamamoto, M. Satō and staff (eds) *Zesetsu Tennō no Sokwirei to Ōnamesai*, pp. 31–2. Tokyo: Shinjinbutsu Ōraisha.

Valeri, V. 1985. *Kingship and Sacrifice: Ritual and Society in Ancient Hawaii*. Chicago: University of Chicago Press.

Waida, M. 1975. 'Sacred kingship in Early Japan: A Historical Introduction', *History of Religions* 15(1): 319–42.

Yamaguchi, M. 1977. 'Kingship, Theatricality, and Marginal Reality in Japan', in R. K. Jain (ed.) *Text and Context: The Social Anthropology of Tradition*. Philadephia: ISHI, pp. 151–79.

Yamamoto, H., Satō, M. and staff (eds) 1988. *Zusetsu Tennō no Sokuirei to Ōnamesai* (Illustrated account of the imperial accession and the *Ōnamesai*). Tokyo: Shinjinbutsu Ōraisha.

Yamaori, T. 1978. *Tennō no Shūkyōteki Keni towa Nanika* (What is the religious power of the emperor?). Tokyo: Sanichi Shobō.

—— 1990a. '*Kakureta Tennōrei Keizoku no Dorama: Daijōsai no Bunka Hikaku*' (A hidden drama of the succession of the Imperial soul: cultural comparison of the *Daijōi*), *Gekkan Asahi*, February 1990: 80–5.

—— 1990b. *Shi no Minzokugaku* (Folklore of death). Tokyo: Iwanami Shoten.

Yanagita, K. 1964 [1945]. 'Sosen no Hanashi' (About the ancestor). *Yanagita Kunioshū* (Collected works of Yanagita Kunio), vol. 10, pp. 1–152. Tokyo: Chikuma Shobō.

—— 1981 [1953]. 'Ine no Sanya' (Parturition hut for rice). *Yanagita Kunioshū*, vol. 1, pp. 178–209. Tokyo: Chikuma Shobō.

—— 1982 [1940]. 'Kome no Chikara' (Power of rice). *Yanagita Kunioshū*, vol. 14, pp. 240–258. Tokyo: Chikuma Shobō.

—— 1982 [1949]. 'Fuji to Tsukuba' (Mt Fuji and Mt Tsukuba). *Yanagita Kunioshū*, vol. 31, pp. 129–39. Tokyo: Chikuma Shobō.

—— 1982 'Kura Inadama Kō' (Thoughts on the soul of rice). *Yanagita Kunioshū*, vol. 31, pp. 159–66. Tokyo: Chikuma Shobō.

Yanagita, K. (ed.) 1951. *Minzokugaku Jiten* (Ethnographic dictionary). Tokyo: Tōkyōdō.

Yoshida, T. 1981. 'The Stranger as God: The Place of the Outsider in Japanese Folk Religion', *Ethnology* 20(2): 87–99.

Yoshino, H. 1986. *Daijōsai – Tennō Sokuishiki no Kōzō* (The *Daijōsaki* – the structure of the imperial accession ritual). Tokyo: Kōbundō.

–12–

Chiefs and Kings in Polynesia

Henri J. M. Claessen

Introduction

There exists an extraordinarily rich literature on traditional kingship, and anthropologists as well as historians have contributed their fair share to this extensive library. Historians and anthropologists approach kingship from rather divergent theoretical backgrounds, however, and base themselves on different sources. Historians, it seems, are interested mainly in particular cases and apply theory only when it is helpful for a better understanding of their particular cases – they are 'ethnographers' rather than 'ethnologists'. Anthropologists are reputed to have much greater interest in theoretical matters and comparisons, and are not averse to developing large, often speculative, global constructs – which is not to say that anthropologists are afraid to study particular kingships in detail. Fortunately, in recent years the situation has changed. Anthropologists are no longer as uninterested in history as they were, and historians have become interested in comparative research. These developments make possible mutual understanding and the exchange of results. Nevertheless it remains difficult to formulate frames of reference that are acceptable and understandable to both parties (Sancisi-Weerdenburg 1995). Agreed definitions can be helpful in moving this dialogue forward, for then at least it becomes clear what we are talking about.

Kingship is a key concept that we need to define, but this is difficult because the word 'king' conveys a wide variety of meanings. The 'King of Swing' was a famous musician, and the 'king of diamonds' is a playing card. In fairytales and musicals kings and queens often play a crucial role. In these the king carries a sword and a sceptre, wears a robe lined with ermine and has a crown on his head. Some kings were wise as Solomon, others were villainous tyrants who would 'trade their kingdom for a horse' and again others were killed in the bath by their queen. In short, the king is a larger than life figure – and not only because in many cases he has the hands of a healer, as in *The Lord of the Rings* (Tolkien 1966: 1129, 1133). Let us begin with the most basic definition: 'king' refers in the first place to the ruler of a kingdom.

Taking this as our point of departure, we can say that – whatever symbols and rituals are found in connection with kings – a king is in the first place a ruler, a specific type of ruler, distinguishable from a chief or headman on the one hand, and a president on the other. It remains to be seen if it also makes sense to distinguish between a king and an emperor. We know of several rulers who were called emperor, including Napoleon, Charlemagne and Nero. Some emperors, such as the Ethiopian rulers, claimed to be 'King of Kings', a pretension also found with German and Austrian Kaisers. There seems to be no reason to consider 'emperor' as qualitatively different from 'king', however, despite such claims. A definition of king, then, might be: supreme, hereditary ruler of an independent stratified society, having the legitimate power to enforce decisions (Claessen 1986: 113).

According to this definition, the distinction between headman and chief on the one hand and king on the other can be readily established: headmen or chiefs do not have the legitimate right to enforce decisions, even though they sometimes do (Service 1975: 16).[1] The distinction between king and president is equally clear: a president is elected, heredity does not play a role. I will return presently to the matter of heredity. The definition enables us to follow Oosten (1981, 1996) in disconnecting kingship from the territorial state. The Germanic kings he described fit this definition, although they had not by that time settled in a specific territory.[2] This tallies with the views of Thapar (1984: 116), who, discussing the formation of the state in early India, states that the development of kingship does not in itself constitute the arrival of the state. The latter requires a number of features of which kingship is only one.

Thus kingship is, or was, a specific type of sociopolitical leadership, distinguishable from chiefship or presidency. But this conclusion leaves important questions unanswered. How did kingship arise? What is the nature of the king's position? How did a king acquire legitimacy? Where did his power to enforce decisions come from? To discuss such questions in a general way would demand a lengthy essay in which various developments in various parts of the world and in different periods of time could be compared and discussed. In Frazer's time, a one volume presentation was perhaps possible, as appears from his *Lectures on the Early History of the Kingship* (1905), but in his more general work, *The Golden Bough*, which started in 1890 with three volumes and ended in 1925 with no less than twelve, he succeeded to solve only one mystery of kingship (Voget 1975). Limitation is inevitable if I am to discuss the aspects of kingship mentioned above in one chapter. I will therefore focus on Polynesia where a wide variety of headmen, chiefs and kings once existed.

Polynesia

Polynesia comprises the islands lying within the triangle formed by the Hawaiian Islands, Easter Island and New Zealand in the Pacific Ocean. The beginnings of Polynesian culture go back about 2,500 years, when a small number of people, carriers of the so-called Lapita culture, left the islands of Melanesia, where they had lived for a thousand years or so (Kirch 1997), and settled on the Samoan and Tongan Islands in the west of the Pacific Ocean. Here, in isolation, they developed the so-called Ancestral Polynesian Culture which spread from there over most of the archipelagos and islands in the Pacific in a few hundred years.[3] Kirch and Green (2001) used archaeological, linguistic and ethnographic data to reconstruct this Ancestral Polynesian Culture in great detail. Their research makes it clear that from its very beginning Polynesian sociopolitical organization was hierarchically structured. The hierarchy was rooted in the kinship system, in which a number of families (lineages) formed a closely connected whole, usually called a ramage. From the very beginning there was a kind of ranking in and among the families. The oldest one was considered as having the highest status. The leader of this family, the oldest male, was called the *ariki*. He fulfilled the ritual and political tasks for the whole group. His position was hereditary, with the eldest son normally succeeding to his father's position. It was believed that this eldest line (the first-born line) traced its descent back to the world of the gods. The ramage would later allow its branches to retain their genealogical interrelations, thus facilitating the formation of larger political units under the leadership of a ranking chief (Kirch 1984: 66). As long as the social units remained small, the tasks of the leader were limited, and mainly of a ritual nature. From the very beginning, then, the concept of the ramage structured the Polynesian societies along hierarchical lines, and the sacredness of the chiefs gave the structure its legitimacy.

The ramage can be defined as a non-exogamous, internally stratified, unilineal (usually patrilineal) descent group.[4] Distance from the senior line of descent from a common (often mythical) ancestor is the criterion for stratification. Succession in the ramage was determined by primogeniture. Problems could arise if the eldest child was a daughter. Usually she was married off to some high-born elsewhere, where she then often played a powerful political role.[5] Within every family brothers and sisters were ranked according to their birth order and this rank was then inherited by their own descendants. Goldman (1970: 20–8) found that the unilineal ramage structure became combined with a non-unilineal principle at a certain moment which meant that people could reckon their descent either along their father's or mother's patriline. This made it possible to include in one's own genealogy highly placed forefathers from both sides to bolster one's claims with regard to hereditary positions. The person with the highest status among otherwise comparable lineage members would then succeed. In this way the rather rigid ramage structure became somewhat more flexible. It seems that this addition only developed after some time, when the rigidity of the system became a burden, and as the prizes to compete for became increasingly attractive.

Recently Thomas (1990: 28–33) has elaborated the ideological background of the ramage system (see Claessen 2000b). As a point of departure he took the position of the *ariki*. The fact that it was firmly believed that the first-born lines traced their ancestry back to the gods or spirits meant that principal gods, spirits, or ancestors were linked in a direct way with the first-born line and only in an indirect way with the rest of the society. Thus access on the part of commoners to the main deities was mediated by the chiefly lines (Thomas 1990: 29). Although in most cases the *ariki* was the first-born male, females who were chiefs in their own right have also been known in Polynesia, for example on Hawai'i (Cook 1967: 578, 599, 1244; Valeri 1985: 167). On Tahiti royal consorts sometimes ruled over a polity instead of their *ariki*-husband (see note 5) and Tonga also witnessed politically powerful women (Campbell 1992: 40–2; Douaire-Marsaudon 1998).

Thomas relates the high position of the *ariki* to the connection he discerns between food production and the ritual activities of the chief in relation to specific ancestors or gods. Without chiefly intervention, all the physical work expended to produce food would be insufficient. This belief became associated with a flow of goods toward the chief (1990: 31). According to Thomas this gift-giving entailed no reciprocal obligations on the part of the chief. At this point, however, ethnographic facts contradict Thomas's otherwise excellent model. Because of increasing population density Marquesan chiefs were no longer able to 'produce' fertility and as a consequence they lost their position (Thomas 1990: 178; Van Bakel 1989; Kirch 1991). The rulers of Wallis and Futuna ran the same risk (Douaire-Marsaudon 1998: 101, 113), and there are reasons to believe that the *ariki* of Rapa Nui (Easter Island) also lost their position because of hunger and poverty on their resources-depleted island (Van Tilburg 1994; McCoy 1979).

Marcus (1989) has analysed the position of the Polynesian *ariki* in a slightly different way. He argues that two aspects are connected with the chiefly office, a 'kingly' and a 'populist' one. The kingly aspect highlighted his ritual character and the exclusive nature of his position: here he is represented as a being of a different order. The populist aspect highlighted inclusion, accountability as an ordinary person and the chief's role as an active embodiment of power (1989: 178). These two aspects are found to play a role in all cases, though with different emphases. Much of Marcus's analysis is persuasive, but I take issue with his use of the terms 'kingly' and populist'. The distinction to which he refers has more to do with the difference between the sacred (or ritual), and the political aspects of chieftainship, and the terms 'kingly' and 'populist' create confusion instead of clarity (for elaboration on this point, see Claessen 1996, note 4).

The data presented thus far enable us to conclude that Polynesian political ideology comprised at least two components: a religious one (the sacred descent of the chiefly lines) and a kinship one (the ramage structure), according to which everybody's place in society was determined by primogeniture and seniority. These closely connected components provided the basis for the hierarchical sociopolitical structure of the Polynesians, and gave it its legitimacy. Conceptually, the chief was the first-born of the eldest line, and everybody else had a lower place in the hierarchy. This made his political position 'legal'. He was considered sacred because of his assumed descent from divine ancestors. His sacredness implied that he could guarantee fertility, and because of that he was entitled to the flow of goods that was handed over to him by his people (Claessen 1996: 343–4).[6] Let us now see how this general model was realized in the different archipelagos, for on this basis large political hierarchies were formed on some islands, and simple structures on others.

Case Studies

The least developed sociopolitical structures are found on the smallest islands.[7] Many of these are atolls with a surface of only a few square kilometers. Examples are Raroia (Danielsson 1956) in the Tuamotu archipelago in East Polynesia and the Tokelau atolls (Huntsman and Hooper 1996) in West Polynesia. Despite their small populations (respectively 116 on Raroia and some 1,600 people on the three Tokelau atolls together), they produced sociopolitical leaders who based their position on birthright, sex, relative age and lineal descent. Their actual power was limited, and there were few tasks for them to fulfill.

A council of family heads existed in Raroia, and it is reported that the chief made his decisions only after having listened to the council. This chief was a descendant of the first family that settled on Raroia, and boasted a long line of forefathers that either had its origin in the world of the gods, or in a person who lived in Hawaiki, the imagined homeland of the Polynesians. The chief led important religious ceremonies himself, but sometimes a relative acted as a priest (Danielsson 1956: 45). In the Tokelaus the situation varied from one atoll to another. The *aliki*, the ruler of the island and priest of the supreme god, lived on Fakaofa, the main atoll. His genealogy went back to one of the founder spirits of the world (Huntsman and Hooper 1996: 155). The *aliki* was chosen from among the mature men of his *kaiga* (lineage). He controlled the gathering and distribution of a number of valued foods, and only at his death was the planting of coconuts allowed. This connected the *aliki* with land and fertility. He was also the sole priest of the principal god; priests of lesser gods were recruited from sororal lines (Huntsman and Hooper 1996: 158). Apart from the sacred chief there was a second in command who was entrusted with civil matters (Huntsman and Hooper 1996: 160). The nearby atoll of Nukunonu was once conquered by people of Fakaofa who established a new sociopolitical organization there which divided the atoll among several lineages. Yet the traditional *aliki* lineage of Nukunonu succeeded in maintaining a position of some ceremonial and administrative importance (Huntsman and Hooper 1996: 166–7). The third atoll, Atafu, was settled around the year 1800 from the two others, and several small, separate lineages inhabit the island.

Looking at the high islands of the Marquesas, a different picture emerges.[8] The archipelago consists of ten small, fairly inaccessible islands (together about 1,000 sq km with 50,000 inhabitants) on which sheer mountains cut off the valleys from each other. Each of the valleys was inhabited by an almost autonomous ramage ('tribe') led by a sacred chief who was the most senior descendant of the 'oldest' family group.[9] His genealogical relations were traced back to the deities, so that the chief was the intermediary between the gods and the people. Because of this, he was connected with fertility and food production. The food situation in the Marquesas, however, was poor. There was little arable land and the cultivation of *taro* was difficult. The chief source of food was the breadfruit tree. Only a very small surplus was produced and this led to a limitation in the number of specialists, who were for the most part dependent on food produced by other people. The political position of the chief was weak; other landholders in the valley enjoyed only a little less prestige. Because of the limited surplus production, the chief received only small gifts from his people. Therefore opportunities to distribute food and gifts to achieve a higher status were limited. His main prerogative was the right to declare something *tapu*, which made it untouchable for other people. This right was only exercised occasionally. Because of the inaccessibility of the valleys, warfare was endemic. This featured raids in which each side tried to destroy the other's bread fruit trees. Because of the repeated destruction of the trees, and the fact that the Marquesas were frequently afflicted by drought and subsequent famines, the chiefs could not live up to the people's expectations that they would use their sacred powers to guarantee safety, fertility and prosperity. And so, as time went on, people lost their faith in the sacred leaders. As a consequence the chiefs lost their ritual status to lower ranking religious leaders, and their political status ebbed away to militant small-scale land owners, who built up a sort of big man position. As they became war leaders, they created the disturbed society, characterized by never-ending hostilities, that was described by their European discoverers.

The Samoa archipelago consists of nine islands, some large (Savai'i 1,707 sq km Upolu 868 sq km), some small (Ofu 23 sq km, and Manono 8 sq km).[10] Despite the fact that the soil is fertile and the climate benign, the size of the population remains substantially below what the archipelago could sustain. No satisfactory answer has been found to explain this. Because of the limited size of the population – and thus the lack of population pressure – the development of the sociopolitical organization followed a different course than on other Polynesian islands.[11] In the Samoa Islands, in practice the highest level of organization was the household group. Its leader, the lineage elder, bore the title of *matai*. His status was high but his power was restricted. He could only reach a decision when he had the consent of all the members of the group. Most of the resulting regulations concerned normal household activities. The same situation was also found at the village level. Here the *matai* of the senior lineage of the village was the village chief, but he was in fact no more than the chairman of the village council. Decisions were only taken when all members reached consensus. In this respect his position was even weaker than that of the headman of Raroia. The same decision-making procedure was followed in higher order councils. This resulted in a weak political structure on the Samoan islands. However, Tcherkézoff (1997) believes that at least in some districts the power of the chiefs was greater than is generally assumed. He connects this with the fact that competition for titles sometimes led to war, and that successful war chiefs gained much power and prestige. This is certainly true.

On the other hand, we also find evidence of weak political structure. Van Bakel (1989) connects this to great individual freedom on the islands. Every Samoan could consider him or herself to be a member of various family groups. When a person did not agree with what was decided in the village, he or she could go to another village and be received there with open arms because of the shortage of people on the Samoan islands. Even within this very loose structure one can identify the same ideas about hierarchical ramage as elsewhere in Polynesia. The strong position of chiefs, based on their alleged influence on fertility and well-being was not, however, realized here. As there was an abundance of good soil, and a benign climate, production of food hardly depended upon the intercession of the sacred chiefs with the gods or ancestors, and thus their power and influence was weakly developed (except, as stated above, when war played a role).This is not to say that titles were not appreciated. Men eagerly tried to acquire some title or other, and most men eventually succeeded in getting a titled position. But, in view of the ease with which their subjects could escape force or obligations, the title holders might well enjoy great prestige, but virtually no power.

Tahiti is one of the islands in which kingship, in the sense of the definition above, emerged.[12] The island is about 1,000 sq km, and about 35,000 people lived there at the time of discovery by the Europeans. From a first settlement in the Vaiari district in the fourth century CE, people gradually dispersed along the coast of the island, the mountainous interior being too difficult to penetrate. In accordance with ramage ideology, it was mainly junior branches of the original ramage that migrated. Ritually they remained bound to the senior branch in Vaiari, and in this way a bond between the emerging separate chiefdoms remained intact. A dilemma for ambitious *ari'i* of the new units was posed by marriage. A man's status was determined by the rank of his mother, so one aspiration was to marry women of high rank. However, a leader could often reinforce his political power more effectually by marrying girls of lower status who came from large families. In most cases, though, men preferred to marry high-born women. Population growth led to a strengthening of the sociopolitical hierarchy (cf. Johnson 1982; Claessen 2000a). The gap between higher and lower ramage members steadily expanded and social differences within the once cohesive kinship groups grew. This brought about the formation of groups of nobles (*ari'i*), of small-scale landowners (*raatira*), and of the lowest members of society (*manahune*). Many of the poor *manahune* chose to surrender their independence and to work on the land of the nobles. The continuous population growth and the mounting tensions this brought in its train served to make the position of a number of political leaders even stronger. As a result, several early states came into existence.[13] The production of foodstuffs was more than sufficient to allow for the existence of complex social and religious structures.

Ruling even these mini states seems to have made it difficult for an *ari'i rahi* (great *ari'i*) to combine his political and ritual obligations. This led to the custom whereby a ruler abdicated as soon as a (legitimate) son was born to him, handing over all his ritual obligations to the baby. He then continued to rule as 'regent', without being impeded by the ritual duties. This was facilitated by the custom of making a brother or an uncle responsible – as a kind of high priest – for a number of priestly duties, including the care for the many temples and offerings. To enforce his decisions the *ari'i rahi* had a number of armed servants, who were never afraid of beating a culprit, or of plundering his house or lands. The judicial system was relatively simple. Most rules and regulations pertained to family matters, and lack of respect for, or neglect of, these rules were corrected or punished by the family heads. In cases of theft or adultery the reactions appear to have been severe, for when the culprit was caught in the act he could be killed by the injured party. However, it is doubtful that such killings happened frequently (Oliver 1974, II: 1058). Chiefs hardly ever interfered in their subjects' quarrels. But in cases of lèse majesté or the infraction of chiefly rights they acted immediately and ruthlessly. The most radical means of disposing of an offender was to select him as a human sacrifice to the god Oro. Such offerings have been witnessed by European visitors (e.g. Cook 1967: 204, 217, 218–20).

The Tahitian *ari'i rahi* sometimes issued decisions regarding the whole population of their princedom. Such decisions were issued only after lengthy discussions with councillors, and were proclaimed all over the country by special messengers. The most important of such laws – for such royal decrees can indeed be considered as real laws – was the *rahui* (Claessen 1978: 460–2; Oliver 1974, II: 632–4). This was a prohibition or restriction laid on hogs, fruit, land etc. by a king or chief who was capable of enforcing it physically. Many European visitors suffered from the consequences of *rahui*s on hogs. Yet, such measures were inevitable at times, if only to restore the depleted stock after selling too many hogs to foreigners. Despite marriages between the ruling families, relations between the Tahitian polities were tense.

The situation became even more complicated at the beginning of the eighteenth century when the Oro religion from the neighbouring island of Raiatea was adopted. Possession of an original Oro image, plus a red or yellow feather belt connected with this god, played a crucial role, for possession of these holy objects gave a ruler the right to make human sacrifices. These sacrifices were essential to win the help of Oro, the god of fertility and war, and bitter conflicts broke out over the right to stage them. Following the introduction of the Oro cult, the connection of *ari'i* with the traditional gods or ancestors was no longer emphasized. From that time the establishment of a link with this new god became a matter of the highest importance (Claessen 2000b: 729).

Shortly after the discovery of Tahiti, missionaries and traders came in great numbers and under their influence traditional Tahitian culture soon began to disappear.

The Tonga Islands of West Polynesia belong to the oldest inhabited Polynesian islands, for already about 2,000 years ago the first settlers (then still Lapita people) arrived there (cf. Kirch and Green 2001).[14] Tongan society was also based on the concepts of sacred chieftainship and the ramage. In contrast to Tahiti, however, an early state developed there, embracing several archipelagoes and islands. These were administered by a central government at Tongatapu, while the outward districts and islands were run by appointed governors. It seems likely that the Tongans used 'strategic marriages' to build their large state (Bott 1981), although the possibility that they acquired the land through wars of conquest cannot be discounted.[15] The position of a governor was usually strongly contested by the members of the nobility from whose ranks the governor would be appointed, while also within the governmental centre different views were sometimes held regarding the candidates.

Traditional history relates that long ago a beautiful Tongan girl gave birth to a son, Aho'eitu, whose father was the god Tangaloa. This Aho'eitu is said to have been the first *tui tonga* – the sacred king. Douaire-Marsaudon (1998) relates another myth according to which Aho'eitu was made a deity by his divine father.

It has been argued that the twenty-fourth *tui tonga* was the one who fundamentally reformed Tongan political organization by delegating his political authority to a younger brother – who was given the title of *tui haa takalaua* – while retaining the sacred authority for himself. There are reasons, however, for interpreting these events slightly differently. The political activities of this *tui tonga* caused great resistance, and he fled (or was exiled) to Samoa, where he, and his immediate successors, remained for many years. His efforts to regain influence in the Vava'u Islands, which belonged to the kingdom, were repulsed, and the ruler finally had to accept the loss of his political power to the, by that time, very powerful family of the *tui haa takalaua,* the descendants of his younger brother (Campbell 1992: 15–17). He was then allowed to return. After his return from Samoa there was some reconciliation between the two competing lines and this resulted in marriages between a daughter of the *tui haa takalaua* and a son of the *tui tonga.* In these marriages the *haa takalaua* bride became the principal wife of the *tui tonga,* and mother of the successor; she was designated *moheofo* – the Great Wife (Campbell 1992: 19).

In this arrangement the highest social and religious rank was held by the *tui tonga,* but the political power lay with the *tui haa takalaua.* Yet some important political prerogatives remained with the king and among these was the right to the *inasi.* This was the ceremonial presentation of enormous quantities of food to the *tui tonga.* The organization of the *inasi* was the duty of the *tui haa takalaua.* He informed the chiefs all over the kingdom of their obligations which were often felt to be very heavy. The underlying idea was the offering of first fruits by the *tui tonga* to the gods and ancestors. The aim was to secure a bountiful harvest and the welfare of the country and the people. After the ceremony the greater part of the offerings was divided among the notables, who in turn handed out the food to their followers. It is clear that this ceremony had important political as well as religious significance (Bott 1982: 46).

At the beginning of the seventeenth century the *tui haa takalaua* in his turn appointed one of his sons as his hereditary deputy, with the title of *tui kanokopulu.* In this case too the appointment had been inevitable: it was the consequence of the emergence of a new powerful line. In the years that followed, the new line took over most of the positions previously held by the *haa takalaua.* Despite being confined to the sacred aspects of his function, the *tui tonga*'s exalted status remained unassailable for quite some time. This comes to the fore not only in the *inasi* and his right to declare things *tapu* (taboo), but also in the fact that it was the *tui tonga* who legitimized the position of all other dignitaries.

At the beginning of the eighteenth century more formalized positions were created for the *tui tonga fefine,* the eldest sister of the *tui tonga,* and her children. These new positions may have been intended to form a kind of counterweight to the increasing powers of the secular political leaders (cf. Campbell 1992: 20). In the Tongan social system precedence of rank was given to daughters above sons. This status difference continued after marriage. This situation required that in the case of the *tui tonga,* precautions had to be taken to protect him against political domination by his eldest sister, while at the same time raising her to a formally high rank. The solution was found by having her married to a foreigner (a Fijian), a marriage which prevented her children from holding political office in Tonga. They retained, however, their social preeminence over the ruler. The daughter of the *tui tonga fefine* married the son of the *tui kanokupolu.* In this way the circle between the three noblest lines was closed (for details, see Claessen 1988: 438–41).

At the end of the eighteenth century, Paulaho, the then *tui tonga*, made an effort to regain his former position, but he lost the ensuing civil war and went into exile. The *tui haa takalaua* line died out, and all power became concentrated in the hands of the *tui kanokopulu*. The ramage structure had become affected heavily by the many 'strategic marriages'. The kinship relations between a local chief and his followers that had once existed had disappeared, and foreigners ruled over the villages instead of members of the kin group of the chief. In the end, kinship ties between the local groups and the ruling elite no longer existed. The ramage had broken down; only obligations to the leaders remained.

As in the other islands, the arrival of European sailors, missionaries and traders brought an end to the traditional culture. In the Tongan Islands, however, a kind of independent kingdom continued to exist, ruled by the descendants of the *tui kanokupulu*, but under the watchful eyes of the British.

Discussion

The Polynesian data make it possible to formulate some tentative conclusions regarding kingship. In the first place, kings, or kinglike figures, were not found in the small island societies. These islands had small populations and, except for some ritual activities, there were no tasks for which a leader was needed. Instead there were only small headmen, and they had limited authority and negligible income. The situation on the larger Marquesas and Samoa Islands differed only marginally from the atolls. One did not find kings there either, though the size of the islands and their large populations might have made kingship possible. In the Marquesas Islands the population was divided over a number of separate valleys, and each of the valleys had its own chief. The various tribes were constantly at war with each other. Soil and climate conditions were too poor to produce much if any surplus. Moreover, during the incessant wars many of the bread fruit trees, which were the main source of food, were destroyed. Small wonder that the chiefs could not live up to their people's expectations that they would procure fertility and well-being. Their failure to do so led to their abolition. The Samoan case is more or less the mirror image of the Marquesas: a low population density and abundant food production made the emergence of a complex, well-functioning sociopolitical system unnecessary. In practice, authority was limited to the village chief, and even he had hardly any power to speak of. A more encompassing hierarchical system of rank existed in theory, but in actuality it barely functioned.

Only Tahiti and the Tongan Islands produced functionaries one might call kings. This type of dignitary was also found in the Hawaiian Islands, which I have left out of consideration for the sake of brevity. Several of the Tahitian sociopolitical leaders fulfilled the requirements of the definition formulated at the beginning of this paper: they were the supreme, hereditary rulers of independent stratified societies and had the legitimate power to enforce decisions. Their legitimation was based upon the ideology of the ramage: they descended from the gods and had succeeded each other in a direct line of first born sons. Because of this descent they had a direct connection with the gods and ancestors, and hence they could influence fertility and well-being. This ideal situation was not always realized. There were sometimes departures from the norm; the successor was not always a first-born son, nor were the *ari'i* always successful in procuring fertility. There have been changes of lineages – but priests and other knowledgeable people could always explain that such changes were wholly in conformity with the traditional norms and rules, so that people had nothing to fear.[16]

On the Tongan Islands the ideal situation of kingship lasted for several centuries. There was one supreme ruler who was backed by long genealogies that connected him with the gods. He was sacred, guaranteed fertility and well-being, and handed out rewards and punishments. Assisted by a number of functionaries, he ruled over a large early state. Only when the *tui tonga* lost the political aspect of his position to a junior line did problems arise. Yet, for quite some time he succeeded in maintaining his exalted status as sacred ruler, and the *inasi* ceremony showed that his worldly powers were not completely lost. In the end, however, the *tui tonga*, and the competing *tui haa takalaua* line had to give way to the aggressive line of the *tui kanokupolu* who succeeded in establishing a new type of kingship, backed by missionaries and colonial administrators.

There are several additional remarks to make. The Polynesian cases indicate that the development of kingship (whether or not in connection with the development of an early state) is a matter of sociopolitical scale. In small-scale societies no rulers who can be called kings emerge. A certain density of population is necessary to fulfill the many functions and jobs connected with a more complex hierarchical structure. There must also be surplus production to 'finance' the sociopolitical organization. Insufficient resources, human and material, simply makes the construction of complex structures impossible.

Secondly, it appears that in the Polynesian kingdoms the combined execution of ritual and political tasks is difficult. In Tahiti a solution was found in the device of the regentship. This enabled the ruler to rule without ritual obligations, while a high priest took over many ritual tasks. In the Tongan Islands the mirror solution emerged. Here the ruler handed over his worldly obligations and concentrated on the ritual ones. This division of tasks seems not to have worked completely satisfactorily however. Seen from a comparative point of view, many rulers – also in Africa and the Americas – shed the greater part of their ritual tasks, reserving only the most important ones for themselves. The African rulers of Dahomey, Buganda and Ashante are cases in point. Where the ritual tasks remained dominant, as among the

Tio, the role of the king as political leader of his society was minor (Vansina 1973). The same is found with the rulers of the Incas, Aztecs and Mayas. Rulers in medieval Western Europe had to shed many of their sacred prerogatives after the introduction of Christianity. However, the way in which the Carolingians were legitimized by the nobility and the Church shows that – within the confines of Christianity – important traces of sacred kingship were retained (Blockmans and Hoppenbrouwers 2002), although they gave priority to political aspects of their kingship.

Finally, in Polynesia the concept of heredity was interpreted in a rather loose sense. In some cases it was not a son of the ruler who succeeded, but a brother or a nephew. This was usually explained within the existing system of rules and customs by 'knowledgeable' people such as priests or diviners. And, speaking in a comparative sense, where there was a polygynous ruler, as was normally the case in traditional Africa, there were usually many sons – or potential successors. Succession, then, depended more on the capacity of a prince to bring together a group of followers, than on the fact that he was a first born son of an important consort (Goody 1966; Claessen 1986).

Notes

1. There is a large literature on chiefs and headmen. Service (1975: 16) states that chiefs have 'no formal legal apparatus of forceful repression'. Schapera (1956) mentions great differences in power between, for example, great Bantu chiefs, and chiefs of small Hottentot groups; some of his Bantu chiefs could easily be considered 'kings'. According to Clastres (1974: 175), 'le chef ne dispose d'aucune autorité. D'aucune pouvoir de coercion, d'aucune moyen de donner un ordre'. His 'chief' is in fact the headman of a small group. Claessen and Kloos (1978: 85) summarize the power position of the chief in nine chiefdoms, and find that in none of the cases was power to enforce decisions found to exist. For Carneiro (1981: 70) law enforcement is the functional requirement for states – though some lines further on he says that in chiefdoms 'rudiments' of law enforcement are found. Pospisil (1984) remarks rather cynically that when really serious matters were at hand, any chief was prepared to use force. Kurtz (2001: 162–8) attributes actual power to chiefs; his chiefs are more similar to the Bantu chiefs of Schapera, than to the chiefs of Clastres. For more general discussions of the maintenance of rules in small societies, see Malinowski (1949); Roberts (1979).
2. Tacitus, in his *Germania*, makes the phenomenon of Germanic kingship even more complex by distinguishing between *rex* and *dux: Reges ex nobilitate. Duces ex virtute sumunt.* Both types sometimes merged, and the so-called *Heerkönige* emerged. These were powerful leaders, and several of these can be called 'kings'. Cf. also Blockmans and Hoppenbrouwers (2002: 44–58).

3. On the dispersal of the Polynesians, see Sharp (1957); Suggs (1960); Claessen (1964); Lewis (1972); Irwin (1992); Cachola-Abad (1993). For the time being Irwin (1992) seems the definitive study on these voyages.

4. See Firth (1963); Sahlins (1958: 140–51); Goldman (1970); Claessen (1978: 442). Interestingly, Kirch and Green (2001) do not use the term ramage, but speak instead of 'conical clan', which is essentially the same; cf. Sahlins (1968).

5. Examples are given by Arii Taimai (1964 [1901]); Claessen (1978).

6. Legitimacy is a complex phenomenon. According to Weber (1964 [1922]: 24ff.), ruling in accordance with the norms and values of a society makes a ruler legitimate. His views are elaborated and augmented by Beetham (1991: 11ff.). Cohen (1988: 3) connects legitimacy with the 'degree of consensus about the rules of the game'. For a discussion of these views, see Claessen (1996: 339–40).

7. The strong hierarchy that existed on the tiny islands of the Mangareva group is an exception to this rule. Van Bakel (1989: 23–52) gives an explanation of this governmental system.

8. Survey based on Van Bakel (1989); Thomas (1990); Kirch (1991).

9. Herman Melville provides a good picture of life in such a valley in *Typee* (1959 [1846]).

10. Survey based on Van Bakel (1989); Bargatzky (1987; 1988); Tcherkézoff (1997).

11. Van Bakel (1989: 57–9), using a number of sources, estimates that in the beginning of the nineteenth century the number of inhabitants was between 40,000 and 60,000. This implies a population density of 14 to 21 people per sq km. As only one third of the surface of the islands is cultivable, the average population density per sq km arable land lies between 48 and 72 persons – a very low number for Polynesia.

12. Survey based on: Claessen (1978; 1995; 1996; 2000b) and Oliver (1974).

13. The early states on Tahiti were only small. According to estimates, Papara, on the south coast, had about 5,000 inhabitants. Tautira, on the peninsula, a good 6,000 and Pare-Arue in the north-west, will also have had 5,000 inhabitants.

14. Survey based on Gifford (1929); Bott (1981); Gailey (1987); Claessen (1996); Douaire-Marsaudon (1998).

15. According to Bott (1981: 42) these were formed when a younger son of a high-placed notable of Tongatapu travelled to another community and there married the daughter of an important local title-holder in order to secure the support of the title-holder and his people. The usual rule of patrilineal succession was waived in favour of the son of the aristocrat and the chief's daughter. In this way leadership of the community came under the sway of Tonga's rulers.

16. Some of the smaller polities in Tahiti, such as Faaa, or Atehuru, remained chiefdoms, while several other, mainly smaller chiefdoms united in coalitions, usually dominated by one of the early states. When talking about kings only the rulers of the early states Papara, Tautira and Pare-Arue are meant.

References

Arii Taimai 1964 [1901]. *Mémoires d'Arii Taimai*. Paris: Musée de l'Homme. Publications de la Société des Océanistes 12.

Bakel, M. A. van 1989. 'Samen leven in Gebondenheid en Vrijheid; Evolutie en ontwikkeling in Polynesië.' PhD thesis. Leiden University.

Bargatzky, T. 1987. 'Die Söhne des Tunumafonos. Dezendenz, Metaphor und Territorialität; am Beispiel der Traditionellen politischen Organization Westsamoas.' Habilitationsschrift. University of Munich.

—— 1988. 'Evolution, Sequential Hierarchy, and Areal Integration. The Case of Traditional Samoan Society', in J. Gledhill, B. Bender, and M. T. Larsen (eds) *State and Society; The Emergence and Development of Social Hierarchy and Political Centralization*. London: Unwin Hyman, pp. 43–56.

Beetham, D. 1991. *The Legitimation of power.* London: Macmillan.

Blockmans, W. & Hoppenbrouwers, P. 2002. *Eeuwen des onderscheids; Een geschiedenis van middeleeuws Europa*. Amsterdam: Prometheus.

Bott, E. 1981. 'Power and rank in the Kingdom of Tonga', *The Journal of the Polynesian Society* 90: 7–82.

—— 1982. *Tongan Society at the Time of Captain Cook's Visits: Discussions with Her Majesty Queen Salote Tupou*. Wellington: The Polynesian Society.

Cachola-Abad, C. K. 1993. 'Evaluating the Orthodox Dual Settlement Model for the Hawaiian Islands: An Analysis of Artefact Distribution and Hawaiian Oral Traditions', in M. W. Graves and R. C. Green (eds) *The Evolution and Organization of Prehistoric Society in Polynesia*. Auckland: New Zealand Archaeological Association Publications, pp. 13–32.

Campbell, I. C. 1992. *Island Kingdom. Tonga Ancient and Modern*. Christchurch: University of Canterbury Press.

Carneiro, R. L. 1981. 'The Chiefdom: Precursor of the State', in G. D. Jones and R. R. Kautz (eds) *The Transition to Statehood in the New World*. Cambridge: Cambridge University Press, pp.37–80.

Claessen, H. J. M. 1964. 'Een vergelijking van de theorieën van Sharp en Suggs over de lange afstandsreizen van de Polynesiërs', *Bijdragen tot de Taal-, Land- en Volkenkunde* 120:140–62.

—— 1978. 'Early State in Tahiti', in H. J. M. Claessen and P. Skalník (eds) *The Early State*. The Hague: Mouton, pp. 441–68.

—— 1986. 'Kingship in the Early State', *Bijdragen tot de Taal-, Land- en Volkenkunde* 142: 113–27

—— 1988. 'Tongan Traditions: On Model Building and Historical Evidence', *Bijdragen tot de Taal-, Land- en Volkenkunde* 144: 433–44.

—— 1995. 'The Oro-Maro-Arioi Connection', in D. Smidt, P. ter Kers and A. A. Trouwborst (eds) *Pacific Material Culture*. Leiden: Rijksmuseum voor Volkenkunde. Mededelingen 28, pp. 282–92.

—— 1996. 'Ideology and the Formation of Early States: Data from Polynesia', in H. J. M. Claessen and J. G. Oosten (eds) *Ideology and the Formation of Early States*. Leiden: Brill, pp. 339–58.

—— 2000a. *Structural Change: Evolution and Evolutionism in Cultural Anthropology*. Leiden: CNWS Press.

—— 2000b. 'Ideology, Leadership and Fertility: Evaluating a Model of Polynesian Chiefship', *Bijdragen tot de Taal-, Land- en Volkenkunde* 156: 707–35.

Claessen, H. J. M. and P. Kloos 1978. *Evolutie en Evolutionisme*. Assen: Van Gorcum.

Clastres, P. 1974. *La Société contre l'état*. Paris: Editions de Minuit.

Cohen, R. 1988. 'Introduction', in R. Cohen and J. D. Toland (eds) *State Formation and Political Legitimacy*. New Brunswick, NJ: Transaction, pp. 1–22.

Cook, J. 1967. *The Voyage of the Resolution and Discovery, 1776–1780*. Edited by J. C. Beaglehole. Hakluyt Society Extra Series 36. Cambridge: Cambridge University Press.

Danielsson, B. 1956. *Work and Life on Raroia*. London: Allen and Unwin.

Douaire-Marsaudon, F. 1998. *Les Premiers fruits. Parenté, identité sexuelle et pouvoirs en Polynésie occidentale (Tonga, Wallis et Futuna)*. Paris: Editions de la Maison des Sciences de l'Homme (CNRS Editions).

Firth, R. 1963. *We the Tikopia. Kinship in Primitive Polynesia*. Boston: Beacon Press.

Frazer, Sir J. G. 1905. *Lectures on the Early History of the Kingship*. London: Macmillan.

—— 1925. *The Golden Bough. A Study in Magic and Religion*. 12 vols. London: Macmillan.

Gailey, C. W. 1987. *Kinship to Kingship. Gender Hierarchy and State Formation in the Tonga Islands*. Austin: University of Texas Press.

Gifford, E. W. 1929. *Tongan Society*. B. P. Bishop Museum Bulletin 61. Honolulu: B. P. Bishop Museum Press.

Goldman, I. 1970. *Ancient Polynesian Society*. Chicago: University of Chicago Press.

Goody, J. (ed.) 1966. *Succession to High Office*. Cambridge: Cambridge University Press.

Huntsman, J. and Hooper, A. 1996. *Tokelau. A Historical Ethnography*. Auckland:

Auckland University Press.

Irwin, G. 1992. *The Prehistoric Exploration and Colonization of the Pacific.* Cambridge: Cambridge University Press.

Johnson, G. A. 1982. 'Organizational Structure and Scalar Stress', in C. Renfrew *et al.* (eds) *Theory and Explanation in Archaeology.* New York: Academic Press, pp. 389–421.

Kirch, P. V. 1984. *The Evolution of Polynesian Chiefdoms.* Cambridge: Cambridge University Press.

—— 1991. 'Chiefship and Competitive Involution: The Marquesas Islands of Eastern Polynesia', in T. Earle (ed.) *Chiefdoms: Power, Economy and Ideology.* Cambridge: Cambridge University Press, pp. 119–45.

—— 1997. *The Lapita Peoples. Ancestors of the Oceanic World.* Oxford: Blackwell.

Kirch, P. V. and Green, R. C. 2001. *Hawaiki, Ancestral Polynesia. An Essay in Historical Anthropology.* Cambridge: Cambridge University Press.

Kurtz, D. V. 2001. *Political Anthropology. Paradigms and Power.* Boulder, CO: West View Press.

Lewis, D. 1972. *We, the Navigators. The Ancient Art of Landfinding in the Pacific.* Canberra: Australian National University Press.

Malinowski, B. 1949 [1926]. *Crime and Custom in Savage Society.* London: Routledge & Kegan Paul.

Marcus, G. E. 1989. 'Chieftainship', in A. Howard and R. Borofsky (eds) *Developments in Polynesian Ethnology.* Honolulu: University Press of Hawaii, pp. 175–209.

McCoy, P. 1979. 'Easter Island', in J. D. Jennings (ed.) *The Prehistory of Polynesia.* Cambridge, MA: Harvard University Press, pp. 135–66.

Melville, H. 1959 [1846]. *Typee: A Peep at Polynesian Life During a Four Months' Residence in a Valley of the Marquesas.* London: Oxford University Press.

Oliver, D. 1974. *Ancient Tahitian Society,* 3 vols. Honolulu: University Press of Hawaii.

Oosten, J. G. 1981. 'De Germaanse koningen', in R. R. Hagesteijn and E. C. L. van der Vliet (eds) *Legitimiteit of leugen; Achtergronden van macht en gezag in de Vroege Staat.* (ICA Publication 41) Leiden: Institute of Cultural and Social Studies, pp. 183–202.

—— 1996. 'Ideology and the Formation of European Kingdoms', in H. J. M. Claessen and J. G. Oosten (eds) *Ideology and the Formation of Early States.* Leiden: Brill, pp. 220–41.

Pospisil, L. 1984. 'Myths in Political Anthropology', *Reviews in Anthropology* 11: 20–8.

Roberts, S. 1979. *Order and Dispute. An Introduction to Legal Anthropology.* London: Pelican Books.

Sahlins, M. D. 1958. *Social Stratification in Polynesia*. Seattle: University of Washington Press.
—— 1968. *Tribesmen*. Englewood Cliffs, NJ: Prentice Hall.
Sancisi-Weerdenburg, H. 1995. 'Medes and Persians in Early States?' in M. A. van Bakel and J. G. Oosten (eds) *The Dynamics of the Early State Paradigm*. Utrecht: ISOR Press, pp. 87–104.
Schapera, I. 1956. *Government and Politics in Tribal Society*. London: Watts.
Service, E. R. 1975. *Origins of the State and Civilization*. New York: Norton.
Sharp, A. 1957. *Ancient Voyagers in the Pacific*. London: Pelican Books.
Suggs, R. C. 1960. *The Island Civilizations of Polynesia*. New York: Mentor Books.
Tacitus 1977 [CE 98]. *Germania*. Translated by H. Mattingly. London: Penguin Classics.
Tcherkézoff, S. 1997. 'Culture, nation, société: changements secondaires et bouleversements fondamentaux au Samoa occidental', in S. Tcherkézoff and F. Douaire-Marsaudon (eds) *Le Pacifique-Sud aujourd'hui*. Paris: Editions CNRS, pp. 309–74.
Thapar, R. 1984. *From Lineage to State. Social Formations in the Mid-First Millennium BC in the Ganga Valley*. Bombay: Oxford University Press.
Thomas, N. 1990. *Marquesan Societies. Inequality and Political Transformation in Eastern Polynesia*. Oxford: Clarendon.
Tilburg, J. A. van 1994. *Easter Island. Archaeology, Ecology and Culture*. London: British Museum Press.
Tolkien, J. R. R. 1966. *In de ban van de ring* (*The Lord of the Rings*), 3 vols. Utrecht: Prisma.
Valeri, V. 1985. *Kingship and Sacrifice. Ritual and Society in Ancient Hawaii*. Chicago: University of Chicago Press.
Vansina, J. 1973. *The Tio Kingdom of the Middle Kongo*. London: Oxford University Press.
Voget, F. 1975. *A History of Ethnology*. New York: Holt, Rinehart and Winston.
Weber, M. 1964 [1922]. *Wirtschaft und Gesellschaft*. Studienausgabe. Edited by J. Winkelmann. Köln: Kiepenheuer und Witsch.

Index